The Package Deal

The Package Deal

Marriage, Work, and Fatherhood in Men's Lives

Nicholas W. Townsend

Temple University Press
Philadelphia

Temple University Press, Philadelphia 19122

Published 2002
Printed in the United States of America

∞ The paper used in this publication meets the requirements of the American National Standard for Information Sciences—Permanence of Paper for Printed Library Materials, ANSI Z39.48-1984

Library of Congress Cataloging-in-Publication Data

Townsend, Nicholas W., 1951–
The package deal: marriage, work, and fatherhood in men's lives / Nicholas W. Townsend.
p. cm.
Includes bibliographical references and index.
ISBN 1-56639-957-2 (cloth : alk. paper) — ISBN 1-56639-958-0 (pbk : alk. paper)
1. Men—United States. 2. Fatherhood—United States. 3. Sex role—United States. I. Title.

HQ1090.3 T695 2002
305.31′0973—dc21

2001057403

To Anita Ilta Garey

Contents

Acknowledgments

The research and writing of this book have occupied much of my attention and have become entwined with my entire life. Although separating individuals and influences for thanks is inevitably selective, it is a pleasure for me to recall the many people who have helped me with this book, to thank them, and to assure both them and my readers that the shortcomings of this book are my own responsibility.

The men from Meadowview High School must remain anonymous, but without their generosity and openness this book would not exist. I am also grateful to the many strangers, acquaintances, and friends with whom I have talked about my research and their lives. Almost without exception they have tolerated my ethnographer's inquisitiveness, and the enthusiasm with which many of them have greeted an interested and sympathetic listener has convinced me that my topic is of general interest and importance. My own involvement in the subject has been given a personal immediacy through my relationships with my stepsons Kelley Garey and Sasha Friedman. With them I have learned a great deal about the connections between fathers and sons.

When I began work on this project, I was encouraged and supported, criticized and instructed by Eugene Hammel, Ronald Lee, and Burton Benedict. Their engagement with my work, from very different disciplinary perspectives, repeatedly pushed me to reexamine the words and lives of the men with whom I talked. The following people read parts of an earlier incarnation and provided comments. I thank them all: Jeanne Bergman, Jay Bernstein, Stanley Brandes, Cecilia De Mello, Roland Foulkes, Cristina Gladwin, Linda Green, Sarah Lamb, Catherine Leone, Jane Margold, Roland Moore, Michael Nunley, Maria Olujic, Robert Priest, Nancy Scheper-Hughes, Frank Zimmerman. Dorothy Brown's experience and advice helped me immeasurably.

From the inception of my research to the completion of this book, Karen Hansen has been a close reader, an insightful editor, an intellectual stimulant, and a wonderful friend. When I returned to this project to write the book, Matthew Gutmann read an early draft with engaged but critical care and gave me helpful comments. Michael Ames, my first editor at Temple University Press, provided the most valuable service an author can receive: He read an earlier draft with a keen eye, not to its many shortcomings (although he pointed them out without sparing my feelings) but to the book that I wanted to write. His comments liberated me to concentrate on presenting the lives and words of fathers with critical sympathy. Sections of the book, in various drafts, have been read by Barbara Andrews, Caroline Bledsoe, Stanley Brandes, Caroline Brettell, Andrew Bundy, Shawn Christiansen, Tom Fricke, Cynthia Garcia Coll, Calvin Goldscheider, Frances Goldscheider, Michael Kimmel, Carolyn Sargent, Barrie Thorne, and Kenneth Wachter, all of whom raised questions, offered advice, and provided encouragement.

I have discussed this work at professional meetings and at presentations at Pennsylvania State University, the University of Michigan, Brown University, and the University of California at Berkeley. Questions, comments, and observations from discussants and members of the audience have repeatedly given me insight, pointed me to references, and pushed me to clarify my position. I am very grateful to all these people whose public engagement has given me so much. And I am also grateful to the anonymous reviewers who have read my work with professional care and attention and have offered collegial comment and criticism. The willingness of other scholars to read and review the work of their peers before publication, a task that brings little glory or profit, affirms the existence of a community of scholars to which it is a privilege and a pleasure to belong.

I have much to say in this book about institutional constraints. It is a particular pleasure, therefore, to acknowledge the academic institutions that have provided me with so much support and a remarkable freedom from constraint. The Anthropology Department at the University of California gave me the freedom to pursue my interests and to explore other disciplines when I was a student there. As a member of the faculty in the Department of Anthropology at Brown University, I have the good fortune of having a job where I enjoy what I am doing a great deal of the time, with colleagues who value one another's varied pursuits. When I returned to Berkeley on sabbatical leave, Ken Wachter, the chair of the Department of Demography, invited me to return as a visiting scholar to what had been my second home on campus. Ken and his colleagues gave me material support, intellectual stimulation, and a room of my own for uninterrupted writing. While at Berkeley, I was also affiliated with the Berkeley Center for Working Families, codirected by Barrie Thorne and Arlie Hochschild, where the weekly seminars attracted an array of outstanding scholars and where the core group of attendees maintained consistently excellent discussions of family life.

Materially, I have benefited from a Dissertation Improvement Grant from the National Science Foundation, from grants from the Lowie Scholarship Funds administered by the Anthropology Department at Berkeley, and from a Research Traineeship from the National Institute for Child Health and Human Development administered through the Department of Demography. Heather Kobal, Michael McGregor, and Cherrie Potts helped with transcription, funded by a research grant from Brown University. I am also very grateful to Brown University and to my colleagues there for allowing me a sabbatical leave, and to the Alfred P. Sloan Foundation for funding my semester in Berkeley.

Finally, I am happy to be able to thank Anita Garey for her unfailing help and encouragement. Her intellectual honesty has not always been comfortable to live with, for it has made me face problems I would sometimes rather have avoided, but my work has benefited immeasurably from her suspicion of glib answers. Twenty-three years of living together, raising children, reading innumerable drafts of each other's work, studying mothers and fathers in the United States and in Botswana, and passing through the crises and celebrations of family life have increased our connection. It is in celebration of our disparate interconnectedness that I dedicate this book to her.

The Package Deal

1 Contradictions and Complications

DAVID: I was a bad father though; we've got to include that. At that time, I mean. I thought I was bad because—

MARY: He didn't do— He was not a participant father.

WE HEAR a great deal about fathers. Dead-beat dads, absent fathers, distant fathers, participant fathers, new fathers, and changing fathers feature in academic and popular discussions. The impact of fathers on children, their influence for good or bad, their central importance, or their insignificance are investigated, assumed, argued over, and mobilized in highly politicized debates. But very few of the participants in these debates have examined what men themselves say about being fathers, about what fatherhood means to them, about what they do and do not do, and about how they explain the place of fatherhood in their lives. What is so often said of mothers is that they were "there" for their children. What is said almost as often of fathers is that they were "not there" physically, financially, or emotionally. The questions that arise are, Where were they? What were they doing? What did they think they were doing?

This book is about the meanings of fatherhood in the lives of a group of American men. Most readers will think they are familiar with the lives of American men. Many of them will themselves be American men or will be their children, wives, mothers, or girlfriends. All readers will have images of them from personal acquaintance or from books, films, and television programs. Given this personal familiarity with the subject, much of the behavior and many of the opinions expressed by the men in this book may seem obvious, natural, and inevitable—hardly worth noticing. When we think we know what we are seeing, however, we often stop looking carefully and stop noticing what is extraordinary. My account examines aspects of the familiar and the taken-for-granted from the perspective of a comparative social anthropologist.

The Package Deal is neither a manual for change nor a polemic. What I hope it contributes to the contemporary debate about fatherhood is a careful, sympathetic description and analysis of the cultural image of fatherhood that is held by many fathers in the United States. This image has internal contradictions and frequently ignores social realities, but it reflects deeply held values, informs a great deal of social policy, and guides the lives of many men. Documenting this cultural image is both an end in itself and a necessary precursor to effective action.

As I listened to the men with whom I talked and studied my notes and transcripts, I came to realize that they saw their lives, and measured their success, in terms of a *package deal* in which having children, being married, holding a steady job, and owning a home were four interconnected *elements*. No single element could be evaluated alone, and success in any one element alone did not guarantee success overall. The four elements of the package deal are in many respects mutually reinforcing, but they are also in tension with one another, so that the package deal incorporates internal contradictions. Being a father is one of the four elements of the package deal. My analysis of the meaning of fatherhood reveals that fatherhood itself is composite. I describe fatherhood, as an element of the package deal, in terms of four facets: emotional closeness, provision, protection, and endowment. Throughout this book, I discuss the complex interconnections of the four elements of the package deal and the contributions that these elements make to each of the four facets of fatherhood.

Research on men as gendered, anthropological research on masculinity, and this book in particular owe a great deal to feminist analyses and formulations of the meaning of gender and of the applicability of gender as a category of analysis. Feminist theory and analysis have opened the possibility of a gendered approach to the study of men and fatherhood. Such an approach sees gender not as an attribute of individuals, but as an organizing principle of social and cultural institutions. Research interest in fatherhood is relatively recent. Motherhood has been a subject of serious social science attention for a longer time, and research on motherhood has opened the way for studies of fatherhood as a set of gendered meanings and activities. The bibliographic essay in Appendix 2 puts my work in the context of some of the important literature in these areas. *The Package Deal* contributes to the popular and scholarly debates about fatherhood by examining closely the life stories of a group of men as they talk about the place and meaning of fatherhood in their lives.

My analysis is directed at understanding a framework of cultural meanings through which men make sense of their actions, circumstances, and relationships as sons, husbands, and fathers. This enterprise is very different from an attempt to discover the underlying motives or internal causes of human action. The anthropologists Dorothy Holland and Margaret Eisenhart made this distinction in their analysis of the role of cultural models in the education of college women and their socialization as adult women. They stressed that the cultural model "is first and foremost an interpretive structure, a meaning system, not a set of prescriptive rules. Actual relationships are not dictated or determined by the model, but rather experience is anticipated, interpreted, and evaluated in light of it" (Holland and Eisenhart 1990: 95). Holland and Eisenhart went on to explore the many ways that behavior can depart from the model, and the ways in which people then deploy other cultural models to make sense of these departures.

This book is not a work of theory, but a theoretically informed study of particular lives in their contexts. The work of Pierre Bourdieu (1977; Bourdieu and Passerson 1990) has influenced my research and my analyses, providing a coherent conceptual framework for thinking about life courses. Bourdieu's theory describes the processes whereby people become imbued with sets of enduring dispositions and obtain access to differential selections of resources. They confront existing situations, with established rules of procedure and patterns of practice, and negotiate outcomes in light of their own dispositions, the expectations of others, and the resources they have available to them. What I find most useful about Bourdieu's formulation is that he depicts the human condition as one in which people have contradictory goals and face conflicting pressures. He presents a theory of culture that is structured and external but is not totally unified and does not determine action. In this endeavor, Bourdieu is reacting against mechanical and directive models of culture, and is building on a tradition of anthropological theorizing that has examined the contradictions and conflicts within cultural settings and situations (Fortes 1949; Gluckman 1940).

I discuss some of the implications of my research in the concluding chapter. To develop either illuminating theory or effective policy, it is crucial to have a clear vision of the lived reality and cultural situation of actual people, so I emphasize what men have to say about their lives and their families, the complexities of their attitudes and the details of their lives, the dominant cultural values they express, and the cultural contradictions with which they deal.

DOMINANT CULTURAL VALUES

Anthropologists have argued about the usefulness and definition of the idea of culture, but at its most straightforward the concept means those beliefs, values, norms, and behaviors that people learn and share by virtue of living in a particular society. Comparative cultural anthropology has documented real cultural difference and explored the human capacity to make sense of the world and human life in diverse ways. Central to anthropological debates has been a tension or oscillation in anthropologists' emphases on variation and homogeneity. At one extreme has been Ruth Benedict's essential identification of personality and culture and her remark that in "primitive" cultures, people are as alike as "peas in a pod" (1934) and at the other has been Edward Sapir's argument that all culture is individual (1956: 151). There has also been disagreement about the extent to which variation should be attributed to structural factors or to individual strategizing and performance.

In any large society such as the United States there is cultural variation, and several sets of cultural values compete or coexist. Some of these values are dominant or "hegemonic" in the sense that difference or departure from them is expected to be justified or explained. The concept of dominant or hegemonic values has a long history and has been applied in many areas besides gender studies.[1] Dominant cultural values are not simply those of a dominant group, forced onto unwilling inferiors, but are those values that shape the cultural landscape for the members of a society. Identifying dominant cultural values is not a way of denying cultural difference but rather of exploring the terrain in which difference can be expressed.

Audre Lorde's invocations of differences among women were decisive contributions to the development of feminist theory because they demolished assumptions of the universality of white, western women's experience. Lorde wrote and spoke passionately about the ways that difference is used to divide and exclude. Differences are used to set one group against another, and differences from a dominant value are used to exclude. Lorde was adamant that feminists, and all who want "to define and seek a world in which we can all flourish" (1984: 112) must recognize our differences and see them as a source of strength, not of division. What all oppressed groups have in common, Lorde said, was that they were excluded and made to feel inferior. The oppressed groups in American society "Black and Third World people, working-class people, older people, and women" (1984: 114) "stand outside the circle of this society's definition" (1984: 112). They depart from what Lorde called a "mythical norm" "defined as white, thin, male, young, heterosexual, christian, and financially secure" (1984: 116). Lorde's emphasis on difference was part of a program to build a better world on the basis of our real differences rather than to compare ourselves with the "mythical norm." Lorde's point, of course, was that the norm had enormous impact on the living situations and inner consciousness of all of us, even though it is "mythical," precisely because it is not a description of the majority but a standard by which all are judged.

Within the study of gender and masculinity, "hegemonic masculinity" is used to describe the way that a certain definition of masculinity is the standard with which other definitions are compared and by which they are judged (Connell 1987: 183–185; Ortner 1990). The particular definition of masculinity that is hegemonic changes over time and varies from society to society. In any particular situation, however, the dominant model of masculinity provides the basic cultural patterns of expectation and outlook that all men and women must confront, whether they accept these expectations, rebel against them, or espouse alternatives.

Erving Goffman argued, "In an important sense there is only one complete unblushing male in America," and described this norm in terms very similar to Lorde's: "young, married, white, urban, northern, heterosexual Protestant father of college education, fully employed, of good complexion, weight and height, and a recent record in sports" (1963: 128). Goffman's norm is no more common or representative than Lorde's. Indeed, Goffman argued, "The general identity-values of a society may be fully entrenched nowhere," but he clearly described the impact of this norm on men's interactions and self-image: "Every American male tends to look out upon the world from this perspective. . . . Any male who fails to qualify in any of these ways is likely to view himself—during moments at least—as unworthy, incomplete, and inferior" (1963: 128). The notions of masculinity and fatherhood, as articulated by the men I talked to, are hegemonic in the sense that all these men have experienced their coercive power and, whatever the differences and divergences of their own lives, have had to take them into account as they tell their life stories.

To talk about cultural hegemony is to talk about power. Dominant cultural values do not become dominant in a vacuum, but because they serve the needs of economically and politically dominant groups. The goals and values of the dominant culture cannot be achieved by everyone and are used to exclude some people from full participation and to judge them as failures. Dorothy Smith, a sociologist whose theoretical work on the sociology of knowledge has its empirical roots in her research on single motherhood, has described the impact of a norm of family life, which she describes as the "Standard North American Family":

> A legally married couple sharing a household. The adult male is in paid employment; his earnings provide the economic basis of the family-household. The adult female may also earn an income, but her primary responsibility is to the care of husband, household, and children. The adult male and female may be parents . . . of children also resident in the household. (1999: 159)

Smith does not, it should be clear, make any claim that such a family form is either morally desirable or statistically dominant. Indeed, her analysis of this norm is an element of her research on single mothers. She does claim that this picture of the family operates as an "ideological code" that informs a great deal of research and policy in such a way as to denigrate or distort any other ways of organizing family life. Smith argues, for example, that the behavior of children is judged and treated very differently according to the kind of family from which they come. The great diversity of mothers who do not fit the cultural norm, and the condemnation they face as a result, is documented in the collection *Mothering against the Odds* (Garcia Coll, Surrey, and Weingarten 1998). These authors describe both the many ways of being a mother and how these ways are judged against dominant cultural values.

Analysis of a cultural norm is something very different from a description of majority experience. To describe a hegemonic cultural model does not exclude the experience of men who cannot achieve success in its terms or who do not share its values. Quite the contrary, this description illuminates how dominant cultural models are used to judge and exclude them and thereby contribute to the material and political oppression so many men also experience. Frequently, men who are found wanting by their culture also judge themselves as failures. Men who cannot find jobs, for instance, may share the social judgment that their situation is a result of their personal inadequacy (Dudley 1994; Liebow 1967; Newman 1988; Sennett and Cobb 1972; Wilson 1996). To see the dominant values of society is to understand what the members of that society must confront in their daily lives. In this book I describe the lives of a particular group of men and analyze them as variations on a dominant cultural theme or hegemonic pattern.

The men I describe were all in their late thirties when we spoke. They varied in educational level, occupation, income, marital status, and number of children, but they all graduated from the same high school in the early 1970s. The school had been in a lower-middle-and working-class area of a San Francisco Bay Area town, in a neighborhood of small single-family homes and modest apartment buildings constructed to house the flood of workers and their families who had moved to the area in the post–World War II boom. These men reflected the racial–ethnic composition of the town when they were in high school: about 70 percent non-Hispanic White, 25 percent Hispanic, and 5 percent Asian American. The racial–ethnic categories are those used by the Census Bureau, which I follow for the sake of comparability. I use the term "racial–ethnic" as it is used by sociologist Maxine Baca Zinn (1991)—to emphasize both that race and ethnicity are intertwined and that membership in racial-ethnic groups is the result of being assigned to socially constructed categories. Assignment to these categories is inevitably arbitrary and the categories themselves do not necessarily reflect either social reality or personal identity. I will return to a more detailed description of these men and their circumstances later in the chapter, but first I will describe a conversation I had with a man and his wife to illustrate the way these men talked about their lives and the way that they expressed dominant values as they constructed culturally appropriate narratives and explanations.

David and Mary: Multiple Interpretations

David Brown graduated from high school in 1972. His father, a blue-collar worker, had encouraged David in his enthusiasm for athletic competition. After high school David found a job in the plumbing section of the hardware store where he had worked when he was in school and started to date Mary, who was a senior in his former high school. When I met David and Mary in 1990, they had been married for sixteen years. David had risen to a middle-management position for the same chain of hardware stores, and Mary worked part time as a secretary for the local school district. They had one child, a twelve-year-old son.

David and Mary had not planned to have only one child, but circumstances and their own actions and reactions had intervened. During my interview, they advanced four explanations for why they were the parents of an only child. As they talked about their lives, they gave accounts that were sometimes internally inconsistent and sometimes different from each other. In their inconsistency they expressed the real and potential contradictions of their various dreams and goals and of the cultural expectations that helped shape these goals. They were expressing the differences that always exist between "his marriage" and "her marriage" (Bernard 1972). This is a point that should always be kept in mind when reading these men's accounts and that leaps out of conversations between husband and wife, even when they are presenting a joint account of their lives. The contradictions, compromises, and constructions internal to marriage are part of men's daily lives. Any one of their interpretations might seem straightforward and adequate, but the juxtaposition of them to explain the same set of circumstances and results brings us face to face with the complexity of their lives, their stories about their lives, and the meanings they bring to parenthood and particularly to fatherhood.

The number of children they had wanted first came up when I asked, "Did you always want to have kids?"[2]

DAVID: Yes I did. Yes. She scared me when we were first going around because she was from a big family. In fact all her family's big and she was saying: "Yeah, I'd like to have nine kids" or something. I'm only [one of] two. I'm like, "Nine kids!" I always thought a couple kids was plenty but even with the one— I mean I'm real happy. I thought a couple of kids would be fine.

MARY: I always said I *wasn't* just going to have one. And that's what I did. I never wanted him to grow up alone. I didn't know what it was like to grow up alone, but because I had so much family around me I figured, "God, how can a kid feel lonely?" I mean, here he is growing up alone— I mean with no brothers and sisters.

At this point in the conversation, David was proposing a two-child family form that matched his own experience and the widely expressed cultural norm. Mary's position was less precise, but neither of them had intended to have only one child. As our conversation continued, I learned about the pattern of events in their lives, and about David and Mary's moves toward a shared story—or at least toward a shared group of stories—about their lives as parents.

They began by telling me that as a young couple they had known what they wanted, believed they could get it, and worked hard to achieve their goals. David told me with pride:

> [Mary] went to work, I remember, when we first started dating and thought about getting married. She got out of [high] school on a Friday and that following Monday she had a job. I thought that was pretty incredible, you know, she didn't even enjoy two days of vacation or anything. She went right to work and worked full time for many years.

From her high school graduation until two months before the birth, Mary worked ten-hour shifts in an assembly plant. A year after her son was born she returned to work and subsequently worked full time until three years before our conversation, when the family had moved and she had taken a part-time job with the local school district.

David gave accounts of his wife's work that were, in their ambivalence, typical of the men with whom I talked. David was pleased that Mary had worked very hard to get them established, but he emphasized that they could now "get by fine" on his income. "She doesn't have to work right now," he said. A few months previously, however, he had been threatened with "downsizing" and had encouraged her to look for full-time work. He was the provider, but her income allowed them to live the lifestyle they wanted. Clearly, to an outside observer, Mary's paid work was an essential part of their family strategy, although both of them spoke of David's job as more important. In the first years of their marriage they had both worked long hours in order to establish themselves so that they could have children.

> MARY: We didn't just have kids because "we're married and we're supposed to have kids" you know.
>
> DAVID: We didn't want kids for at least three years. We kind of put our heads down and worked for a couple of years before we thought about—

> MARY: We had our lives when we first got married. We knew what we wanted. Where we wanted to be like ten years down. We were setting goals basically. We knew we wanted—
>
> DAVID: A car. We knew we wanted a few material things and we just didn't go out and always buy 'em. We kind of set a goal like: "Well, we'll save a couple thousand here, put a couple thousand there, and we'll try to get these things."
>
> MARY: Because we always said we wouldn't have kids unless we owned our house.
>
> DAVID: Yeah, I thought the timing was right. This was our second house, mind you, we were moving to when we decided it was time for a kid. We wanted a bigger house. We could afford— We had the new car and everything was right. And she was pregnant at the time too, but we knew a couple of months later. But everything was perfect, I mean things were just perfect timing. But that's the way we wanted it. That's the way we got married. We didn't want kids at the beginning. We wanted to get some things, and things went fine. And we bought our first house, and things were fine. And I got promoted, things got better. And we just— And the time was right, and we could afford everything we wanted, and comfortable, and give our kid— We thought we could give him the best.

For David and Mary the basic structure of their story at this point was one of couple self-sufficiency and hard work to provide the suitable material conditions for the children they both regarded as inevitable. The sequence of their lives did not depend on a particular length of time between marriage and birth, but on achieving a particular set of circumstances. Changing circumstances, not the simple passage of time, dictated the pace of their lives.

While they reported strong agreement on what they had wanted to achieve before they had children, David agreed with Mary that control over the timing had been hers. I asked David what would happen in a relationship in which one person did not want children. Mary leapt in:

> MARY: Who doesn't want children? If I really wanted to have a child earlier than we did, I would have had a child earlier.
>
> DAVID: She could have stopped the birth control.
>
> MARY: I always felt, "The guy doesn't want the baby, then that's not the time to have a child." Because I saw it as, "He was the breadwinner, he's the one that's going to be working, it's up to him to say:

'OK. Now I'm ready to be a parent.'" But if I wanted to I would have done it. I would have just stopped taking the Pill. I wouldn't have even asked him.

Mary and David agreed about the appropriate pattern for their lives and about the gendered division of labor and of decision making because they shared basic cultural notions. They agreed, specifically, that the timing of children and the responsibility for birth control was up to women in general, and to Mary in particular. Their ideas about how parenthood should be gendered extended beyond birth control and provided, as we shall see, the context for their reaction to an unexpected turn of events. Gendered parenthood was also an important element in their further explanations of why they had only one child.

Although it has become more common in the United States for married couples to have only one child, such couples often feel they need to explain their situation. The more closely behaviors and situations conform to cultural norms, the less people feel the need to explain, account for, or elaborate on those behaviors. Male corporate executives, for instance, do not talk much about why they wear suits, but there is considerable discussion about "casual Fridays." The cultural norm in the United States is for a married couple to have two children.[3] This norm is not, of course, a description of actual family size: Norms and behaviors are not the same. Some departures from this norm are within a normative range and need little explanation; others require more elaborate accounts. Having an only child, or having more than four, requires more cultural explanation than having two or three. The amount of scholarly and popular attention applied to the only child is itself an index of departure from a cultural norm. David and Mary's need to account for and normalize their having only one child is not a response to overt criticism and does not indicate that they think there is anything wrong with this. Their attention to the issue is, however, a recognition that the outcome of having an only child needs to be situated in terms of cultural values and cannot be so easily taken for granted as can the normative outcome of having two children.

At first, David attempted to normalize the fact that he and Mary had only one child by referring to his own childhood:

The way I grew up in my childhood there with my father, I was almost like a single— It was always me and my dad, me and my dad,

> me and my dad. So I could almost look at my son and think, you know, "He's growing up the way I did," which I have no regrets over. I think it was fine.

David actually had a sister five years older, but she never featured in David's accounts of his childhood, and he remembered himself as being the focus of his father's attention. While David and Mary said they were content to have only one child, they acknowledged that they had not planned to do so, and they moved on from David's memories of his own childhood to recounting the story of their son's birth and infancy.

Their son was born with an undiagnosed digestive obstruction, which is how they explained having only one child. When David's son's medical condition came up in our talk, David assured me, "It's minor, it's minor," but Mary immediately contradicted him, which reflects the very different impact their son's medical condition had on their lives. It was Mary, with the help of respite care from her mother and sister-in-law, who had borne the brunt of daily caretaking, and it was Mary who told me about her son's surgery:

> Prior to him having the surgery, for weeks I'm dealing with this. I'm not sleeping at night and getting up in the middle of the night because I hear him and then see his face in just a puddle of milk. He could choke had I not gotten up. I was doing that. Well, the weekend prior to taking him in on a Monday, my Mom had him that weekend, because I needed the sleep. I needed to rest and she took care of him. She brought him home and he's still acting up and that's when I took him in [to the doctor]. So right then they knew: "Well we're going to have to do surgery tonight." I'm a new mother and I'm thinking, "I don't want this. I can't go for this," and then they tell me they have to do surgery tonight. Ten thirty. So it's like: "Oooh." New mother. Crying. Call my parents: "This is what's happening." They rush to the hospital, and here we are. Little baby that— They have him in intensive care, in a little room where you could see— And they're taking blood out of him and he's looking at me, and I'm thinking he must be looking at me saying, "Why are you letting them do this?" You know, all of these things, and you remember— I thought it was colic, and all that whole time it was because he was starving to death. Until we finally had the surgery. Then he was fine. He ate good after that. But that was scary. And to know that if I had another child I would go through that same thing. I thought, "I don't know if I'll go

through that right away." So we figured— three years go by, four years go by, well twelve years have gone by. [laughs] I don't want to go through diapers again. But no— we were thinking about it about a year ago.

There was more to this story than a wrenching tale of medical complication and maternal distress. After he and Mary had agreed that their son's medical problem was the reason they did not have more children, David raised the issue of his own participation. Even as he tried to explain his behavior, David acknowledged his own failures as a father and provided another reason for having only one child. In his acknowledgment, however, he still presented himself as dedicated to one of the facets of fatherhood, that of being a good provider:

DAVID: I was a bad father though; we've got to include that. At that time, I mean. I thought I was bad because—

MARY: He didn't do— He was not a participant father.

DAVID: And even the first couple years I was so wrapped up in—

MARY: *Five* years [with emphasis].

DAVID: —in my being promoted and managing. I had to go in at four, five o'clock in the morning. Those were my hours. So I'd be getting up at three, four in the morning and then I'd be in bed at nine. And that was it. That's all I did is I went to bed at eight, nine o'clock. And if anybody called, I was mad: "Don't bother me," you know. I had to get a few hours sleep before I go to work, and I just let that too seriously take over. And I regret that I didn't really help her a lot or do little things that I should've done as a father in the younger years.

David's acknowledgment that he could have done "little things" as a father is very far from questioning what he and Mary both saw as the basic division of labor in parenting or saying that he should have done half the childcare. David did recognize his own shortcomings, but he went on to explain and minimize them in terms of his own father's behavior and the cultural norm of the father as breadwinner:

But then again I look at the way I grew up and I didn't know my dad until I was like five or six years old, until I was able to play ball and get in with the go-cart. Then my dad just took me and we were two buddies. But you know until then I guess he was always working. I found out where I didn't know much about him. I guess I went in with that too. I was just trying to make sure I had the extra income

> coming, and that things were all settled, you know, things for the kid and the bills were— things we were going to need. And put too much emphasis on the work and not enough into what she needed. And that caused problems between us, down the road. And maybe she thought if she had another kid, that I'd be the same way, not really participating until he was five years old, where she's got to do it all.

Mary confirmed David's suggestion that his lack of participation in childcare contributed to their decision not to have more children: "I didn't think I could want it. I didn't want to raise another child by myself." And David went on with regret, knowing that there was no going back to do it again: "And I didn't see it. Now I do. Now I know if it was going to happen over it would be totally different. Now it's awakened me. Now I could see it, but it didn't happen at the time."

Mary was sure she also would do things differently. She saw herself as a different person than the new mother of twelve years ago:

> As strong willed a person as I am, now I wouldn't put up with it. . . . But then I know he wanted to move up in the business. I knew that's just the type of person he was. Plus he didn't understand his part. I felt badly. I had to sleep in the back room because he had to get up so early that when the baby woke up in the morning I had to— But (and I've told David) I can see where a parent, a new mother, can abuse. Because I remember several nights being in that back room and— because I could not be in the same bed as David because the baby would cry—and when that baby would wake up it was like you know you almost wanted to put a pillow over the head. And then there's where reality sets in and you get the baby and, "God, how could I think like that." Then I'm crying, you know, because. . . .

"Wow!" she said, wiping away her tears, "I didn't want to go into that. But that's probably why those years went by without— I told him so many years later, 'I don't want to have another child with you.' Because he didn't participate."

In responding, a subdued David gave a glimpse of his part in daily life when his son was an infant and of the way he had avoided his wife's distress. Although he said he understood Mary's position about not having more children, it seemed to me that David was still minimizing the impact of his wife's experience in a way that was not so different than it had been twelve years before. David's perspective on the gendered division of labor went beyond the division of domestic and childcare tasks to a gendered division of attentiveness to the activities and lives of others that contributes to the invisibility of women's work.[4]

> DAVID: Well, she kept a lot into herself, you know, crying by herself in the room with the baby, and stuff. And like she said, she slept in the other room a lot not to bother me, and I'd get up and go to work and I'm working. I don't know that there's anything wrong, and come home, and she'd have dinner ready, and I'd eat and fall asleep on the chair, and go to bed, and she'd be there with the baby. And I didn't really participate in doing a lot when he was real young, those first couple years. So I think that put a big damper on her thinking of having another child. Knowing another one would have the same thing and then thinking, well, I was in the same job— in the same rut at work. So she kind of figured I'd be the same way.
>
> MARY: [laugh] You *would* have. [with emphasis]

In their joint narrative, David and Mary elaborated their reasons for having only one child by appealing to David's own childhood, explaining it in terms of their son's medical condition, and blaming it on the physical and emotional burdens placed on Mary by David's failure to be a participant father. But their story did not end there. They had agreed that it was the husband who was to be the primary breadwinner, and the wife who was primarily responsible for caring for the children and for domestic work. They also agreed that the wife was responsible for birth control and thus for the timing and number of children. They agreed, in other words, on the gendered division of labor in parenting of children in general. Children, however, are born with particular physical characteristics, and those characteristics lead them to be placed in a specific sex category and to face certain gendered expectations (Fausto-Sterling 2000; Goffman 1977; West and Zimmerman 1987). Immediately after he and Mary told me that she would not have had another child with him because he was not a participant father, David raised the issue of his child's sex, and their previously clear-cut certainty that they would not have another child was called into question:

> DAVID: But I was content with the one myself. It was fine with me. Because he was a boy, too. Maybe if it was a girl, I think I would've really wanted a boy right away. Just something inside me. I wanted a son. I think—I don't know—some, a lot of, guys say, "No." Whatever. But I think most men would really honestly say—

MARY: Had we had a girl we probably would have had a second child.

DAVID: Yeah. Most, most men I think always want to have a boy, always want to have a son.

MARY: I didn't want to have girls, I wanted boys. So I was glad.

AUTHOR: So, you were OK with one? In terms of having a girl would you have wanted to try again?

MARY: Probably.

DAVID: I think we would have. I would have enforced it more than probably.

MARY: [laughing] He would have, yeah.

DAVID: Probably, yeah, yeah.

MARY: Yeah, most, most likely.

David and Mary gave, between them, four explanations for why they had an only child when their original plan had been to have at least two children: (1) it just happened, but it was alright because David's childhood had been like that of an only child; (2) their son was born with a medical condition and they did not want to go through that experience with another child; (3) David did not participate as a father of a young child and because of this Mary refused to have another child with him; and (4) their first child was a son and they would have had another if their first child had been a daughter. From one perspective these four stories may appear to contradict one another or to be successive approximations to the truth, but I see them rather as linked elements of a complex whole, as stories that David and Mary told me, told each other, and told themselves in order to make sense of their lives. Berger and Kellner (1970) described how couples work together to construct a story of "our marriage," a construction that feminist scholars have further examined in terms of gendered relations of power (Hackstaff 1999: 11–12). The carefully crafted shared story is often shattered by divorce and by the reassertion of the individual experiences of the spouses. Both David and Mary were trying to bring together sets of contradictory expectations in one life, in one marriage, and in one account of that marriage.

Their stories are not simply presentations of fact, but are cultural productions that make several points about the meaning of fatherhood in the United States: A man's experience of his own father is crucial for his sense of what it is to be a father, sons and daughters mean different things to fathers, women are the default caregivers, home ownership is a material condition for and expression of family life, and work and breadwinning are central to fatherhood. The generalizability of David and Mary's images of appropriate parenting comes not only from the similarity of their circumstances to those of many other Americans, but also because they are deploying the images, ideas, and terms of the dominant culture. The dominance and uniformity of basic cultural notions about gender relations and parenthood has been reported by writers about motherhood, who describe variations in emphasis and deployment rather than differences in norms (Garey 1999; Hays 1996; McMahon 1995; Walzer 1998). Mary did not invent the term "participant father," and David is not the only man to justify his absence from home with the importance of his work.

The Study: A Particular Time and Place

It is a basic tenet of ethnography that in important ways the universal is expressed in the particular—the generality of human experience is illuminated by examining the particular lives of particular people in particular places. The core group of men I describe in this book were born in the mid-1950s and graduated from the same northern California high school in the early 1970s. In my descriptions of these men I have used pseudonyms and have described their work and family situations in terms that protect their anonymity. I have changed the name of the town and high school to Meadowview and have left the county unnamed. The descriptions and statistics of high school, town, and county are, however, accurate representations of real places.

By the end of the twentieth century, Meadowview was a city of about one hundred and twenty-five thousand people in the global center of computer development and manufacturing known as the Silicon Valley, but in previous decades Meadowview was typical of the suburbs and suburban communities that were developed after World War II, matching baby boom with housing boom. Originally an agricultural town and canning center, Meadowview had a population of fewer than ten thousand in 1950. In the next ten years, during which the men in this study were born, the population grew to five times that number, and by 1970 it had doubled again to almost one hundred thousand.

I lived in the same metropolitan area as Meadowview from 1980 to 1992. Between 1989 and 1992, I visited Meadowview many times, studied the history of the high school, the town, and the surrounding area, traced men who had graduated from the high school, and conducted a series of in-depth interviews. Like any ethnographer, I learned a great deal from informal conversation, observation, and interaction. The quotations in this book are all drawn from tape-recorded conversations I had with thirty-nine men who had graduated from Meadowview High School in the early 1970s. I also interviewed eighteen men from other schools in the area who were their contemporaries, some of their female classmates, and some of the men's wives, parents, and former teachers. Most of the interviews were conducted in people's homes, but about a quarter took place in restaurants, parks, and offices. Of the thirty-nine men from Meadowview High School with whom I had extensive conversations, six were Hispanic and three were Asian American. Thirty were non-Hispanic White of various European ancestries. I describe the men I quote most extensively when they first appear and in Appendix 1. Three of them were Hispanic and two were Asian American. All spoke English as their primary language and all who had children spoke English in the home.

In 1970, when the men I describe were in high school, the population of Meadowview was almost 95 percent white and less than 1 percent black. In terms of the great bifurcation between black and white that dominates discussions of race in the United States, the town was overwhelmingly white, but in terms of racial–ethnic category, ancestry, country of origin, and ethnic identification, it was certainly not homogeneous.[5] More than one quarter of the population was either foreign born or had at least one foreign-born parent, and 23 percent of the population of the Meadowview High School enrollment area was either Spanish speaking or had a Spanish surname (United States Bureau of the Census 1972).

The heterogeneity of the community was reflected in the graduates of its high school. Of the two hundred and forty-seven young men who graduated from Meadowview High School in 1972, one hundred and seventy-five (71 percent) could be categorized as non-Hispanic White, fifty-six (23 percent) as Hispanic, thirteen (5 percent) as Asian American, and three (1 percent) as African American. The non-Hispanic White students included young men who had been born in Europe as well as the children, grandchildren, or more remote descendants of immigrants from a dozen European countries, as well as men whose parents had moved from various regions of the United States and North America. Similarly, the Hispanic students included young men whose immediate families came from Spain, from several countries in South and Central America, and from Mexico, as well as some whose ancestors had lived in California for generations. The thirteen Asian American students were descendants of immigrants from at least four countries.

Mary Waters (1990) combined analysis of responses to the 1980 census questions on ethnicity with interviews conducted in Pennsylvania and in the California county that includes Meadowview. Waters examined the ethnic identification of people whose parents were from different ethnic or national backgrounds. She described ethnicity as "optional" in two senses: as a supplement to identities based on other characteristics, not a core identity, and as a choice for people with several possible ancestral identities who can select between them or combine elements of several. So a family may eat corned beef and cabbage on St. Patrick's Day to mark their Irish heritage and celebrate Columbus Day to show that they are Italian American. Waters's analysis of the census data showed that this type of ethnic optionality is not only a local, but also a national phenomenon.

In describing their own ethnicity, the men I talked to spoke in the same terms as Waters's informants and frequently described strategic and situational choices. One man told me that until recently he had always listed "White" for his children's ethnicity. The elementary school district in which his children were enrolled was implementing a program of busing the children from his neighborhood in order to achieve desegregation of enrollment. However, minority children from his neighborhood would not be bused, since they were living in a "good, white neighborhood" and attending a "good, white school" already.[6] As a result of a conversation with his neighbor, a school counselor, the man recalled his wife's mother's Hispanic heritage and reregistered his children as Hispanic so that they would not have to be bused. I heard an almost identical story from a man who had always described himself as white, but had just discovered the category "Pacific Islander" and now used that.

In my interviews, the racial–ethnic category was not associated with different fundamental values about the place of fatherhood and family in men's lives, although some men did invoke their particular ethnic or cultural background to explain adherence to values that were in fact widely shared. I was struck by the way that men whose ancestry was Italian, Chinese, Irish, Portuguese, Filipino, or Mexican (none of whom spoke their ancestral language to their children) invoked, in almost identical terms, the "old country values" of their fathers as a support for the importance of family life, loyalty, and respect for the older generation. I found a remarkable degree of uniformity in men's depictions of the central elements of fatherhood, a discovery that mirrors the similar findings of a dominant image of motherhood by researchers who have studied diverse groups of mothers (Garey 1999; Hays 1996; Segura 1994; Walker 1990).

My study is not one of the racial–ethnic patterning of difference but is an investigation of the composition of, and internal contradiction within, a cultural model of successful male adulthood and fatherhood. While labels such as "Hispanic" and "Asian American" certainly point to important aspects of discrimination in the United States, they also accept a particular racializing division of people and obscure other crucial dimensions of difference. Denise Segura (1994), for instance, discovered that Latinas did not share a uniform orientation to motherhood, but rather that there were important distinctions between mothers who had immigrated from Mexico and Mexican American women who were themselves born and raised in the United States. To use the categories Hispanic or Latino to include Californians of Mexican descent whose families have been in the United States for several generations as well as immigrants from Mexico, Guatemala, Argentina, and other countries in Central or South America; or to classify as Asian American third-generation Chinese Americans as well as people who have themselves immigrated or whose parents immigrated from China, Japan, Vietnam, Korea, and the Philippines is not so much to recognize cultural difference as it is to impose dominant American patterns of discrimination and difference.

My interviews, which I quote in detail, revealed a basic pattern of goals and tensions that was shared by the men with whom I talked. I did not find that the Asian American or Hispanic men I talked to, or the men whose parents, grandparents, or more remote ancestors had come from various parts of Europe, had different visions of what it means to be a successful man and a successful father in the contemporary United

States. My conclusion is supported by the research of many others on parenthood in U.S. culture. Every specific study is, of course, subject to the limitations of its specificity, but, as the authors of so many of these specific studies point out, the findings of specific studies reveal a broadly shared and general picture.

Although I have not treated racial–ethnic categories as explanatory variables, I refer throughout this book to the pervasive racism and discrimination of U.S. culture and to the ways in which the dominant values of the culture exclude members of some groups from participation in the supposedly universal "American dream."

The men I talked with reflected the heterogeneity of the community, but they are a particular group, not a representative sample. The group does not include all types of men, it is class specific, all the men were avowedly heterosexual, and none of them was African American. Within the group, however, there was variation in opportunity and in outcomes. I deliberately chose men who were the same age and who went to school in the same town because it allowed me to learn about the circumstances of their lives in a way that would have been impossible if I had talked to a random sample of men from different parts of the country or of different ages.

My approach has been to examine the lives and words of people who accept the dominant values, who judge themselves by those standards, and who occupy social positions that enable them to realize those values to an extent that they can find acceptable. These men are "typical" in the sense that their lives and values represent the dominant cultural norms. It is worth noting that for men in the United States who were born in 1950, 95 percent were in the labor force at the end of the twentieth century, more than 90 percent have married, and almost 90 percent of their wives have had at least one child.

These men who had attended high school together had once been part of a shared face-to-face community. They no longer met daily at the same place, nor did they form their social groups and choose their activities in front of one another, as they had in high school. Almost twenty years after high school graduation they no longer all lived in the same town or shared the same experiences. They did, however, still form a community of sorts because they continued to share parts of a past (Ortner 1989, 1995). Some of them were married to former schoolmates, and many had friends with whom they had gone to school. Most important, all the men *knew about* and *talked about* other men who had gone to high school with them. The high school graduating class functioned as a reference group, a shared cast of characters who had "made good," "gone bad," or were "like me," and who provided a scale or standard against which to judge their own achievements.

While high school graduation is a common rite of passage in the United States, it is neither universal nor evenly distributed across racial–ethnic groups. The student body at Meadowview High School, for instance, had higher percentages of Hispanics and African Americans than the graduating class. African American and Hispanic students are less likely to complete high school than are non-Hispanic Whites.[7] The salience of high school graduation as a rite of passage and of high school classmates as a reference group varies. But the fact that they are very important to many people is indicated by the considerable industry devoted to organizing high school reunions and tracing high school classmates and by the frequency of references to high school classmates, graduations, and reunions in everyday conversation and popular culture. Vered Vinitzky-Seroussi (1998) observed several high school reunions and talked to people who attended them. She emphasized the ways that reunions function as occasions for comparison with the reference group of fellow graduates and the ways reunions function for individuals as "autobiographical occasions" at which people are expected to provide, for themselves as well as for others, culturally acceptable narratives and accountings of their lives. People's lives may be very different from, and are always much more complicated than, the narratives produced.

College graduates, who acquire new reference groups based on college attendance, credentials, and occupation, frequently underestimate the significance of high school attendance and graduation in the lives of the two-thirds of Americans for whom the high school diploma is their highest formal credential. In 1995, only one in ten of the men in the United States who were the same age as the men I talked to had not graduated from high school, and only one in four had a bachelor's or advanced degree. More than 60 percent of men of that generation had graduated from high school but not from college.[8] The men from Meadowview High School were, in their educational experience, typical of their generation. Many of them had attended a community college for some time, had an associate degree, or had taken vocational or work-related college classes. Those who did not have a college degree all hoped and intended that their children would attend college.

Several of the men had kept in close touch with a number of friends from high school, but it is not necessary for people to be in frequent or direct contact to form a reference group (Merton 1968: 337–42). Several men told me at our first meeting that they had not kept in touch with anyone from their high school, but many of them subsequently modified this. In the course of conversation they would mention someone from the high school who played on another team in their softball league, or was married to a coworker. Frequently, when I was talking to a man from Meadowview High School the mention of a classmate's name would elicit not only a memory but also current news. That person, I would be told, had "got divorced and moved to Modesto," "married Bill's sister," "had cancer," "is doing well in his business," or "died in prison." Men's knowledge of their former classmates was not formal and organized, but was embedded in a matrix of associations and could be retrieved to make a point or a comparison. This process is familiar to all of us: We meet someone whom we have known in another situation and remind each other of our respective histories by running through a mental list of the other people involved, reminding each other about them, and sharing our recent information about them. In the process our memories are refreshed and new information is contextualized. Repeated, even occasionally, these conversations keep us informed about a scattered group of people.

Even though this group of men are approximately the same age and from the same place, the choices they faced and the resources they could deploy differed significantly. The variety of their family backgrounds and the changes they have lived through have combined to cause variation in their experiences and in their current situations. Some had been only children and others had many brothers and sisters, some had married parents and others had been raised by single mothers, some lived with their parents into their twenties and others were autonomous at age sixteen. Some had been dedicated students and others had barely graduated from high school. Some of their parents were deeply religious Catholics, Baptists, Methodists, Lutherans, or Jews, whereas others were agnostic or uninterested. Some of their parents had been abusive or alcoholic and others had been encouraging and involved. Some lived in owner-occupied single-family houses and others in rented apartments. Their fathers had a range of jobs and incomes. Some had faced discrimination and others had received the benefits of invisible privilege. They were European American, Hispanic, or Asian American. Almost twenty years after graduating from high school, some had been married for almost that long and had teen-aged children, whereas others were newlyweds, had infant children, or did not have children. Some had gone to college and had advanced degrees and others had only their high school diploma. They lived in a variety of neighborhoods, in houses of different sizes, and earned different amounts of money at jobs ranging from delivery driver to doctor. I have resisted typologizing these men in terms of their current situations or their backgrounds because such typologies conceal as much as they reveal about variation, and because I want to pay attention to their lives as complex wholes.

Regardless of their differences, the men I talked to echoed David and Mary in their expression of the dominant cultural view of family life. All the men believed that the couple was the basic unit that should make decisions about reproduction and child raising, men should work outside the home and provide for their children, material success was an important indicator of success as a father, childcare was the primary responsibility of the mother, and the nuclear family living in a single-family home was the preferred residential and family arrangement.

I did not select these men because of their attitudes or because of any outstanding characteristic of their lives, but because of the apparent "ordinariness" of their lives as members of the middle class in the United States. I did not choose them because of where they were in their lives, but because of where they had begun—and because they had started together.

Meadowview's economic history has had a direct effect on the life courses and life chances of its high school graduates. Few of them were from families that had lived in the town for many years—at least 90 percent of the population in 1970 had arrived in the previous twenty years. During the men's childhood and adolescence, the town was growing very rapidly, high-paying manufacturing jobs were available, and houses were affordable. Their parents, as young couples, were riding the crest of the prosperity of the United States. Their fathers worked as salesmen, truck drivers, and construction workers, and as machinists and assembly workers in the factories of one of the nation's aerospace centers. Many of their mothers were also employed, but their employment histories had usually followed the common pattern for mothers of leaving the labor force or drastically reducing their hours when their children were young, and then resuming employment, often part time, as their children grew older (Moen 1985).

The young couples who flooded into Meadowview during the 1950s saw a good place to raise a family. Mike Martin, the California-born son of immigrants, had moved to Meadowview in the early 1960s with his parents. He remembered how his father had talked about the place and about his own first impressions:

> In those days, the late 1950s and the early 1960s, [my father] called Meadowview "the country." "We've got to move out to the country, so you can grow up in the country." I never really understood it. I was kind of excited, and when we got out here I can remember nothing but orchards, seeing orchards and "Wow, this is really the country." And it was great because there was a ton of fields around us where we could play.

In 1950, there were one hundred and thirty-five square miles of fruit, nut, and berry orchards in the county. By 1974 only 27 percent of that was left. Over the same period, almost half of the forty-one square miles of vegetable fields were built over.

The men I interviewed were born into the new houses and prosperity of the post–World War II "American dream." They were born in the 1950s, grew up in the 1960s, and came to adulthood in the 1970s. Their life stories should be understood in the context of their childhoods in the new postwar suburbs of California, the economic boom in military manufacturing that employed so many of their parents, the civil rights and antiwar movements of the late sixties when they were in high school, the women's liberation movement and changed expectations for women's lives of the seventies and eighties, the explosion in real estate prices that ruptured the relationship between work and home, the creation of a new technology and economy of which their community was at the epicenter, and the transformation of the southern San Francisco Bay Area into Silicon Valley.[9]

While these changes did cause some problems for them, and exacerbated some tensions, the men I talked to had in general benefited from the circumstances of their births. Men with similar aspirations living in regions such as the older industrial cities of the Northeast and Midwest that have declined economically have had very different experiences. In studies of those areas, Katherine Newman (1988) and Kathryn Dudley (1994) have written about the experience and meaning of downward mobility in the American middle class, about people who have been swept out of the American dream by the forces that have, in general, lifted the men I talked to and that have transformed Meadowview from a cannery town to the epicenter of unprecedented technological change and financial concentration.

In many ways the men from Meadowview were fortunate to have grown up when they did. Unlike their slightly older peers, they did not face the draft and military service in Vietnam.[10] And unlike their fathers, who were born before 1930, they did not have memories of growing up during the Great Depression (Elder 1974). When they graduated from high school they were able to find union jobs in construction or entry-level positions in the new computer industry, which allowed them to buy houses in neighborhoods like the ones in which they were raised and to live at a material level higher than that of their parents. Men ten years younger than they were in a very different position, for rapid rises in the price of houses, stagnation and decline in real wages, and higher educational requirements for jobs meant that their younger cohort have had to scale down their dreams (Goldscheider and Goldscheider 1993, 1994). Men who graduated in the early 1970s frequently told me that they would never have gotten the jobs they had, or risen as fast, if they had graduated from high school in the 1980s or 1990s.

That the men I talked to knew one another had two major implications for my research. The first was that introductions and personal references carried me easily from one person to the next. I was careful to start the process of introductions from several different people, so that the contacts I made were not all with members of a particular circle of friends or high school "clique." Only one of the men I contacted declined to talk to me. The second implication was that the men I talked to had a shared body of examples and references when they were talking about schoolmates who had done well or badly, significant events, and important influences. As a consequence, I frequently had additional perspectives on what I was told.

When talking to these men, I found that the similarities and differences between my life and theirs helped me to understand them and encouraged them to explain themselves to me. In many ways I was both an outsider looking in and an insider sharing important aspects of their experiences. To begin with, like those I spoke with, I am a man born in the middle of the baby boom. At the time of the interviews, I had lived and worked in northern California for twenty years, so I knew the places and the events the men talked about. I was familiar with, even if I did not always share, their cultural perceptions. But I was born and raised in England, which my accent makes obvious, so it seemed appropriate for me to ask some apparently naive questions about life in the United States that would have seemed strange coming from another American. Similarly, I had worked for several years in construction before I went back to college, so I understand blue-collar work. As an academic and a researcher, I could relate to the professional men I interviewed. In addition, I am the parent of two stepsons, so we could talk about our common experience of child raising. But the fact that my children were stepchildren gave me something in common with men who did not have biological children, and allowed the men who had biological children of their own to explain why they believed this was a special link.

Many of the men from Meadowview told me that they never talked about their feelings about family, fatherhood, and work, and several said that their wives would be amazed to hear them talk at such length about these things. Several men told me that talking to me was "like therapy." Regardless of the therapeutic value of our conversations, these comments indicated that these interactions were out of the ordinary. I do not doubt that these conversations were uncommon in their lives, but the issues that I raised are "in the air" for these men: Television programs, talk radio, magazines, and newspapers are full of images of family life, fatherhood, and success. These men may have produced longer and more elaborate stories when talking to me than they had in other situations, but their stories are crystallizations or condensations of existing attitudes and reactions.

In describing these men's lives I have tried to convey their points of view. This does not mean accepting uncritically what they said about their lives, or taking their self-defense or their condemnation of others at face value. Their accounts of their lives are selective and characterized by omissions and internal contradictions, but this is the human condition. What people say is inescapably partial and frequently self-serving. It is easy to identify the contradictions in their accounts, whether these are contradictions between accounts given at different times or for different purposes, contradictions between the values they espouse, or contradictions between their accounts and our perceptions of their lives. But the contradictions do not invalidate what they say, and simply identifying contradictions is not analysis. Tightly coherent accounts should be treated with skepticism, and, on the other hand, incoherent accounts should be treated sympathetically and analyzed carefully. Regardless of whether their accounts are coherent, people are telling us about the strains and conflicts in their values and their lives. Since these strains and conflicts are what make choices necessary, they are also telling us about the circumstances of their decisions and actions. It is these strains and conflicts, sometimes unexamined and buried deep beneath the details of everyday life, sometimes forced to our attention, that require us to engage in cultural work to create for ourselves, and for others, coherent and acceptable accounts of our lives and actions. By paying attention to what people say, and to what they do not say—to overemphasis and to passing mention, to hesitation and to word choice—we can see how they are negotiating cultural values (Mishler 1986; Plummer 1995).

Taking people's point of view enables us to see how they deal with complex and contradictory situations and values by doing cultural work to make sense of their lives. A man who feels that he is a financial failure, for instance, may attribute his failure to his own lack of ambition and ability or to the malevolent conspiracy of others. Without taking his account at face value, we can take his point of view in order to grasp his understanding of the situation in which he is living, the things he is trying to achieve, and the resources available to him. One effect of this shift of focus is to change the level of analysis from individual characteristics to a system of interactions in which individuals are enmeshed. A feeling of personal inadequacy is an individual sentiment, but the distribution of men's incomes, the correlation between income and class or racial–ethnic background, and the notion that a man's worth is to be judged by his income are features of social structure and culture. The individual sentiment, in other words, must be seen in relation to a set of circumstances that transcend any individual. None of this is to excuse cases of personal hypocrisy, self-deception, or abuse of others. Sometimes the men's comments clearly show the impact of their child-rearing practices on their sons and daughters, or the impact of their ways of being husbands on their wives, and sometimes the impact can be surmised, but my central concern is to comprehend how they construct themselves as men and as fathers in order to better understand their actions.

"Dominant cultural values" and "material circumstances" have specific and concrete referents. Discussing dominant cultural perspectives is a way of talking about the values, hopes, memories, and fears of specific people. The material circumstances of their lives include their houses and neighborhoods, their employment, the schools their children attend, and the opportunities they face. When men say they want to raise their children in a good neighborhood of single-family, owner-occupied homes, they are expressing a dominant cultural vision of what family life should be like. When they discover that their incomes only allow them to buy a house in that kind of neighborhood if they move miles away from their work and commute for several hours a day, they are being constrained by their material circumstances. It is in order to see how dominant cultural values about fatherhood are embodied and negotiated in individual lives that I have concentrated my description on men from a particular time and place.

The Pattern of the Book

In the next chapter I describe the package deal as it appeared in the lives of the men I talked to and explain how they tried to achieve their composite goal by following a culturally approved life script. In each of the following four chapters I examine one of the four elements of the package deal.

In Chapter 3 I describe the four facets of fatherhood: emotional closeness, provision, protection, and endowment and list the contributions of each element of the package deal to each facet of fatherhood in Table 1. The figure at the end of Chapter 3 depicts the relationships between the four elements of the package deal and the four facets of fatherhood. Together the table and figure encapsulate the argument of the book.

In Chapters 4, 5, and 6 I explore marriage, employment, and home ownership as elements of the package deal and examine their different contributions to the four facets of fatherhood. I situate fatherhood in the context of the cultural systems of kinship and gender in Chapter 7, showing how the cultural constitution of contemporary fatherhood in the United States contributes to the reproduction of gendered social relations. In the final chapter I suggest some of the implications of my analysis for understanding and changing fatherhood.

2 Package Deals and Scripts

> I just always kind of imagined myself grown up, being married, having two kids. Ever since I can remember. I never thought I wouldn't want kids. Never even gave that consideration, that I would just be married and not have kids, it was just all part of the package. —*Phil*

To BE a father is to reconcile competing ideals, demands, and responsibilities: time spent with children against money earned, the kind of house you live in against the length of your commute, your responsibility as a husband against your responsibility as a father, and within yourself the reconciliation of being simultaneously your father's son and your own son's father. To be an adequate father is to put together a "package deal" of work, marriage, home, and children.[1] Not every father is married or works outside the home, but every father constructs, for himself and for others, a story about his life that takes into account the four elements of the package deal.

For the men I talked to, plans and projects were directed toward a composite goal, their decisions about one element took into account their situation with regard to the other elements, and their judgments of their own success were multidimensional. The idea that fatherhood is a part of a composite goal or package deal is not as obvious or trivial as it may at first appear, and it needs to be restated and acknowledged in our everyday thinking, in academic research, and in policy. Too frequently, discussions of fatherhood separate paternity from the rest of men's lives and treat decisions about children, marriage, and work as if they were independent. Although human goals may always be composite, the particular composition of the package deal of successful fatherhood expressed by the men from Meadowview High School and the particular approved way of living that it embodied was specific to a place and time. That the composition of the package is widely understood and hegemonic should not conceal the fact that in practice it is neither inevitable nor universally achieved.

The dominant vision of successful fatherhood as embodied in the package deal can oppress and exclude men in the United States in three ways. First, even when the men are successful this dominant cultural image traps many of them in lives of "quiet desperation." We hear this desperation in men's comments about their sense of being caught in the "rat race," of hurrying all the time to keep place, and of not measuring up to their own expectations even when they appear to be doing the right thing. Second, the dominant cultural image portrays men as failures when they cannot meet the expectations of the package deal (Dudley 1994; Newman 1988; Rubin 1994; Sennett and Cobb 1972; Wilson 1996). Third, the dominant cultural vision is actively deployed as a tool of exclusion. Exclusion from one or more elements of the package deal is a way to exclude men from full fatherhood, full masculinity, and full personhood. In a precursor to his famous "I have a dream" speech, given in Detroit in 1963, Martin Luther King addressed the issues faced by African Americans in the North. Even in the absence of the legal segregation of the South, he identified three key areas of exclusion: in jobs, in housing, and in schools. In terms of the package deal, African American men were being excluded from three key elements: employment, home ownership, and the ability to endow their children with opportunities. These exclusions extend to gay men when they are denied contact with children or when they are denied the culturally approved definitions of closeness by not being allowed to marry.

That the package deal comes so naturally to mind as an image when we think about men's attitudes indicates its cultural fit. Ralph Colson, who had risen through the ranks to supervise safety procedures for a large manufacturing plant, was a calm, soft-spoken man who was described with respect and admiration by everyone who remembered him from high school. His account of his marriage, the birth of his first child, his career development, and buying his house illustrate how these elements of the package deal (marriage, children, employment, and home ownership) were integrated in his thoughts and actions:

> So I was gonna start in July. So my wife and I planned our wedding. I told her we'd get married as soon as I got hired by the department because it was a much more stable job. And so we planned our wedding for June and I started working here as a [temporary worker]. I was here two months and they had an interview and I went through the interview process and was selected and had to start July 1 and

> our wedding was set for June 25. So we got married four days before I got hired. Cut the honeymoon short and reported for duty July 1. That's how I got started. We were married. I got through my probation and we bought a house. And we started discussing about having children and at the same time we discussed that I needed to start preparing myself for a promotion. So I went to the local community college and signed up and we discussed the time it would take. And then I was enrolled in the classes. Everything was set to go. And the very first class started on September 9. The reason I remember that was because my daughter was born at eight that morning and I was in class at one that afternoon. I remember going to the class and passing out cigars to everybody and stuff. And the instructor says, "What are you doing here? If my wife had a baby I wouldn't be here." I said, "I talked to her. The baby is fine. I was driving my wife nuts and the nurses nuts because I was holding my daughter so much." I was right there when she was born because I was so excited. We continued on and then I got promoted.

Ralph's story illustrated clearly how his decisions about work, marriage, buying a house, and having children were interrelated both practically and in his own thinking. It also illustrated that the elements were combined in an appropriate sequence. This interrelationship also came out in the account I was given by Skip Barnes, a design engineer with two children who sat forward in his chair and concentrated all his attention on me as he explained how his family worked. Skip's narrative expressed his ideas about child development and the gendered division of labor, as well as his knowledge of the realities of mortgage payments, commuting, and the scheduling of everyday life, presenting a composite picture of how life should be:

> Well, [my wife] originally was working in the electronic industry with me. That's when we met. But after we got married, we decided the best thing for her to do was to spend time with the children and to raise the children so they don't grow up in a baby-sitter environment. Because most of the time, when they're awake, they're at the baby-sitter and the baby-sitter has a very large influence on their life and how they are being brought up. And we really didn't want that to happen. So we made the decision that she would quit work, stay home, and we'd try to make it as best we could. It's pretty tough giving up one complete income. But it worked out for the better. She

> stayed home and took care of my daughter and when my son was born, the same thing, she stayed home so she could influence them the way that she wanted to. I personally think it's very important, when children are first born, they are very influential [easily influenced], to mold them the way you want to. I know a few people that I work with are single parents or they're a married couple with small children, but their mortgage payment is so doggone high that both parents *have to* work. So the child goes to daycare all day. And they're exposed to all these different things, and all these other little children, and they're a little older and they are pulled and pushed and shoved, and throw things. So they grow up not knowing, "Jeez, is this the way life is going to be? Picking on me all my life?" . . . You have these poor children who have to get up at five in the morning to make it to the baby-sitter, that's really rough on them. That's where I feel pretty strongly. They need their sleep. You have to get them to bed at seven if you're going to get them up at five.

Skip told a complicated story about how his life had been and about how family life should be. Some of the complexity came from the number of topics he addressed simultaneously, and some from the many implicit assumptions he made. One of his basic assumptions, the centrality of work in men's lives, was explicit. Skip made it clear that the decision he and his wife faced was whether she would quit work to stay home with the children. That Skip should be a "stay at home dad" or a full-time homemaker was not an option that the Barnes had considered. If only one of them was going to work, it would be him. Other men presented the decision to have one spouse work and one stay home as a much more open choice, even though their "choices" resulted in the same outcome. The assumption or assertion that their lives were governed by their choices was a central element of these men's life stories, but it was an assumption that obscured the cultural and social realities that impose a remarkably uniform division of labor. Even widely held attitudes were described to me as the personal opinions of autonomous individuals, as when Skip said, "I personally think it's very important, when children are first born . . . to mold them the way you want to." With a different view of the origin of values he might have said that this was a fact, or a religious duty, or a custom of his people, but instead he presented a commonplace and unexceptional position as his own personal belief and responsibility.

The assumptions behind Skip's account of the combination of elements in his family life are so widely accepted that they are frequently taken for granted, but cross-cultural comparison and recognition of variation within a setting show that they are, indeed, cultural assumptions and not facts of nature. Among these assumptions are that if a couple is to live on one income it will be that of the husband, the first years of a child's life are crucial,[2] a mother's influence on her children may be consciously directed, making arrangements for the care of children is the responsibility of the couple acting alone (not, as might be expected elsewhere, of the children's grandmothers or other senior kin), and, in general, the married couple constitutes an autonomous unit.

In his presentation of the autonomous couple as a decision-making unit, Skip was in accord with a great deal of social science research on family and parenting that builds on a "rational actor" model of human behavior and that emphasizes the determinants of decision making and the costs and benefits of outcomes, including children (Becker 1976; Easterlin 1978). His assumptions allowed him to move easily from one topic to another, presenting a picture in which marriage and the division of labor between husband and wife, child development and childcare, mortgage payments and wages, commuting and daily scheduling, all fit together.

The life stories of the men I talked to and their discussions of work and fatherhood revealed individual variation but also a general agreement about the appropriate place of fatherhood in a man's life, about what it means to be a successful father, and about the preferred sequencing of events over the course of a life. The normative sequence of life events, or "script," allowed men to incorporate into a life course multiple activities and lifestyles that could not be combined simultaneously.

Scripts and Sequences

The script as a description of a life, whether it is the narrator's own life story or an account of another person's life, should include the important events of that life. But the script differs from a mere list of events in that the narrator *makes sense of* these events by connecting them in a plausible account of cause, effect, and motivation. The idea of the life script has a long history and a wide application in the human sciences. For some writers drawing their inspiration from Freud (1965: 294–99), the script is internalized early in life and becomes something to "blindly follow" (Steiner 1974: 64). The interactionist use of the term, however, derives from Simmel's observation: "Our inner life, which we perceive as a stream, as an incessant process, as an up and down of thoughts and moods, becomes crystallized, even for ourselves, in formulas and fixed directions often merely by the fact that we verbalize this life" (1971: 352). In this view, which has been elaborated in the United States by a range of researchers influenced by George Herbert Mead (Prus 1996), the script and the life are mutually constructed in a sequence of interactions. The interpretive task becomes not to assign priority to script or action, but to understand the meanings and normative directions embedded in the life stories we tell (Mishler 1986; Plummer 1995). The sense of the script as both directive and descriptive, as embodying cultural ideals and simultaneously being deployed to influence behavior, has been developed in its application to family life in an influential article, "Kinscripts," by Carol Stack and Linda Burton (1993). They show how kinscripts ascribe specific roles and express particular expectations people use to justify their own behavior and to affect the actions of others. Scripts, in this sense of the word, speak to specific instances at the same time that they embody general cultural norms.

Jim Mitchell, for instance, included the normative idea of stable monogamy and a cultural notion about the needs of young men into the chronology of his own life:

> I thought when I got married I would stay married to one woman the rest of my life, and only one woman. I knew if that was going to happen I wouldn't be able to get married at a young age because I was too into playing sports and too into having fun. What I figured was I'd probably get married about twenty-five, wait about three to five years, make sure the marriage was sound and then have kids, starting at about thirty.

Physically strong and vigorous, Jim spoke quietly in our conversations. A skilled artisan, he had moved from job to job, supplementing his regular income by working as a gardener and handyman. When I met him he was separated from his wife, Monica, who was living in the family house where their two young children spent most of their time. Jim set out a sequence of life events that he thought was both likely and appropriate. I describe this as a "script" to mean both a description of what has happened in a man's life and a set of directions for what should happen. In this double aspect, the script is typical of cultural productions, which are simultaneously descriptions of and rules for behavior (Geertz 1973; Hammel 1990).

The life story or sequential narrative of events is a culturally specific production. What it means to make sense of one's life, or to find a life morally justifiable, varies from situation to situation. The pattern I am describing here is, however, of long standing and wide distribution among cultures originating in Europe. The life script these men were following had enough flexibility that considerable variation in life course could be justified and reconciled. But there are limits to the flexibility, and in cross-cultural comparison those limits are quite narrow. There was, for instance, no room for polygamy or polyandry, for long-term extended family coresidence, for many more than three children, or for very large age differences between husband and wife, all of which have been elements of other systems of family and reproduction and elements of other male scripts (Townsend 2002).

When people talk about their lives, they do not give exhaustive lists of everything they have done. Rather, they select events that seem to them significant and connected and weave them together into life stories that they find coherent and morally justifiable. They also produce life stories that they want other people to find understandable and acceptable.

Greg Turner's discussion of why he got married and had children when he did was very similar to Jim Mitchell's and illustrated both the descriptive and the prescriptive aspects of the script. He described what happened in his life and provided an explanation or justification of what he had done:

> Well, I was twenty-nine when I got married. And I waited. Kind of got everything out of my system before I got married. And then, when I did get married I wanted it to be forever, as they say, and I was ready to have kids. When I got married I was ready to have kids. I probably had it planned in my mind: "We'll get married and we'll have children." I think you just get to a certain age and you just kind of know that you want to settle down. And I didn't want to be forty years old and start a family because I didn't want to be real old when

> my kids were growing up. I mean I still consider myself quite young and I didn't want to— I still want to be able to do things with my kids as they grow older. That was a big factor. . . . But that was my limit. I didn't want to go beyond thirty and then have to worry about feeling, you know, dealing with getting married and having kids. I just sort of stretched it out as long as I wanted to, I think.

Waiting to get married until he had "got everything out of his system" and was "ready to have kids" but also not wanting "to be real old when my kids were growing up" were two potentially competing desires that interacted to restrict the timing of his marriage to a culturally appropriate period within the much larger range that is physically possible. Greg's desires seemed natural to him and struck him as giving a satisfactory explanation for what he had done. He expected others to find them acceptable, and his reference group (his peers, his family) also found them acceptable. They were part of a "vocabulary of motives" or "normative repertoire" that operated within his social situation.[3]

The reasons people give for their actions are socially situated in the sense that they must be accepted by the participants in a particular social setting. There must be a shared understanding of these reasons and an agreement about when they are appropriate, so that reasons are not independent and arbitrary expressions but are linked with one another. The people involved, whether they are in direct interaction or members of a reference group, agree that there is a set of motives that can be deployed to explain a particular kind of action and another set that would not be considered as explanations or motives and would be questioned if presented. The narratives or scripts that people give as explanations of their lives simultaneously direct, justify, describe, and rationalize action. But they do none of these completely, and through their ambiguity and vagueness allow a range of interpretations. They are, in fact, pragmatic productions brought forth for particular purposes and elaborated and systematized only so far as is necessary for the job at hand.

The sequence of life events described to me as both an expectation and an achieved reality will be familiar to most Americans. These men had an image of the male life course that is generally held in the United States (Buchmann 1989; Cooney and Hogan 1991; Elder 1974; Hareven 1986; Hogan 1981). The basic ordering of events in this culturally approved life course for a man is to complete an education, to get a job, to move out of his parents' home and live independently, to date a number of women, to meet the woman he wants to marry, to spend time as a couple, to set up a home together, to buy a house, and to have children.

CULTURAL SPECIFICITY AND VARIATION

The morally approved sequence of life events varies from society to society and, within the United States, from class to class. Successfully achieving this particular sequence of events depends on a combination of circumstances. Getting a job and becoming financially independent as a young man, for instance, depends on an economy that is generating enough good jobs, just as buying the home he wants depends on the state of the real estate market. The basic order of life events is culturally variable and variably evaluated. In rural Botswana, to take an example with which I am familiar, if a young man in his early twenties set up a household with his wife and his own children and supported them alone, thereby following the Meadowview script, he would be considered totally irresponsible and would be described as "lost" by his parents. A young man in Botswana was expected to help supoort other family members and to rely on them for vital resources (Townsend 1999; Townsend 2002). His well-being over his life course depended on his access to the land, cattle, and social support controlled by his elders, and his responsibility as a young man was to work and remit his earnings to his parents, to his mother's brother, and to his wife's or fiancée's parents. So the script of events in the life of a Tswana man reflects a fundamentally different evaluation of the needs and capacities of people of different ages and of the pattern of responsibility for children.[4]

This southern African example, which is just one of a multiplicity of different patterns, disrupts our sense that the Meadowview script is somehow natural and inevitable. Not only is that script only one among many cultural variants, there is also patterned variation within the group of men I interviewed. A clear-cut example of variation is that dividing men for whom high school graduation was the terminus of their education and those who intended to earn a college degree. Earning a degree involves, for most men, a delay in financial independence and blurs or complicates the sequence of stages. The difference between having a high school diploma and a college degree is strongly connected to the difference between having a job and a career—a difference that has an impact on marriage and fathering, as I discuss in Chapter 5.

There is also a great deal of variation among men in the details of the sequencing of their lives and in their adaptation to contingencies. The men whose lives I describe have not each experienced all of the events listed in the script, and many of them have experienced these events in an order other than the prescribed one (Hogan 1978). One man, for instance, got married in high school because his girlfriend was pregnant, while another did not get married until he was over thirty and had his first child at age thirty-six. Frank found well-paying work while he was in college and never graduated, while Jack completed his college degree but has since worked at jobs that did not require it. Some of these men bought a house while they were still single, while others, married with children, rented their homes. Some men's search for the right woman was ended by the pregnancy or insistence of their future wives; others married women who they subsequently divorced. Some had children when they planned to; others had early, unexpected, or "accidental" births or acquired "instant families" through marriages to women with children; and some had no biological children. Some married before they completed their education, others before they had jobs. Some had children before they were financially secure, others were well established before they even thought of marriage and children. Underlying all these variations, however, was a broad notion of the appropriate sequence, and departures from that sequence were generally justified in terms of the script itself. For example, getting married while still in college was justified by the expectation of secure employment after graduation, having children before buying a house on the grounds that the house was already planned, and so on. Just as these men's statements about the normative value of fatherhood were variations on a theme, so too were the sequences of their lives variants of a common script.

Within this general pattern the script provides room for alternatives or variations. For example, when Barry Richards said of having children: "You can either have them when you're real young and that way they're grown and out of the house while you're still young, or you can wait until you're older and have fun first," he expressed two alternative sequences. Either one is justifiable, and both justifications acknowledge the desire for a period of "fun" in an adult life and assume that "fun" is incompatible with the day-to-day work of raising children. Both alternatives also assume that a man will have a few children whose births will be relatively close together, so that he will be the parent of young children for only a few years.

SCRIPTS IN PRACTICE

Greg Turner was the only man I talked to who had taken on the primary day-to-day care of his children, who were then aged six and eight, and even for him this pattern was described in terms of a temporary departure from the norm and one that contributed to his overall progress through an approved sequence. Greg had taken a job in a manufacturing plant right after he had graduated from high school and had developed specialized skills. Technological change, however, had made his skills obsolete, and although he had kept his job he had not received pay raises and had no prospects for promotion. His wife, Maggie, who had also gone to work after high school, had developed skills and abilities in office administration that had led her, when she returned to full-time work when her youngest child was three, to rapid promotion to a relatively well-paid position of responsibility. While her supervisors valued her ability, Maggie had reached the highest level she could without a credential. Greg and Maggie had decided that it made sense for Maggie to devote herself to completing the coursework for a credential and that, while working full time, she could do this in one year if she had only minimal domestic responsibilities. Greg had, therefore, quit his job to take care of house and children, with the understanding that once Maggie had her credential and promotion, she would return to her maternal duties and he would return to school. So Greg described his role as the stay-at-home father as a temporary departure that would allow him to "get back on track" with a new career.

Greg elaborated on the overall sequence of life stages when he talked about what it meant to have children. The alternation of phases and orientations was striking in Greg's account:

> You know we [my wife and I] talked about this just the other day. We can't remember not having them. Once they're here it's almost like your life stops at that point and you start a new life and you kind of forget a life before. I mean, not completely. I mean you still remem-

ber. It's like it starts at the point where we had the child and we just don't remember not having them, you know. I think that's going to be a hard day to have your children leave your home, but if you have the right attitude toward life you can start a new— almost like another section of your life that you and your wife can pick up. And then, "Hey I don't have the kids here, we can go there or if we want to go to the Bahamas or something." Hopefully then you'll have money and stuff and you can do that kind of stuff, you know, and kind of start another new section of your life, and go have fun for us. You know, we've spent eighteen or twenty years raising these girls and we've put all of our time and effort into them and, like I said, we still have a life of our own, and someday once we get our children raised I want to be able to take my wife and have fun. We may be fifty years old, but you know, I still don't consider that too old to go out and have fun, do a lot of fun things. But, I think the initial moment of them walking out the door and leaving your home is going to be like shattering, but you gotta have the attitude, "Well, OK, fine. This gives us a chance to do what we want to do."

In the accounts I was given, major life events and transitions were often presented as "overdetermined" in the sense that they were seen as natural or inevitable but equally often seemed "undermotivated" in the sense that they had not been the result of conscious deliberation and were not justified with specific reasons. Because moving through the sequence as a whole was taken for granted, the individual steps did not have to be considered anew, but seemed to follow naturally one after another. Greg, for instance, told me he had always wanted to have children, but when I asked if he and Maggie had talked about having kids he replied, "Sure. Yeah. I mean in a roundabout way. We didn't— We didn't say, "OK, next week we're going to start having kids" or something like that. We both knew that we both wanted them, but it wasn't really a specific thing we talked about before."

Just as Greg and Maggie had approached having the children they knew they wanted without much conscious planning or deliberation, Jim said he knew he had wanted to be married but was imprecise about his reasons for marrying: "I think it was just the time in my life I knew I wanted to have kids and be married—not just *have* kids and marriage but I wanted to *be married*." Jim did, however, have a clear sense of the sequence or script to follow after marriage. At that point, his expectation was explicit and concrete enough to be a guide for action. For Jim, marriage meant not only commitment to one woman, but also the responsibility of home ownership. Jim was very clear on the connection of those two elements of the package deal: "We started making marriage plans and talking about where to live." The requirements for a house were affordability and staying in the area. They bought a three-bedroom, one-bathroom house in an older neighborhood and put a lot of work and energy into fixing it up—refinishing the hardwood floors, painting inside and out, replanting the yard, and buying furniture and drapes. Their intention, when they bought the house, was to "make it nice" and move up to something larger after about five years:

> We were just extending ourselves like anyone else at that time of our marriage, and working hard and doing overtime so we could recoup again. Just doing our little ups and downs, buying and saving, buying and saving. We both felt, like, that we had reached a point in our lives when we had made the house comfortable and we wanted to add a child to that house— to our lives.

For Jim, marriage meant both emotional and material stability, and it meant preparing a home as the material expression of readiness to have children.

Jim made a direct comparison to others as he described what he did and what he expected. The phrase "like anyone else at that time of our marriage" worked in retrospect to explain the course of his life, and we may suppose that it worked at the time to justify to the young couple why they were working hard and "extending" themselves. This appeal to the universality of the script, to the idea that "everyone does it," is an example of a frequent rhetorical device these men used in telling their life stories.

Mike Martin was as driven and ambitious as Jim was easygoing, but Mike, too, explicitly denied the need to make plans for children because "that's everybody's plan":

> We didn't talk about having kids. Well, we talked about we'd have cute kids because they'd be half and half. That's the kind of talk we had. But we never talked about having them. We assumed we would end up having children, because if you're going to get married, that's everybody's plan.

By making a distinction between planning and the kind of conversations that couples actually have, he gives us an idea of how couples who talk together about having "cute kids" come to "know" that both want them.

The kind of conversation in which a couple says they will have cute children because they are themselves a cute couple only makes sense if they assume they will have children, but it does not require that they have ever had an explicit discussion about children, or that they have made explicit plans or decisions. In fact, as with so much human interaction, this is just the kind of conversation that allows people to "know what each other think" without either of them saying it. It is a way of finding out, establishing, or assuming a position without having to have the potentially disruptive or confrontational interaction that direct interrogation would involve.

Mike's story included other glimpses of the specific interactions between people that take place all the time and are subsumed under the general heading of "finding the right woman and getting married." Mike told me that in his early twenties he had partied heavily and dated widely. When he became engaged, he made some changes—quitting his job in the entertainment business because he and his fiancée both knew that he met a lot of women at work and would be tempted to resume his party lifestyle. Nevertheless, the engagement ended because Mike's fiancée thought he had no prospects. Mike started dating again, but with the aim of getting married. Speaking of his wife, he said:

> We were only acquainted for about two months and then we got engaged. I was kind of in the position where I wanted to be married. I was engaged once before. But it was a neat feeling, because I always wondered after Samantha and I broke up, "Well, who's going to be that person, because it's definitely not going to be her now." And that was exciting, even though it was heartbreaking, it was very exciting. And it was exciting to meet those new somebodies. There was maybe ten or twelve or fifteen somebodies in between that I thought that I could possibly get married to. I was always looking for a wife. I wanted to settle down.

Like the other men, Mike was vague about why he wanted to get married in the first place—"I wanted to settle down"—but this vague sense of what he wanted nevertheless directed his actions.

Through social interaction, dating, and casual conversation, individuals who are following cultural scripts become sorted into couples who "just know" that they want to get married and have children. They do not simply follow a script, they reinforce it. We can see how this process works if we consider the issue raised by Jim and Barry about the appropriate age for a man to have children. These men constructed a relatively narrow age span in which they felt it was appropriate to become fathers: old enough to be ready, not too old to be able to have fun with their children or to be old when their children are grown.

Many men explained the narrow age range in terms of the age they would be as their children grew up. Roy Warner's wife wanted to have another child, but Roy did not. Roy, who was thirty-six and married for the second time, with a six-year-old son and two stepdaughters, expressed a common sentiment:

> You keep thinking of how old you are, and how old your children, your son or daughter, are going to be when you're this age, or this age, because I want to involve my kids. One of my fantasies is— I play a lot of sports, mainly softball. I play about four nights a week. I'm really into it. And one of my fantasies is, when my son is old enough to play ball, hopefully I'll still be active to where we can still play. It's a normal fantasy. I'm sure lots of fathers have the same ideas.

Having talked to a number of fathers, I can confirm that Roy's fantasy is normal, at least in the sense that "lots of fathers have the same ideas." His sense of an appropriate age to have children, so that he would not be too old when his children were growing up, is culturally and historically specific. In colonial America, and in many other societies, men routinely continued to father children into their fifties and sixties. Not only did they not worry that they would be too old to play sports with their children, but even the knowledge that they might well die before their children reached adulthood was not a deterrent to fatherhood. What mattered to them was that their children be provided for.

The cultural norm that Roy expressed so clearly was born out in practice: Ninety-two percent of the children born in the United States in 1982 (when the class of 1972 was ten years past graduation and its birth rate was at its highest) were born to men between twenty and forty and 82 percent were born to men aged between twenty and thirty-five (National Center for Health Statistics 1986: 95).[5] When men, following the script, start having children in their twenties and stop in their early thirties, they contribute to a society in which fathers are, on average, twenty-eight years older than their children. When the men look around them, they see this age difference, and their sense that it is appropriate is reinforced by their perception that it is universal.[6]

The flexibility of the script allowed men to construct coherent accounts of their lives as deliberately planned even when many of the events of those lives were the result of idiosyncratic circumstances. Frank Smedley, a design engineer, was typical in the way he talked about decision making and about the way his life had unfolded. On the one hand, Frank wanted to present himself as a planner and to take credit for having made sensible decisions; on the other hand, many of the features of his life were the result of "accidents" that had turned out well or that Frank could at least describe as having turned out well. After high school, he had not been sure what he wanted to do. He drove a delivery truck for a couple of years, then went to community college and started working nights as a machinist. He had the opportunity to go to college for a professional degree, but the training was long and the eventual prospects seemed poor. He decided to continue working as a machinist and stay in school to get an engineering degree but moved within the company to a position in design, stopped attending college, and has worked since in positions of increasing managerial responsibility for the same company. In his twenties he was "too busy with the guys and messing around" to think about having children, but just before he met his wife he "started thinking about settling down and having a family." His parents helped him buy a house when he got married. Went I met Frank, he and Carol had been married for six years and had three children.

The number of children and the amount of schooling that Frank had, the work he did, and the house he lived in were in a sense things he had chosen or decided on, but in another sense were things that had happened to him. They were all, however, within the range of what his script could embrace, so it was relatively easy for him to tell me, and himself, a life story that made sense as a series of appropriately timed decisions leading toward the realization of the package deal. Frank expressed the common connection between marriage and children:

> I wasn't necessarily looking for somebody that *just* wanted to have children, but that was definitely a piece of the puzzle that *had to be there*. And if that piece of the puzzle wasn't there, I probably

> wouldn't have committed to the marriage. That was a *very important piece*. That was just a percentage of what had to be in place. Definitely had to be there.

When Frank switched between "definitely" and "probably" as he wondered whether he would have "committed to the marriage" if his wife had not wanted children, he was doing more than expressing the difficulty of answering counterfactual hypothetical questions or of conveying a high probability. His image of "the piece of the puzzle that had to be there" is indicative of a way of looking at life choices as interconnected parts of a whole. A piece of a puzzle is not simply additive to the other pieces. A puzzle with a piece missing is incomplete, it does not work, the picture cannot be seen, and trying to put it together is pointless. And a piece of a puzzle on its own is without value. The pieces do not have their own separate fractional worth; they make sense only in combination. In this image of life, decisions are made sequentially, but always with an eye to how they fit into a pattern of other decisions and reactions, past, present, and future. Frank's life story, and the life it was about, was not so much assembled piece by piece as brought into focus.

When I interviewed Frank and Carol at the same time, they agreed that they were "absolutely" sure that they would have no more children. I asked if they had thought about how many children to have before they started, and Frank replied:

> Yeah, we talked about it before we got married. We discussed family and it was important how many kids we felt we wanted to have and what we wanted to do with our lives before we made that big step. We had planned on having two. And we were hoping to have a boy and a girl.

Frank explained that their decision to have two children was made in the light of their judgment of how long they could afford to live on one income while Carol stayed home with the children:

> We wanted to be financially stable enough that we could survive on one income, for that five- or ten-year span, depending on how many children we decided to have. And that was the main concern with having children. We felt that was important: to bring up our own kids, not somebody else. That's a responsibility that I think the parents have: to bring their kids up. And unfortunately that's not the

> view of a lot of people, but it was our own personal feeling. We wanted to raise our own children.

In spite of their plan to have two children, Frank and Carol ended up with three:

> We had planned on having two. And we were hoping to have a boy and a girl. The first two were girls, so the third one was a boy. Ideally we would have liked one of each. But we're not complaining with three. Really didn't plan to have three children. At the time we had the two girls we were planning to stop then and having our son was an accident. And luckily the accident ended up working out good in the long run.

Interested in the possible gender preferences behind Frank and Carol's desire for "one of each" I asked Frank if he had actively wanted a girl. "Yes," he said. My next question, "If you had two boys would you have wanted to try for three?" elicited a response of real uncertainty: "I don't know. I really don't know. Probably. Probably." This was understandable. After all, I was asking a deeply hypothetical question and was probing a potential contradiction in his story. However, Frank's hesitation evaporated at the next question: "Would you have gone on if you'd had three girls?" Frank's emphatic "Yeah" was interrupted by Carol's only half joking answer: "If we'd had three girls he would have killed me." Having a son, although it was concealed by his wanting two children, by financial considerations, by concern that his wife could stay home to raise the children, and by his fondness for girls in general and his daughters in particular, was central to Frank's vision of the good life. He went on with animation: "Yeah, that was a real concern for me. I was the last male with our last name in our family. And so the boy was real important. In fact, at least for me, I wanted a son to carry on our name." He explained how his great-grandfather had come from Europe and his only son (Frank's grandfather) had had two sons and a daughter. The daughter could not carry on the name, and Frank's paternal uncle had a daughter, so it was up to him, his father's only son, to produce a boy.

Frank's script incorporated two goals. On the one hand he wanted to achieve the package deal of male employment and financial security, homemaker wife, and two children—a boy and a girl. On the other hand, he deeply desired a son. The two were not in necessary conflict: If Frank's first or second child had been a son, his script would have carried him seamlessly to his first goal while also achieving his second. As it was, an unplanned pregnancy and the fortuitous birth of a son had allowed Frank to avoid a direct contradiction. He was spared the cultural work of reconciling himself to having daughters only, or the financial and emotional burden of having many children in order to have a son. The script, which appears at first to have directive power, is realized as a flexible story with ample scope to incorporate departures. The package deal is sufficiently general to allow a variety of concrete manifestations, and Frank's circumstances were such that he could manage the material costs of departing slightly from a personal and cultural ideal.

The Script as Metaphor

The flexibility of the script, its essential quality of being renegotiated in changing circumstances, suggests that the word "script" is perhaps too directive in its connotation of either a dramatic script to be acted out or a computer program's script, determining identical responses to identical situations. But performance is always more complicated than the simple following of a script—we know that there are better and worse performances of plays, pieces of music, or songs where the script is identical. We also know that performances of a piece will be influenced by previous responses the performers have received and by previous performances they have witnessed. Performance of a jazz standard exemplifies what I mean by acting out a "script." The melody—the notes and the order they come in—is given. Also provided (although always provisionally) is the range of variants that may be applied. But the final performance, although it should be recognizably a performance of the standard, is not predetermined. While improvisation on a theme is the key to a jazz performance, good improvisations do not exist in isolation but refer to other performances. Good performers not only know how to play their instruments, they also know what others have played. Their improvisation is original and creative within a tradition and in the context of a range of existing exemplars. A successful performance reproduces the original standard, reproduces (echoes, modifies, pays homage to) other performances, and sets itself up as an exemplar to be copied, modified, referred to, or rejected in its turn. Each varied performance also helps establish the underlying melody as a standard.[7]

The metaphor of life as a performance is venerable in literature and social science because it suggests vital truths. The notion of a script conveys that we are giving performances of something external and preexisting. Our performances are cultural rather than exclusively personal productions. The use of the word "script" also has the advantage of reminding us that the accounts we give of our lives are essentially verbal.[8] The script provides, by prescribing an approved sequence of life events, one way of reconciling contradictions. It simultaneously emphasizes men's departures from cultural norms and provides them with a narrative framework within which to explain and justify those departures.

3 The Four Facets of Fatherhood

> Especially in this area, it's a lifestyle not to have children. A lot of people don't. They'll be old and gray and I'll have my children around Christmas day. I don't determine success in life as financial or monetary or anything like that. My success in life is when my kids leave and go out and make their own lives; they'll come back and say, "Dad, you did the best job you could. Thanks." And they'll come back and see me. And to be a good husband to my wife. I consider that a successful life. —*Howard*

FATHERHOOD IS one of the four elements that make up the package deal (fatherhood, marriage, employment, and home ownership). The elements are interconnected and mutually dependent. As a complex whole, they can be viewed from a number of different perspectives. An analysis of men's lives from the perspective of employment, for instance, would examine how fatherhood, marriage, and housing are affected by the structure of work and the employment opportunities available to men. It would also examine how men's employment prospects, experiences, and histories are affected by being (or not being) fathers, husbands, and home owners. In this book, I examine the elements of the package deal through the prism of fatherhood. My primary interest in men's employment is in its impact on their fatherhood, and my primary interest in their marriages is in the connections between marriage and fatherhood. This approach illuminates the tensions and complications within the package deal that have implications for fatherhood.

The fathers I talked to recognized that fathering was a complex activity with no guarantee of success. They were all concerned with ensuring their children's current well-being and future life chances. "Life chances" is used to describe the fact that the ability to obtain goods, living conditions, and life experiences differs between people according to their social position (Weber 1978). The idea of life chances is at the forefront of my descriptions of men and their lives. For me it captures simultaneously (1) the real possibilities and limits to what they can achieve, (2) their subjective perspective that life unfolds by presenting opportunities, (3) the fact that life outcomes depend on both the existence of opportunities and the availability of the resources to take advantage of them, and (4) the notion that social position or class is about consumption or "lifestyle" as well as production or income (Bourdieu 1984).

Most fathers saw successful parenting as doing the right thing but avoiding extremes. They wanted their children to be disciplined but still to have fun, to have opportunities but not to be forced into particular directions, to respect their parents but not to be afraid of them, and to make their own choices but not to make too many mistakes. Even though they saw no unquestioned rules or role models to follow, they were sure that the kind of relationship fathers have with their children was vitally important.

Knowing that the stakes were high but that there was no guarantee of success, the fathers repeatedly returned to the question of why some people turned out well and others did not, and of what fathers could do to make a difference in their children's lives. These discussions inevitably involved comparison with their peers who were also fathers and with their own experience of being fathered. Men talked a great deal about their own fathers and about the fathers of their friends.

Ralph drew on his memories of his friends' childhoods to muse on the importance of fathers, but also on the unpredictability of growing up. He was sure that social background made a difference, but not an automatic one. Surely a boy's father could help him to turn out to become a good man, he thought, but this was not guaranteed. Character seemed to count also, but he wondered where it came from. Ralph's high school companions and their parents served as a reference group for him as he considered what good fathering was, and what he should do as a father:

> When I was a kid, I remember I was a real hard worker. Always had two paper routes and always hustling to make a buck because I never had money. So I was determined to have money when I got older. I envied a lot of my friends whose parents were well off. They had motorcycles and they had the nicest bike. We had a ten-year reunion in high school and when I went to it, I saw some of these guys that had all the breaks in the world. They had everything given to

> them and now they had mediocre jobs and weren't going anywhere in life. It was just unbelievable. One guy had been divorced twice. One guy was a janitor. One guy was working in electronics. And I shocked them all that I was doing well. And then there were guys like Mark who had the ideal father, I thought. His dad coached Little League and Mark was a big kid. He was like the biggest kid around, the strongest kid around. Could throw a baseball harder than anybody. Was best pitcher in the Little League. And he turned out alright. He turned out real good I think. So where's the balancing act? I think it was because his father was real involved and didn't just give him stuff, but actually took time with him. I learned a lot from watching people like him. But there was another friend of ours, Tom, his dad was really a great dad. He had four kids and two of them turned out OK and one didn't. I wonder about that often. With my kids, am I giving them too much? What can you do to make them better?

Part of the reason Ralph paid particular attention to his friends' fathers was that his own childhood had not given him direct examples of effective parenting. His parents had separated when he started high school and his father had moved out of state. Ralph did not want to live with either his father, who had married a woman who was "an alcoholic," or with his mother, who "drank too much," so he had lived with friends in an apartment of their own for the last two years of high school. Years later, a high school counselor who had helped him at the time told Ralph, "I thought you'd either be dead or doing time by now." Remembering his own high school years, Ralph said,

> That was tough, but it made me tougher down the road because I was having to worry about bills and rent, everything. I was that much more prepared when I got into my early twenties than other guys in their early twenties. They were having to learn all the ropes. I was twenty-four when I started here [at this job], but it felt like I was thirty-four by all the life experience I'd had. And that helped me greatly. Some people pay their dues early. Some people pay their dues late. I paid mine early and so that's why life is pretty easy for me right now, or seems to be.

Ralph was proud of himself for having worked hard and risen to a responsible position, for being married to a popular girl from his high school, and for having two children for whom he could provide a good life. Ralph's account was typical of those I heard from other men in the way it paired hardships and benefits, transforming, in retrospect, obstacles and disappointments into challenges and opportunities. These men's transformation and reinterpretation of their own life-stories complicated their task of deciding on what was important for children. Since indulgence might make children lazy, and hardship could build character, it was never clear that doing the right thing by children was not simultaneously depriving them of important lessons.

Under these conditions, the men from Meadowview constructed their accounts of their own fatherhood within the context of cultural expectations and in comparison with, imitation of, or reaction against, their own fathers. Judging their fathers and themselves by the standards of their culture, they took one or more of three positions: "He did well, and I do as he did"; "He did not do well, so I do differently"; or "He did badly, but I don't know how to do differently." In every case, there was a striving to meet a culturally approved and personally acceptable level of parenting. In their accounts, men talked about fathering, about what they did for their children, what they wanted to do for their children, what they wanted their children to be, and what they feared for them, and thus illuminated what fatherhood meant to them. As they talked about the similarities and differences between their own and their children's childhoods and about the things they did or wished to do differently or the same as their own fathers, they drew a picture of fatherhood as multifaceted.

Fatherhood, as one element of the package deal, is itself composed of four facets: emotional closeness, provision, protection, and endowment. Of these four, men said the most important thing they did for their children was to provide for them. This identification of fatherhood and providing is crucial, reflecting the central place of employment in men's sense of self-worth and helping to explain many of the apparent anomalies in men's accounts. Because holding a job and earning a living are so important for American men's identity, I return to the place of work in men's lives in Chapter 5. But there are other things, not directly material, that fathers want: to be emotionally close with their children; to protect their children from threats, fears, and dangers; and to endow their children with opportunities and attributes that contribute to their life chances. As I describe what I was told about each of these facets of fatherhood, it will be clear that they merge and overlap, that no one of them can be achieved in isolation, and that protection and endowment depend on being a good provider. It will also become apparent that being close to one's children and being a good provider are in tension and that fathers have to do cultural work to make the case that they are doing both.

EMOTIONAL CLOSENESS

> The way I was brought up, my family unit were close. But individually, one to one, person to person, it's like—how to say this? But I never heard my dad say that he loved me. We're a close-knit family. It's just when it comes down to the one on one, we don't really communicate or tell each other our feelings. And it's known. It's known, but we just don't get really down to it and tell each other that. I don't remember my dad ever saying that to me. So I make it a point to tell my kids all the time. Because for some reason, I don't know why, that sticks in my head. I know he does. By the things he does. Couldn't ask for a better parent than I have. It's just something that sticks with me. —*Roy*

Emotional closeness—intimacy or the lack of it—was the dominant emotional theme in my conversations with fathers. That their concern is widespread is indicated by the amount of attention that advice books directed at fathers devote to connecting to their children. In a typical example, James Levine and Todd Pittinsky appeal to men's memories of the absence of expressions of affection:

> To understand how much a hug, and expressions of affection in general, can mean to your kids, think back to how much it meant (or would have meant) to you when you were a child. A study of 300 male executives and mid-level managers found that "when managers were asked what one thing they would like to change in their relationships with their own fathers, the majority indicated they wished their fathers would have expressed emotions and feelings." (1998: 173)

Some of the men from Meadowview spoke with deep feeling about the love they had known from their own fathers; others talked about the distance they had felt from them. Many of them spoke about their own difficulty expressing emotion and about the joyful and transforming effect of children, who brought love into their lives and opened the way to their expressions of affection. The men of Meadowview High were well aware of the multiple positive contributions fatherhood made to their own well-being and sense of themselves, as well as the contributions they could make to their children's happiness and success. Phil

Marwick, who had married for the first time at thirty and had two young sons, expressed the optimistic sense in which becoming a father allows a man to make a fresh start emotionally, to overcome the experience of his own childhood, and to be a warm and loving presence in his children's lives:

> Of all my friends growing up, I don't know anybody who really had a good friendship with their father or mother. I'm trying to think. I must have seen it because it appealed to me. I do remember that kids that had a household that's open and a lot of communication really appealed to me a lot. Love wasn't real big in my house, so I wanted to be around a lot of love. And I had so much love to give because I never gave it growing up. And it's funny, I had such a hard time growing up telling anybody that I loved them, I just could never do that. And even to this day, with my wife, it's difficult for me to show feelings towards her. That's always been an issue in our relationship, that I hide my feelings and I don't express them enough. Because that's how I dealt with it when I was young. But with my kids, gosh, I can tell them I love them five hundred times a day and it feels so natural. I come home from work, they run out of the door and "Hi daddy!" And give me a hug and a kiss. And that just makes my day good. I love that part of it.

Phil clearly expressed the anguish of distance and the joy of closeness, but his comments were also significant for what he left unsaid. It is noteworthy that Phil attributed his delayed marriage, and the issues in his relationship with his wife, to his own upbringing. Explaining one's adult situation in terms of one's childhood experience is a common practice in the contemporary United States, but there are other possible explanations for Phil's predicament. We might, for instance, consider male privilege that allows self-absorption, the pressures on masculinity that militate against emotional expression, and defects of character such as selfishness or lack of empathy.

It is also significant that Phil selected the moment of his return home from work as emblematic of the emotional rewards of fatherhood. Providing a home is a central element of the package deal that makes symbolic and material contributions to all the facets of fatherhood. By returning to the home he had provided and to his waiting children, Phil was performing one of the essential acts of fatherhood. The moment of return home is also significant because it reminds us of the invisible woman in this story. For the children to come running out of the door when Phil came home from work there had to be someone at home with them. Someone watched and prompted the children in their display of affection: "Daddy's home!"

Levine and Pittinsky stress the importance for fathers to reconnect with their children when they return from work. Their advice assumes that the children are already at home when fathers arrive. This assumption is explicit in their example of Michael Johnson, a man who has

> an extremely clever way of cutting "to the chase" and connecting with his son. Before he comes home, he calls to ask his wife what their five-year-old son, Will, is up to. When Johnson comes home, he's able to be specific: "I'll say, 'I hear you were running around with an eye patch playing pirate today.' It lets him know I have been thinking about him." (1998: 175)

This example is paradigmatic of what I call, in the next chapter, women's mediating position between fathers and children.

Phil knew about the gendered division of labor in parenting and recognized that it was his wife who would make possible his vision of "a household that's open":

> I know my wife's gonna be the one that all the neighborhood come over and have my wife drive them somewhere. You know how you have certain moms and dads that take all the kids to the show? That's what my wife's gonna be. She's already kind of like that now. All the kids kind of hang around at our house because my wife is always doing something for them.

Phil certainly *felt* that he was closer to his children than his father had been to him, but all the examples of closeness he gave depended on the presence and full-time parenting of his wife.

While Phil remembered that his father never told him that he loved him, Barry remembered feeling close to his father although they did not talk about it very much:

> I always felt fairly close to my dad, especially when my mother left him. That's why I chose to live with him. I had my choice. My mother said, "Make your choice; live with him or live with me." And I chose my dad because she had somebody. She had the person that she left my dad for, and he basically had nobody. We were fairly close as it is. He'd come over. He was real handy and he could build things and he was crafty with wood. He'd come over and help me build something. Or if he needed some work at his house, I'd come over and help him. We weren't real buddy-buddy, but we were close. I don't

> think we ever had any fights or arguments that I would say, "Hell, I'm not going over there anymore." We never were like that.

The point of this comparison between Barry and Phil is that the closeness of a boy's relationship to his father is not an objective fact of his life, but is a creature of memory and interpretation. In a review of studies on father love and its influence on children's well-being, the conclusion of study after study is that *perceived* paternal warmth and acceptance is an important and significant factor in explaining a whole range of adult children's characteristics, outcomes, and attitudes (Rohner and Veneziano 2000).[1] Amato (1994), for instance, found that young adults' *perceived* closeness to their fathers made a unique contribution to their level of psychological well-being, while Barrera and Garrison-Jones (1992) conclude that it is adolescents' degree of *satisfaction or dissatisfaction* with the support they get from their fathers that is related to their depression. Rohner and Veneziano multiply the examples in their review, and the tenor of their conclusions is supported by the recent summary statements of long-time researchers of fatherhood. Both Pleck (1997) and Lamb (1997), for example, conclude that it is the *perceived quality* of paternal relationships, rather than the more easily observed amount of time that fathers spent with children, that matters to children's outcomes.

Phil felt that fathers should tell their children that they love them. He missed being told that and told his own children he loved them "five-hundred times a day." Barry, on the other hand, found closeness in doing things together with his father and did not feel they had to be "real buddy-buddy" to be close. Barry valued his children as people to do things with, to "share your life, and share different things, and take them to a ball game." His emphasis was on what fathers *do* with their children, more than with what they say, but, like Phil, he wanted to improve on his own father's record: "He really didn't have a lot of time for me. That's something I'd try to do differently."

Mike Martin, by contrast with both Phil and Barry, felt that his father had been both physically and emotionally close to him. His father had been considerably older than his mother and had been the person who was the home presence. Mike felt that he had developed the skills and drive he used in his own work from spending time with his mother at her business. Mike shared with Phil the great value he put on expressing affection between father and son, but while Phil was anxious to do this because his father had *not* done so, Mike felt able to be affectionate because he had the example of his own father: "I had good examples from my father, because he was so loving with all of us. I mean, it wasn't any big deal to run up and hug him and kiss him, even when I was eighteen. And that's how my son is with me." Mike told me how happy he was that, when his son forgot his lunch one school day and Mike delivered it to his classroom, his son had overcome his shyness and "jumped out of his desk and ran over to me and hugged me and kissed me. . . . And it made me feel good, that he's proud of his father, you know? That really made me feel good."

Significantly, Mike described his relationship with his son in terms of fun and friendship rather than of paternal supervision, direction, or protection: "We have a lot of fun together. It's almost like he's my little brother instead of my son. It's like talking to a regular person." I suspect that Mike stressed the fun and equality of his relationship with his son because he structured his life and his time very differently than his father had. For years, he had been totally absorbed in his work and his business, returning home only to snatch a few hours of sleep. His wife had been totally responsible for the day-to-day care of their son. He claimed that his pattern was changing, but admitted that the next few years would be critical for his business and that it would take all his effort and attention. Mike talked more enthusiastically, and in more detail, about his work life than any of the other men I spoke with. He remembered the details of deals and decisions he had made years before, and recalled the tensions and triumphs of building his business in vivid detail. Although he felt he was following the example of his own warm father, Mike's inclination did not translate into the actions and practices that would have allowed him to be a close and present father.

Howard Garbett shared Mike's desire to be close to his children, but unlike Mike he had not had the example in his own family. And also unlike Mike he did not feel blithely confident that he was doing the right thing, but instead dwelt on his own inadequacies. Howard described his family of origin as characterized by alcoholism in three generations, teenage pregnancy, violence, and early deaths. His experience of emotional distance shaped his desire for closeness with his own children:

> I don't want their childhood to be like mine was. I see people who when they hug, they grab each other and stand far away. They don't want to really embrace. I don't want that. When I was growing up, I

> used to see a lot of that. I come from a cold family and I know the way I want things to be. I want to be fun for them. I don't remember a lot of things about it being fun. I really and truly cannot remember. I can't remember too many things about my father. I don't remember— See, I can't remember *good* times. What was a good time with my father was probably just getting drunk.

There were two intertwined aspects of Howard's life that stood in the way of his dream of a different future: his job took up too much of his time and he felt personally unable to be the kind of father he wanted to be. I found our conversation painful, for Howard's repeated themes were "I hope it's not too late" and "I don't know how."

One of the joys of fatherhood for Howard was seeing himself in his children, but even this was a mixed pleasure:

> I like seeing them because I see myself a lot. I see [my oldest] do things and I used to do the same thing. And then I hear Margie say, "Gee, he's just like you." That's kind of neat to see. But what I'm trying to do when I see them, I try to change, so he doesn't end up the way I did. I think I ended up with a lot of selfish traits.

Howard certainly felt the pressure of time, an issue to which he returned repeatedly. Working for a small but very busy construction company, Howard put in long hours of hard physical labor:

> I think that one of my main things is respect. I want them to look up to me and I want them to think of me as being somebody really good. The oldest one is nine. I hope it's not too late to show him a lot of good things. I just hope my job slows down. I keep going back to my job. I get tired of that. That's an excuse. Well, it's not an excuse. I'm tired of it. All day long I'm thinking of them, getting home and seeing the kids. I want to come home happy and play catch. But as soon as I get in my truck and come home, I just want to sit down or lay down or whatever. I feel burned out.

It was not only time pressure that made Howard feel that he was not a good father. He felt he had no patience, that he put off being with his children, and that his own quiet or "selfish" personality did not equip him for opening up to others:

> I want to teach them the things I know. Things I know about being a parent or— I wouldn't know too much about that. But baseball or things like that, that's not all there is. Teach them things you know

> about being a father, or just being loving or being not selfish, being really open. I don't really know about those things. But I do know that's what *should* be done. Kind of I *know*, but I don't know *how*. I gotta prove it to them and show them how. Actions speak louder than words. I have a picture of what a father should be and there's a lot of things I can picture about being a father, like going to a ball park, playing baseball, reading a book together, showing interest. And I didn't have all those things. So I know what I want to do. It's just getting to it. That's why I say I hope it's not too late.

The consistency with which men expressed their shared vision of what makes a good father—warmth, involvement, doing things with his children, playing with them, teaching them good values, taking pleasure in them—was accompanied by a very variable sense of their own success at realizing that vision. Emotional closeness was a crucial facet of their vision of good fathering, but it was not the only one. These fathers wanted to experience emotional closeness to their children for its own sake, but they also saw emotional closeness instrumentally, as something that would make it more possible for them to protect their children from harm and to endow them with opportunities and character.

PROTECTION

> I don't like to think I'm overprotective and I don't want to be. They've got to go out and do their own thing. But I want to keep them out of harm's way as much as possible. I don't know. It's tough. —*Paul*

Protecting their children was an important part of what fathers felt they had to do. Paul Watson, a transport worker with two sons aged six and eight, was not exceptional in his sense that the world was a dangerous place for his children. Paul expressed the impact of this sense of danger when he told me about a recent incident:

> Just the other night I blew it. I came home after working out and my wife asked me if our youngest was with me. I go, "No, he's not with me. Where is he?" So she said, "Well he was supposed to be at his friend's house. We checked there and he's not there. We thought he was with you." I'm just real emotional when it comes to my family. So the first thing that goes through my mind is worst-case scenario. So I start screaming in the courtyard out here: "Where is my son?"

> And I come in the house. I look at all the places where he's supposed to stay. Under his brother's bed, on his bed, on my bed, on the side of my bed. And he's nowhere to be found. So I go back outside and I'm screaming again. And I started to add some profanity and I'm just going nuts out there. So come to find out that my screaming wakes him up. He had been in my closet asleep with the lights off, hiding from his brother and he woke up and came out and finally told me what it was. It was good because I was rusty on panic. I don't think I'd ever panicked. And that was the first time I'd ever really panicked. And my blood pressure went up. My heart tried to break through my rib cage. I had an adrenaline surge like you would not believe. I had all the classic symptoms. My mouth was dry. I was racing around. But that's just the way I am about my family.

So protective was Paul of his family that he had determined to live in the community where he worked:

> The goal for us was to get a house. That was my big goal. Like a maternal instinct for me. To get a house after we have the kids. The second goal was to move into the town I worked in. So we've got into the town so I could keep close tabs on my boys while they're going to school, while I was raising them. So if they screwed up, I was there and could go take care of stuff.

Paul was, compared with his peers, at an extreme in his desire to be physically nearby and in his perceived ability to monitor his children's lives. But his underlying perceptions of the world and motivations for action were very generally shared. Most men I talked to expressed their fear about the dangers of the world. Most of them also said it was important to live in a safe neighborhood and to protect their children by distancing them from dangers and bad influences.

The men who had themselves been children in Meadowview remembered playing in the fields and orchards that have since been paved and built over. The landscape of their childhood was not only physically different, it was also a different social landscape. They remembered playing, alone and with groups of their peers, far from home and without adult supervision. They told me how they rode their bikes all over the neighborhood and the town and played baseball and other games in the public parks. None of this was part of their children's experience. In informal conversations many adults from a range of backgrounds have said that their own childhoods were less supervised than are their children's. Bicycle helmets, car seats, playgrounds that charge by the hour, careful checking of Halloween candy, suspicion of adults who interact with children, and keeping children indoors or under the eye of adults are some of the many ways in which childhood has become increasingly circumscribed. This change has made the work of parenting more labor intensive at the same time that public provisioning for families and children has been systematically dismantled. Public space for children has been replaced by privatized extra-curricular activities; children's sociability is organized by adults. It is not only privileged children who are supervised and protected from what is seen as a dangerous world. Parents living in inner-city neighborhoods also feel forced to restrict their children's freedom in order to protect them, though they find themselves without the resources to provide the alternatives they would like (Kotlowitz 1991; Kozol 1991; Macleod 1995; Suskind 1998).

Fathers expressed two kinds of concerns about social dangers to their children: they were worried about what others might do to their children, and they were concerned about protecting their children from what they described as bad influences. Not one of the many men who admitted their own youthful drug use was sanguine about his children's ability to emerge as unscathed as he had. Their general attitude was that they had grown up in what was seen as a tough neighborhood but that, first, it was not as bad as outsiders thought, and, second, they had survived anyway. Thinking about their own children, they tended to agree that the world had become more dangerous and violent, and in any event they had no intention of letting their own children sink or swim in a similar environment.

While all fathers shared the perception of increased danger, different men emphasized different steps they had taken to protect their children. They all perceived both physical and moral dangers, and in their accounts they frequently conflated the two. Some hoped that moving to "good" neighborhoods would isolate their children from bad influences and harmful people; others tried to achieve the same goal by sending their children to "good" schools or inculcating them with "good" values.

Roy and Sarah Warner emphasized the moral dangers of bad influences and Roy worked to earn enough so that Sarah could be physically close and protective of their children. Roy and Sarah had met at the electronics company where they both worked. She had stopped working there to stay home with their three children and had done childcare at home until their youngest was old enough for preschool. Sarah then worked at her children's school for much less than she could have made on the assembly line.

Roy and Sarah were also concerned about their children's schools. Roy attributed the initial concern to Sarah:

> When she grew up it was a minority-type scene, low riders and Mexicans and this and that and she sees all the minorities and this and that and all the tough kids and all the news and she's really got this thing about sending the kids to public school. It's like she's deathly afraid. The two schools my wife went to, like I said, she had a tough time. She hung out with the wrong crowd and she's just afraid that our oldest will get swallowed up into this. And then end up with the wrong crowd and doing the things that she went through. I mean the whole thing.

Roy said that Sarah insisted that the children go to Christian schools, and Roy said, "the thing is they're pretty well protected now because they go to this private school where my wife teaches." It was very clear that Sarah's concern was not simply about what others might *do to* her daughter, but also about what their influence might *make her be*. Roy had initially reacted to Sarah's anxiety with the feeling that his own childhood had not been a problem. It is interesting to hear, in Roy's account, the change in his attitude to his own schooling as his experience of alternatives led him to reevaluate his childhood:

> When we first talked about sending [our eldest] to a private school, I was, "If the school was good enough for me— Look at how I—" I kind of had these arguments, and as I look back at it, you argue, "My whole family, everyone I know—" *I didn't know anyone that went to private school.* So how did we turn out? I tried to use examples and I was thinking about how she's done this and all these activities [at public school]. But when they did start to go to private school I saw the different advantages of it.

Roy and Sarah removed their children from the public school system. Other parents moved to neighborhoods where they did not see the same problems in the public schools. All shared a concern with protecting their children from bad influences as well as from immediate dangers.

Frank Smedley shared much of Roy's characterization of the dangers, but he emphasized parent–child communication as the solution:

> I think it has actually gotten a little worse now in certain areas than what we had. We have stabbings and that kind of stuff. The drugs were a big influence back then and they still are. Things have changed drastically in the last ten or fifteen years. But I think I see a lot of the same problems. Different minorities now, but still the same social problems that we've always had. Pot was a real big deal back in the late 1960s early 1970s. And now it's no big deal. Now we get the cocaine and crack problem. And that's the scariest thing about bringing kids up is trying to give them the proper influence to stay away from those and educate them in that section. Hopefully they won't have to experience the pains that some people have. My parents didn't talk to me about anything: drugs, sex, or nothing. I guess I considered myself "street wise," I guess they call it. Hate to say, "You learned it on the streets," but that's more or less the way it happened. My parents were very quiet and shy about those type of things. Never really talked to us about it. That's why I try to communicate to my kids more than my parents communicated to me.

Frank shared the widespread belief that parents must talk to their children about making good decisions and staying away from drugs and other bad influences. Barry Richards shared Frank's hope that emotional closeness with his children would foster the open communication between parents and children that was believed to be an effective strategy for protecting them from harm:

> You have to think how you felt when you were growing up. Your parents were never right. They were always on your case. I think back on it and I did some crazy things when I was growing up. And I think, "Jeez, if my kids did that, I don't know what I would do." If my parents found out some of the stuff that I did (I mean, it wasn't malicious or got me into any trouble) but it was the Friday night go out and get drunk and go to the basketball game and stumble home, try to sneak in and not wake them up. And you have to think about that. Decide, "Well, jeez, what would you do if your child did that?" That's real difficult. But what we're trying to do is create a buddy system, a good friend-type system. Not only us being their parents but us being their friend, so if they do have any problems, they can come to us and talk with us about the problem. We can kind of see that at their age now, where something will happen at school and they will come home and

> they will tell us. They are not afraid to tell us. That's the kind of rapport we would like to have with our children. We'd probably just sit down and say, "That's not a good idea, you shouldn't do this or that." You don't want to come down on them like a ton of bricks because you then ruin the so-called friendship.

By referring to the relationship between parent and child as a "so-called friendship," Barry recognized that the "friendship" was not an equal one. The "good friend-type system" was an attempt at emotional closeness with an instrumental purpose. By keeping communication with his children open, Barry hoped that they would tell him about dangers he might otherwise not see.

While Barry reacted to the dilemmas of parenthood with uncertainty and hope in the effectiveness of open communication, Tom Douglas responded with conviction and faith in his religion. Tom worked as a construction foreman while his wife stayed at home with their two children and home-schooled them. Tom's born-again Christianity colored his every utterance. This meant that some of his opinions struck his friends and acquaintances from high school as extreme, but he kept preaching to them because he saw it as his duty to save them from hell. He explained how he talked to one of his friends from high school who had not accepted Jesus:

> "You better listen to what I'm saying because it's like what you're doing right now is walking on the handrail on an overpass. And you're great as long as you don't fall. But as your friend, I'm supposed to stand there and watch you and let you do that? No! As your friend, I'm supposed to take you off the handrail because you're gonna get killed if you don't. This is the same thing. I've gotta, as your friend, help you to understand that what you're doing and the way you're thinking is dangerous." And the Bible goes into great detail to explain hell, and it's scary stuff. Total, total, total darkness. Priority one is that my family is safe. That when we go to heaven, we go together.

His vision of life and the afterlife had direct implications for Tom's view of family and fatherhood. To protect his children from the immanent dangers he saw in the world, such as New Age religion with its worship of the self, Mormonism and fairy tales and all forms of blasphemy, and the daily absorption in material life that leads to hell, Tom and his wife drew back into the community of fellow believers and homeschooling parents. Tom explained his priorities as a father through comparison with another man who attended high school with him:

> Lewis, he's a nervous type. And he will freak completely out if his kids get hurt. If they fall down and get hurt, he gets angry because he should have been there to protect them. And I stop him and I say, "You're so concerned with a skinned knee. What about their salvation? What have you done? Your job as a dad, as head of the household, what have you done to guarantee their salvation? Nothing. Squat. You're worried about skinned knees and you haven't done anything about forever."

Tom told me that he and his wife were homeschooling their children because the books children read in public and Catholic school are "demonic" because they were full of magic and witchcraft. He was articulating a position widely shared among some fundamentalist Christians who object to fairy tales and stories about talking animals and characters that change from one form to another on the grounds that they usurp the power of creation, which is a divine monopoly. In holding this position he was definitely distinctive, although not unique, among his peers, but when he moved from the desensitization brought about by magic stories to the desensitization brought about by media violence, he was articulating a virtually universal opinion:

> Look how many kids are watching these bloody horror movies and the kid will sit and watch somebody's head be completely blown off his shoulders in graphic detail and won't even blink. That's how desensitized they are. Nothing matters anymore because they've had so much exposure.

Every father I spoke to was concerned about his children's exposure to potentially harmful outside influences. Losing interest in school, using drugs, being violent or the victim of violence, and, for daughters, being the object of sexual attention (even in this era of AIDS no man volunteered concerns about his own sons' sexual activity) were seen as influences from the larger society, from other people, and from "the media."

While Tom was at an extreme in the vehemence and persistence with which he hammered home his religious message, he was similar to many men in his instrumental view of religion. Particularly when talking about the role of religion in their children's lives, the men I talked to emphasized its practical or behavioral aspects and never mentioned transcendence or fulfillment. For many people in the United States, religious observance is imposed on them as children, dropped when they are young adults, and resumed once they become parents (Hout and Wilde 1999). Parents of young children enlist religion as a source of values to inoculate their children against danger. Their motivation is in line with their view of children as malleable. Greg, the father of two daughters, put his finger on the responsibility of parenthood:

> I feel I'm doing something very important raising two human beings that start out as not knowing anything, and it's almost like you're responsible for programming these children. They're like sponges. Whatever they see and hear that's how they're going to be when they grow up. That's how you're molding them. So it's a big responsibility to try and mold them the best way you can.

Given this image of children as sponges, and a sense of the world as full of bad influences, it is hardly surprising that many parents turn to the churches as allies in their struggle to protect their children. Even though his family members were all Baptist, Ralph and his wife were raising their children as Catholics because, he said, "It meant a lot to her parents, grandparents, and her." What was important to Ralph was that his children have the guidance of some kind of religion:

> I did want religion to be part of their upbringing. I think in today's world, you have to give your children a foundation to build on and teach them at a very early age about God and what He stands for. And if you want your children to obtain high morals, you have to start early—by teaching, by having high morals yourself and letting them see what you do. They know that it's not OK to drink and drive. They know that it's not OK to ride without your seatbelt. Just the same things. And if you do it yourself, and adhere to those rules, then hopefully some of it will be ingrained in their thinking.

religious

Ralph's examples were typical of the men I talked to, who equated "high morals" with not using drugs and with wearing a seatbelt rather than with thirsting after righteousness, sacrificing for the common good, or speaking truth to power.

In what they saw as a dangerous world, many men felt called upon to be protectors of their wives and children, and also felt that being a protector involves closeness and love. Jim expressed his version of this feeling:

> There're so many things about being a man. Being a man, your wife looks at you for strength and support as a protector. Kids definitely want you to be the protector. It's like, "Hey daddy, Joey just hit me, go beat him up." He really wants you to be the protector. But I know my kids want me to be a very loving father too because they come to me.

Protecting children, as a facet of fatherhood, was very closely linked to emotional closeness. Protecting children meant, to the fathers I talked to, not only physical protection but also being able to talk to them about the dangers they faced and about the consequences of their actions. In teaching values these men were filling their children with good influences and inoculating them against bad. At this point the protective facet of fatherhood merges into the facet that I call endowment. While protection is directed against harm from the outside, endowment aims to give children encouragement and opportunities and the inner qualities of character necessary to take advantage of opportunities. As they talked about the opportunities they could give their children, the fathers I talked to again reflected on the shortcomings of their own fathers, and on the changed circumstances their children faced.

ENDOWING CHILDREN WITH OPPORTUNITIES AND CHARACTER

> They never pushed me to do anything except leave. My mother pushed me to leave the house. That was it. "Don't cause any problems and be a good boy." And that was the extent of it. "Get good grades." But they never once sat down and helped me with my homework. I don't say that out of exaggeration; they never once did. They were too busy doing what they had to do. Maybe in the fifties that's the way things were. I don't know. —*Paul*

In both protecting and encouraging their children, fathers need to strike a balance. On the one hand they did not want anything bad to happen to their children, but on the other they did not want to be overprotective and deprive their children of the opportunities to learn from their mistakes. Several men claimed that they were better people for the hardship or adversity of their childhoods. Indeed, it is hard to know how they could claim otherwise, for the alternative seemed to be to admit that they were damaged, as very few did. Similarly, they said they wanted to support their children in doing what they wanted to do, but they did not want to force them in any particular direction.

Sometimes even the most self-assured men did not persuade me that they had managed to maintain this balance. Mark Baxter, for instance, expressed the strain between competing values that makes child rearing a process of negotiation, alteration, and concealment of contradiction. His explicit position was unambiguous: "I don't want to push them into anything. I feel they'll do whatever they want to do. I can guide them in certain areas, but whatever they decide is fine with me." But Mark's general attitude that his children should make their own decisions, follow their own aptitudes and preferences, was in tension with his aspirations for his children. He was able to reconcile the contradiction through his use of "guidance."

Just how firm his guidance could be came out in our discussion of his son's academic performance. Then in the eighth grade, his son was in a program for the gifted and talented. Mark said he had to keep him "geared in" to school, and that in Mark's judgment, if he got below a B grade he was not trying. Mark helped his son to achieve by reviewing and correcting his homework, setting times for study, and setting high standards. The strain that this put on his son became clear to me as Mark described what happened when his son got a D in a math test and became so distraught that his teacher sent him to the school counselor. There it came out that his son was terrified of Mark's reaction: "My dad's going to kill me." As it turned out, Mark's son received a D because he had inadvertently skipped one question, so each of his answers was recorded on the answer sheet against the previous question. Mark denied that his son's distress was evidence that he was "pushing" his son, but interpreted the entire incident as confirmation that the "parameters" of the parent–child relationship were intact.

In all aspects of his parental relationship, Mark, like so many of the men I talked to, said he was steering a course to avoid what he perceived as outmoded, rigid, and authoritarian fathering, while not abdicating his parental responsibilities. The difficulties of the distinction came out particularly when Mark was considering whether he wanted his children to look up to him: "Looking up to me is not important. If they respect me, that is important." The difference between "looking up to" and "respecting" one's father is slight at best, and not easily defined. Mark explained that he did not want fear or obedience just because he was the father, and would always try to explain his actions to his children: "I want them to know I gave it some sort of logical thought before I yell." Mark, in fact, wanted his children to obey and respect him because they recognized his greater experience and because they thought he was right, not simply because he was their father. The distinction was blurred because it did not occur to Mark that his essential values and orientation could be incorrect. Since he saw himself as both his children's father and as correct on the issues, the practical consequences of the distinction were minimal. Whether they obeyed him because he was their father or because they recognized that he was telling them the right thing to do, Mark expected his children to do what they were told.

Since he was convinced that success in school was something that would open opportunities for his children, and that doing one's best and fulfilling one's potential were both means to an end and ends in themselves, he did not hesitate to demand effort, application, and success from his children. His major concession in this area was that he tried to explain to his children why his demands were reasonable. These explanations, both to his children and to himself, were frequently couched in terms of sports: Certain activities are necessary for athletic success; others are damaging. It was Mark who told me, "I would love [my son] to be a professional athlete. . . . I just keep him aware of the fact that if you want to play sports there's certain things you have to do. Being smart is one of them."

There is an enormous expenditure of parental time, energy, and financial resources on children's sports. Both mothers and fathers were involved in their children's athletic activities, though their involvement was gendered (Lareau 2000; Messner 1992) in ways I describe in the next chapter. Little League, soccer leagues, swimming teams, gymnastics classes, skating lessons, martial arts classes of all kinds, all required that the parents chauffeur their children, buy equipment, and pay memberships fees and tuition. Significantly for the relationship between parents and children, these activities also involved parents as experts and participants. In sporting equipment stores I observed children stretching their parents' technical knowledge and finances by influencing the buying process with what their friends and the media pressured them to buy. And the sales staff helped the process along by pushing certain brand names, trying to make a sale, and consequently needing to combine the excitement of youth with the appearance of adult levelheadedness. In order to navigate through these purchases, and also to understand their children's comments and questions, to offer encouragement, and to help their children succeed, parents perforce became, at least to a degree, experts in their children's activities. Frequently they mastered a technical vocabulary, and many of them became actively involved as coaches, league secretaries, equipment managers, starters, timers, linesmen, and assorted support staff.

The parents' commitment of money and time was complemented by a commitment of thought and emotion, so that their participation in their children's athletic activity was something they did *with* as well as *for* their children. Parental participation was most strongly and widely expressed in *watching* children's activities. And, as one man typically described, in recording their activities for later watching by parents and children: "At times they can be really fun. In fact, we love our video camera for that. You can catch them doing the weirdest things. And that's great. You don't really realize how funny they are until you catch them doing something and then you sit down and see it." It was here that the emotional direction of the parent–child relationship in the contemporary United States came out very clearly. The relationship of adult and child described to me by the men I talked to was not one in which the child watched the parent and learned how to perform adult activities, but one in which the parent watched the child perform, expressing through watching both approval and encouragement.

This direction of watching was particularly true for fathers and sons, for sons rarely see their fathers at work. To the extent that women were watched doing domestic work by their daughters, another pattern would hold, as it would when men worked around the home, either at domestic work or at do-it-yourself projects of home repair and improvement. The paid work of both parents is almost always physically and socially "invisible" to their children (Christiansen and Palkovitz 2001) though the paid work of fathers is culturally emphasized.

Jim, like Mark, wanted to encourage his children to fulfill their highest potential and to pursue their ambitions. Jim made a very explicit comparison between the "wrong kind of encouragement" he had received from his father and the kind of encouragement he gave his son:

> My dad was the type: "Oh, you can't do that." And he thought by doing that I would say, "Oh, yes I can," and go out and do it to prove him wrong. I didn't catch on. When he said, "Oh, you can't do that," I thought: "Oh, OK, dad told me I couldn't do it." So I was kind of frustrated a little bit. When I graduated from high school, he goes, "I don't know why you didn't go on to college or get into a program somewhere. With the right training you could have been good." And I said, "Well, I wasn't helped, or pushed, or talked to, or encouraged that way."

Jim said that his father was never there to talk to and communicate with. From the time he was twelve he had never wanted to talk to his father and, rejecting his father's model, was determined to be a new kind of father. In his stress on open communication with his five-year-old son, Jim was absolutely prototypical of the men with whom I talked. He was also typical in the twist he had given to his father's form of "encouragement." In both cases, Jim represented as a personal discovery and intention what was at the same time a general social and historical process. When he said, "Kids I don't believe are limited. They're only limited by their parents," he was expressing a historically specific but widespread view that has faded in and out of fashion during the twentieth century and that would have been incomprehensible to, for instance, a colonial parent. When he contrasted his father's style of "encouragement" with his own positive attitude, he was the exponent of a more facilitating, less directive approach to child rearing that has expanded its influence and acceptance in the United States since the 1950s. Although Jim emphasized the difference between his style of parenting and his father's, his account of his "totally different" way of encouraging his son illustrated the continuing salience of paternal influence toward achievement, physical activity, and competition.

Jim told me how he had taught his son to ride a two-wheeler when the boy was four years old, and that he had said to him:

> "You're better than daddy, because daddy was five years old when he learned to ride a two-wheeler. His daddy taught— my daddy taught me when I was five, but you learned when you were four. That shows you how much better you are. I'm real proud of you."

When his son heard this, he "got all giggly and smiley and then told mom, 'Mommy, I'm better than daddy.'" As outsiders, we may question whether Jim was really applying any less pressure to his son than his father did to him, even though the pressure was of a different kind. We may notice that Jim's son was being encouraged to compete in just those physical activities that defined Jim's own masculinity, and we may wonder what he would have to say about fatherhood in thirty years.

There is, however, no doubt that Jim was actively involved in his children's lives or that his involvement as a father was consciously intended to be a contrast to his own father's actions. Jim described how he encouraged his son in values, academics, and masculine work:

> When he ever says he can't do something the first time, I say, "Daddy couldn't do this the first time. Never say you can't, because you don't know because you haven't tried, or you haven't practiced long enough." So he's finding out and it's working. So now I haven't really heard him say, "I can't do it."
>
> And anything that I do, he wants to do too. Which is neat. And I let him. At two years old, he was pushing a lawn mower with me. I did some dangerous things with him. I let him get in with me with the chain saw. I had my hands on it, but his hands were on it. I was doing everything, but his hands were on it. And we were splitting logs in the backyard for firewood. I'd let him hold the cone. He'd hold it and I'd tap it a few times and then I'd say, "OK, now stand back." I knew it was dangerous, but we worked together real well. And never any incident.

Jim's encouragement of his son was not simply a neutral fostering of his talents. And this was also true for the other men with whom I talked. Jim's deliberate interaction with his son was directed toward endowing him with particular values such as determination, skills such as arithmetic, and activities such as splitting wood. Jim might have tried to endow his children with quite different values, skills, and activities, as fathers around the world and throughout history have tried to do. Closer to home, Jim's wife, Monica, had rather different ideas about the kind of encouragement their children should receive. She had objected when Jim played exuberantly, exposed their son to the dangers of sharp blades and power tools, and took their son to work with him. Jim characterized Monica's attitude as infantilizing: "She hates to see them grow up. She wants them to always be babies." He contrasted this with his own view, which he defended while admitting that he might occasionally have overstepped the bounds: "I think if the child says, 'I want to try,' with the right supervision and— I probably shouldn't have let him do the chain saw and maybe some other things, but I feel that I can keep things under control." But the differences between husband and wife went deep, and had been the occasion for conflicts over the years. Jim described his frequent job changes as a reasonable attempt to learn new skills and to avoid boredom, but he reported that Monica had criticized him for not "sticking to one job" and "making something" of himself. Monica's objection to Jim's teaching their son his skills was at least partly that she wanted her son to have different skills, to go to college, and to be a different kind of man than his father. "Endowment" is, after all, directed not only at the current happiness of children by giving them praise and validation, it is also directed at how those children "turn out"—at the kinds of adults their parents want them to be.

Education was the one area in which there was a very clear and definite and universal change in both attitudes and practices between the men I talked to and their fathers. The men from Meadowview High School all agreed that their children's success and happiness as adults depended on their education, and they were involved in making sure that their children were successful in school and had opportunities for higher education. Some of the men's parents had expected them to go on to college, but for many finishing high school had been the summit of their aspirations. Their higher goals for their own children reflected changes in the distribution of wages. Adjusted for inflation, the average entry wage for college graduates was 2 percent lower in 1997 than it was in 1979. For high school graduates, the entry wage had dropped by 24 percent. A declining real minimum wage, more workers earning the minimum wage or little more, declining union membership, and the shift from manufacturing to service jobs have all contributed to these changes. The growing differential between wages for college and high school graduates underlay the realization of the fathers I talked to that going to college was more important for their children's financial well-being than it had been for their own. In 1979, about 18 percent of young people obtained four year degrees, by 1999 the figure had grown to 27 percent (Mishel, Bernstein, and Schmitt 2001).

The job market in 1972 had been such that many high school graduates had been able to find jobs and earn promotions without any additional credentials. Greg Turner had been one of these, and he took a certain pleasure in telling me in detail about how college graduates had been hired by his firm making less than he did, and how their "book learning" had not benefited them in the world of work. However, he had, after fifteen years in the labor force, come to see that his job was a dead end, that his company was vulnerable to downsizing, and that he did not have the credentials or skills to transfer to another position. As mentioned earlier, his wife, Maggie, was going to evening classes to get her bachelor's degree, and his plan was to do the same as soon as she graduated. In spite of all his scorn for "book learning," he realized that he had missed something valuable:

> My parents never— actually it kind of bothers me that they did not push me. They never discussed education and all this kind of stuff. If they had I probably wouldn't have to be worried about doing it now. They didn't even really make the attempt to make sure that my grades were good or even ask, "Well, Greg, what are you going to do after high school?" I was kind of on my own, in that respect. I didn't even know what a GPA was, you know what I mean. They just never ever explained anything to me. Basically because I don't think they even knew. And sometimes I'm a little upset when I— Especially in the last few years I kind of resent that they did not give me the opportunity at a younger age. I know it's not too late, but you know it probably would have been a lot easier for me to do it then.

He differed from his parents in both his aspirations for his children and in his belief that it was part of his parental responsibility to ensure that they had the credentials he knew were necessary in the changed job market. Regarding his daughters, he said, "See, what I didn't have, these girls— I mean we're going to try to make sure they have good schooling and we want to encourage them to go to college."

Similarly, Roy compared his own lackadaisical attitude when he came out of high school with his own effort with his children. He told me that his parents had no plans for him, or any idea of what he ought to do:

> They came from poverty to here and built all these things for themselves. And they did it all on hard work. And I guess I was fortunate my dad got that job and he did stick with it for thirty years. And things worked out. But he never had any real ideas or expectations of what I should do or what I should look for or how I should do things. Not at all. I didn't get the exposure. I didn't even think about

> college. I never did. My schoolwork in high school, I just wanted to get out of high school. I had no goals. And they might have asked me what I wanted to be and I had no idea. Gosh. Not a one. And they never pushed me. When I was going to junior college I signed up for the Navy. I think I remember the first thing they said when I signed up for the Navy was they asked me if my girlfriend was pregnant. (laughing) "No, not pregnant. I'm just going in the Navy."

He had definite ideas, however, about what his daughters should do, he had the knowledge to guide them, and he worked with them to achieve:

> My ten-year-old girl, she's already talking about college and I'm already instilling in them at this tender age about their grades and GPAs. As a matter of fact they're taking SATs this week. So it's a little different. And you want to try to tell them about the different occupations. They're at a point now where they like to go shopping and buy clothes and you try to explain to them about jobs and how much people make and what it takes to get a good job. So hopefully they'll have an idea early in their lifetime so they might see something they want to achieve.

The fathers I talked to wanted to endow their children with opportunities and skills and also with aspirations and qualities of character. In this cultural model of fatherhood, providing children with their immediate material needs and ensuring their future life chances are aspects of the same activity. Endowing children with opportunities is inextricably bound up with nurturing in them the qualities of self-reliance and persistence necessary to take advantage of those opportunities. And giving children the qualities of character they need to make good decisions is at the same time protecting them from bad influences.

The Facets of Fatherhood in the Context of the Package Deal

All the men I talked to denied that establishing one's virility or masculinity was any reason for having children—at least in their own cases. Frank made the typical exception of himself from the general rule when he said, "I think everybody has a big ego trip with having children. I don't think that was really the case with me." These men did, however, explicitly value having children as an affirmation of who they were, of their purpose in life, and as representations of what they fou important. Frank elaborated on his personal sense of accomp... on becoming a father:

> I think the first time Carol got pregnant, with our first child, I felt a sense of accomplishment. But as far as changing my manhood, I didn't really feel any change. I just felt that positive feeling that we could have kids. Everybody has that question: "Can I have kids? Will I have kids?" Just made me feel a lot better. Didn't feel like I had any more power or anything, but I felt a lot better knowing that I did have children.

Becoming a father was a moral transformation in that it shifted men's priorities and sense of responsibility. Within their script, marriage marked the end of a period of fun and responsibility only for oneself, and having children marked the shift from couple time to family time. The responsibility for children found its focus in working to provide for them, but was also expressed through the other facets of fatherhood.

In the next three chapters I describe how marriage, work, and home ownership each contribute to every facet of fatherhood. These contributions are summarized in Table 1, in which the elements of the package deal are arranged in columns, and each row contains the contributions of the different elements to a particular facet of fatherhood. Home ownership, for example, contributes to the provision facet of fatherhood by providing shelter, physical amenities, and a surrounding standard of living. It contributes to protection by physically separating children from bad influences, and endows them with opportunities by giving them access to good schools and approved peers. Home ownership contributes also to the emotional closeness of fatherhood because it gives concrete expression to the symbolic importance of "home" as a site for the intimate relationships of family life.

One striking feature of the picture in Table 1 is that the typical contributions to emotional closeness are all symbolic or indirect—they all require cultural work to be interpreted as expressions or manifestations of emotional closeness between fathers and children. It is a major revelation of my research that the emotional closeness men value so highly is, within the context of the package deal, not achieved directly through prolonged intimate association with their children, but is mediated by the men's wives and expressed symbolically through employment and home ownership. It is not so much that men lack the capacity or desire

TABLE 1 The Contributions of Each Element of the Package Deal to the Facets of Fatherhood

Facets of Fatherhood	Elements of the Package Deal		
	Marriage	Employment	Home Ownership
Emotional closeness	A mother to mediate the relationship between father and children	Expression of paternal love	Symbolic "home"
Provision	Mother for children, family life	Material well-being and maximum maternal care	Shelter and standard of living
Protection	Maternal care, two parents to watch over children	Security and safety, housing and neighborhood	Separation from "bad" influences and danger
Endowment	Values, character, self-esteem	Schooling, activities, lessons, aspirations, options	"Good" schools, peers, and reference groups

for emotional closeness, but rather that, if they are to achieve the package deal, they are in a situation in which direct emotional intimacy with their children is in tension with other elements.

In particular, the continuing cultural primacy of providing for children means that men's time and energy are devoted to, and consumed by, their paid work. In important ways employment and fatherhood are mutually reinforcing, for having children provides a motivation for dedication to employment, and supporting a family is crucial to successful fatherhood. But there is tension within the system. The tension between dedication to employment and the desire for emotional closeness to children is addressed, if not resolved, by the cultural work men and women perform within the confines of the package deal. Looking at the row titled "emotional closeness" in Table 1, we can see that the contributions of marriage and work to men's emotional closeness to their children are symbolic and indirect. The men I talked to recognized that their employment took them away from intimate relationship with their children, but they defined their work as an expression of their paternal love. They also used their earnings, in conjunction with their marriages, to ensure that their children had a mother who was at home, or was at least represented as being at home. In many cases the trade-off was explicit: Men told me that they worked longer hours so that their wives could be home with the children. These men's employment did nothing to contribute to their own, direct, emotional relationship with their children, but it did make sure that the culturally appropriate person, their mother, was there for them.

Figure 1 illustrates how each element of the package deal is linked to all the others. The elements are mutually reinforcing, but this is not a system that returns to a stable equilibrium. Men's employment, for instance, enables them to achieve appropriate housing, but also removes them physically from home and makes them more dependent on their wives to mediate their relationships with their children. The dark arrows emphasize that every other element motivates and reinforces the importance of employment, thus concentrating men's energies on the

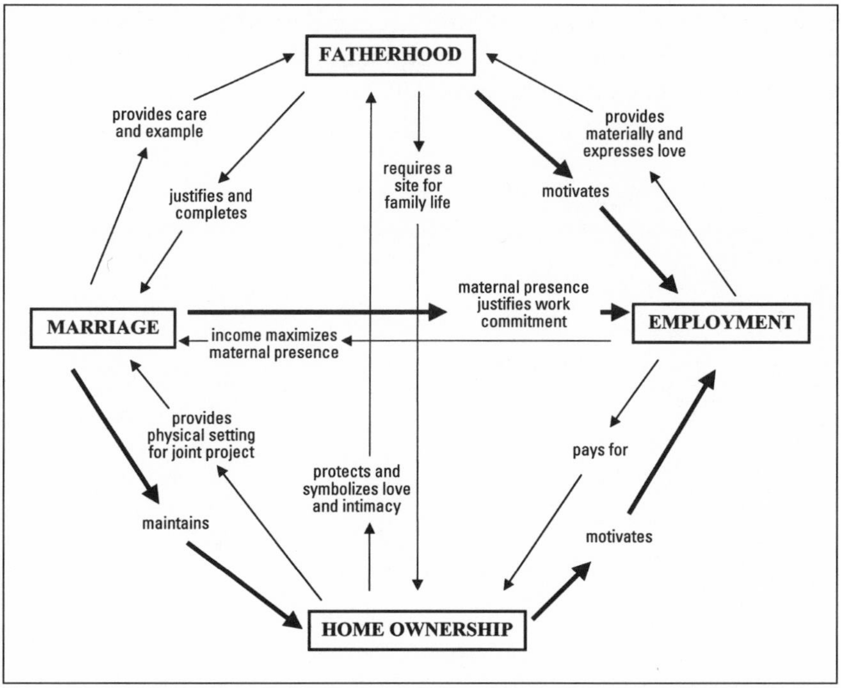

FIGURE 1 The interconnections and tensions among the elements of the package deal.

one element that does not contribute directly to emotional closeness to their children. Within the system, reducing the commitment to work in favor of any other element increases the tensions. Changing the experience of fatherhood involves transforming a cultural system, not just altering emphasis within it.

None of the sources of tension are fully resolved by the cultural work men perform. First, the surrogate closeness provided by mothers and the symbolic expression of paternal love through work and home ownership do not fully satisfy these men's yearnings for emotional closeness with their children, nor, to judge by their comments about their own fathers, do they satisfy children's cultural expectation of paternal intimacy. As we shall see in Chapter 7, these adult men have to do further cultural work to address the tension between expectations and achievement in their relationships with their own fathers. Second, the trade-off between fathers' earnings and mothers' intimacy is further strained by men's declining real earnings and mothers' increasing labor force participation. This contradiction can be addressed through cultural work, but it cannot be resolved within the cultural system defining what men must do to be successful fathers.

4 Marriage

The Women in the Middle

> When we had them, it was always very important for my wife to stay home with the kids. I see a lot of people at work that their wife gets pregnant, has a baby, and two months later they're back at work. And they never see their kids. They don't see them walk or crawl or anything like that. And that was always real important for me that my wife be able to stay home and raise the kids and not have to worry about things. She likes it but it's hard. It's hard raising two small kids. All day long. I don't know how she does it. I couldn't. —*Phil*

WHEN I asked men about their parents, they talked mostly about their fathers, but when I asked them about becoming fathers, they talked about their wives. What emerged from my conversations is that, for the men I talked to, the father–child relationship could not be described or thought about independent of the relationship between husband and wife. Some of the paradoxes of men's relations to their children may be understood by appreciating the relative positions of men, women, and children, and specifically the crucial linking or mediating role of women.

Appreciating the linking role of women is not to say that men do not care about children, or that they think that children are entirely women's business. Certainly becoming a parent is more separated from biological reproduction for men than for women. One can scarcely imagine a woman saying, as one of the men I talked to did: "Actually I have had a child before, although through very strange circumstances I didn't know I had a child before he was a year old and someone sent me a Christmas card saying. 'This is your baby.'" Equally certainly, men consider childbearing and child rearing to be predominantly women's responsibility. In an investigation of the attitudes toward parenting of men whose wives were pregnant with their first child, some men were distinguished by their intention to be "involved" in their children's lives (Angell n.d.). That some men express this intention may index a change in attitudes and behavior, but pregnant married women are not likely to see being involved in their children's lives as a matter of choice. Walzer (1998), who examined the relationships between new parents and their babies, also notes the distinction between mothers' and fathers' expectations of themselves as parents. Other studies of the transition to parenthood also show that mothers and fathers have different expectations of themselves and each other and that gender differences in behavior are increased by having a child (Belsky and Kelly 1994; Cowan and Cowan 2000).

There is also an asymmetry in the ways that men and women *think* about becoming parents. For instance, many women are prepared to consider single parenthood as a possible, though usually less desirable, route to motherhood; the men I talked to, on the other hand, did not even register it as a possibility. This is not to say that men are indifferent to having children. They have strong feelings about the number, timing, and characteristics of the children they want, but at crucial points in their lives they find that their paternity depends on the cooperation of women. Many single childless women are able to consider and talk directly about whether they want to have children. In doing so, and in reading the advice and examples they are offered in books and magazines, it is clear that they see having a child on one's own as a possibility. It is an option with definite emotional, social, and financial drawbacks as well as opportunities, and it is an option that they may well reject, but it remains a possibility. Because of this, women are able to weigh and articulate their specific desire for children outside the matrix of family and relationship with a man. They can think directly and in isolation about the relationship between mother and child, the activity of mothering, and the transformation of self into a mother. The men I talked to did not talk about having children without talking about "having a family" or "being a family man." For these men, "having children" was part of the package deal of "being married and having a family." They could only conceptualize the relationship between father and children within the matrix of a marriage.

The relationships between husbands and wives are, of course, very important in their own right, but my focus here is on the way that marriage, as an element of the package deal, is structurally important for men's relationships with their children. Women, as wives and mothers, mediate and facilitate men's ability to fulfill the four facets of fatherhood. I use the word "mediate" to describe women's role in the relationship between men and children because it captures, in its various meanings, some of the complexity of that role. Women make possible the reproduction, both biological and social, that is at the heart of fatherhood—as wives and mothers they facilitate the relationship between men and their children. Women also frequently mediate in the most literal sense of operating as go-betweens or negotiators between their husbands and their children—they are literally in the middle of the relationship.

Women are often in the position of structural mediators in social relationships. Using the example of domestic and reproductive labor, Glenn examined the differences in position, interests, and standpoint among women, and drew out the complex relationships between race and gender. She described how race and gender are constructed—the categories used to distinguish people "are positioned, and therefore gain meaning, in relation to each other" (1996: 145), and observed that: "White professional and managerial men are the group most insulated from dirty work and contact with those who do it. White women are frequently the mediators who have to negotiate between male superiors and racial-ethnic subordinates" (1996: 144). Looking at patterns of caregiving outside the home, Naomi Gerstel found that women provided "an average of fifty hours a month giving informal care outside the home, men an average of twenty" (Gerstel 2000: 472), but, more than the difference in amount of care, Gerstel found that married men followed their wives' lead in the kinds of kin they helped and the kind of care they gave. Gerstel concluded that "wives link husbands into families and the caring that sustains them" (2000: 473; cf. di Leonardo 1987).

Marriage and Children: Wife and Mother

"We always knew we wanted to get married and have a family" was a frequent comment of men who married women they had known in high school. For the men I talked to, marriage was almost always considered to be a relationship that would involve having children. In most first marriages, husbands said they either "knew" or "assumed" that their wives would want children.

As is often the case, it is when obstacles to meeting a norm arise that its existence is made most clear. Several men told me that they did not marry women with whom they had "good relationships" because those women did not want or could not have children. Conversely, men who had actually wanted to have children told me that they had ended relationships with women they did not want to marry by telling them that they did not want to have children. That this was an excuse was made clear by the rapidity with which these men had subsequently met, married, and had children with other women. Regardless of whether the particular men or women in any relationship or marriage really wanted children, the point is that the cultural idea that marriage and children go together was so clear to all that it could be used as a reason to end a relationship without saying, "I don't want to marry you." Men were making a simultaneous decision about "a wife and a mother to my children."

Greg Turner was the temporary stay-at-home father whose views on the appropriate age to get married I quoted in Chapter 2. Greg had married at twenty-nine, a fact to which he returned repeatedly. To him, twenty-nine was old to be getting married, and he did not want to be too old to be a vigorous father to his children. Although Greg linked marriage with having children, he said that he and his wife had not talked explicitly before their marriage about having children, but that it was, "Just something you kind of know":

> I had seen a lot of women over a period of years. You see all kinds of women out there. I mean, there are some smart ones, but most of them are— they don't know if they're coming or going, you know. Maggie's very intelligent, which I like, very kind, and very funny. That's very important to me, a sense of humor. It is kind of hard to explain exactly why you know that that's the person, but she had all the factors that I was looking for. I remember telling myself: "I can live with this girl for the rest of my life. I mean I can actually do it through the day to day." I just had the inner feeling that I could be comfortable with her for basically the rest of my life.

Greg's choice of a wife was, however, not based simply on personal compatibility. Although he had said that he knew that Maggie was "the person" he wanted to spend his life with, he added, "If I knew that she did not want to have children, I would not have married her."

Gordon Mackenzie, an engineer with three sons, had married his wife two years after they met, and two years later, while he was still in college, his first son was born. Gordon told me early on that: "before we got married we had a goal of three and when we finally got three, I just said, 'I don't have enough for any more.'" Later, when I asked him if he had always wanted children, he replied, after a pause, "I never felt that I would *not* have children. But, you know, up until I found the person I wanted to marry and live with, I never thought, 'I really want kids.' I don't think I consciously said that." And when I asked him if children were needed to complete a family he immediately responded, "That's not the reason we had children, but I believe that's a true statement. Not to say that a couple is incomplete, but I think you're *more married* if you have children." His predisposition to have children, and his affection for children (he had worked with a youth group before he was married) had not settled into a firm plan to have children of his own until he met the person he wanted to marry. Marriage and children were inextricably linked in his thinking, as they were in another man's comment: "Getting married and not having kids at all seems kind of incomplete. I can see you being a single person and not having kids. I can understand that more now. If you're married, it would be odd not having children."

A deliberately childless marriage is definitely something to be negotiated beforehand. At least normatively, inability to bear children is not grounds for divorce, but one partner's unwillingness to have them might cause the other partner to hesitate or to refuse to enter into marriage in the first place. Several men said that in order to marry a woman who did not want children "you would have to love her a lot." There is an implication here that a marriage without children requires a stronger love than a marriage with children. But I think it is closer to these men's meanings that children provide structure and cohesion to a marriage, and that romantic love alone, without the cement of shared parenting and the economic partnership of working to support home and family, is a slender thread on which to hang a lifetime together.

During the 1970s and early 1980s, when the men I interviewed were between eighteen and thirty years old, the divorce rate for childless couples was higher than for couples who had children (Wienberg 1988). Divorces of childless couples also proceeded more rapidly than the divorces of couples with children (White, Booth, and Edwards 1986). Conversely, the birth of a first child within marriage drastically reduced the divorce rate for the next year (Waite, Haggstrom, and Kanouse 1985). Although subsequent births did not have this effect, the presence of children in a marriage did appear to slow the process of divorce

(White, Booth, and Edwards 1986).[1] Of the men I talked to, those who had been through divorces in which children had been involved reported more protracted divorces, with separations and reconciliations, whereas the divorces that had not involved children were more rapid and clean cut. The direction of causation in these relationships between having children and divorce is not always clear. It may be that having children makes a marriage less likely to end in divorce, but it may also be that couples who think their marriage is in trouble are less likely to embark on childbearing.

The men I talked to recognized that having a child may either strengthen or undermine the relationship between husband and wife. On the one hand, they understood the problems of fatigue, busy schedules, and restrictions on shared leisure that children create for marriages. On the other hand, they stressed the responsibility they felt toward maintaining an intact family and also mentioned the new connections with their wives that came from enjoying their children and from sharing activities with them. Having children certainly made divorce harder to consider. They would, they said, stay married through hard times and routine times.

These men depended on a marital relationship with a woman for a paternal relationship with children. In the contemporary United States, the availability of effective contraception and a relaxation of the standard of sexual chastity for brides means that a man's girlfriend, his premarital sexual partner, the woman he lives with, and his wife are not necessarily the same person, though they may be so—the roles and the individuals filling them are uncoupled. A wife, however, is unique in the formalization of her social position and in the way that she links a man to other social persons by virtue of that social position and not merely by virtue of her personal qualities and associations.

George, balding and hospitable, lived in a new house in a new subdivision. As we sat on his deck, watching his young children from his second marriage play in the wading pool, he told me a story that encapsulated the connection between marriage and children:

> It's funny, I knew this one girl that I worked with. She was living with her boyfriend. She never took any birth control. For probably years, she never did. Never got pregnant. But they finally got married, and like their wedding night, she got pregnant. It was kind of a psychological thing, you know? Like, "Jeez, I can't get pregnant, I'm not married. Well, now I'm married, it's OK."

Barry, talking about his own marriage, drew the same distinction between living together (and therefore not having children) and being married (and having or planning children).

> We both had our own separate homes and lifestyles when we first met and we spent a lot of time together. We decided we had a pretty lasting relationship going and that we should live together and consolidate. That way we could really tell, by living together, whether or not we could live together forever. Because you just don't know people until you actually live with them. So we lived together for a while. And then we decided to get married and have children. In fact, that was kind of interesting. My wife— one of her comments that kind of surprised me was, "Jeez, we don't need to get married to have children." And that really kind of took me by surprise because I've kind of had different morals than that. If you're going to have children, at least *plan* children, then you need to be married. Obviously there are times when things are not planned and you're not married. But the way I believe, if you're going to plan to have children, you should be married. She was very insistent that that didn't need to be the case. . . . She likes children, and I like children, so it was kind of a— We discussed it and decided: "Let's get married and we'll have children" instead of just having children and not getting married.

Barry attributed his surprise at his wife's suggestion that they did not need to get married before having children to "different morals," but when his comments are taken as a whole, we can see that his association of children and marriage is not so much moral as conceptual. His picture of family life, his conceptual framework for social relationships, was one that included the possibility of living together and that separated sexual relations from procreation, but equated having children with being married. In this, and in the difference between him and his wife, Barry was typical. In order to be a father, he had to be married. His fatherhood, therefore, conceptually depended on his having a marital relationship with a woman. Once married, the timing of his children's births would depend on his wife's willingness and initiative.

"The Driving Force": Women, Timing, and Birth Control

In general, the men I talked to assumed that, in their own lives, conception and birth could be controlled. They assumed that sexual intercourse without pregnancy was a reasonable expectation, so that premarital sex, a space of time between marriage and their first birth, a controlled space between their children's births, and a cessation of childbearing were all things to be reasonably expected and planned for. Their confidence in their ability to plan was, to a certain extent, justified by the technological innovations of the birth control pill, the IUD, and safe and easy techniques for male and female sterilization.

Previous fertility declines and birth control have depended on a mix of methods, including heavy reliance on abstinence and withdrawal (Schneider and Schneider 1996). These methods involve at least the participation, if not the initiation, of men. The pill and the IUD, by contrast, are methods that women use and that do not require contraceptive action by men or women at the time of intercourse. For men in the United States, these methods have had the double effect of enabling a conceptual and physical separation between sexual activity and reproduction and of moving control over reproduction to women.

Barry did not say that the decision about when to have children was his wife's alone, but he did put the primary responsibility on her:

> She was probably the driving force. Again, I wanted children too. So it wasn't like: "OK, I'll just give in. If you want children, we'll have children." But she was probably more the driver of that issue than myself. I could have been content to wait a couple years. But again, we both wanted children. It wasn't just because she wanted children. If she would have been very insistent against it, it would have been something we probably would have had to talk about. It's really hard to say, but I think I wanted to have children also, but not to the same degree as she did.

Notice that while Barry made it clear that he too wanted children, he placed the initiative with his wife.

Marvin Middleton, a large, easygoing man, who worked in purchasing, told me that he and his wife had children sooner than he would have liked. His plan had been to graduate from college and buy a house before having children. His wife had taken the initiative and had persuaded him that they should have children while he was still in college:

> I wasn't all that hot about the idea. I was not sure I could handle all the responsibilities. I probably thought, in fact I did think, about how they develop and how you grow along with them. It's "Oh gosh, what am I gonna do when they're teenagers?" that sort of thing. So I wasn't all that hot about having kids. My wife convinced me that

> yeah, it's probably not all that tough. I should say now *I know how tough it is*. It's very hard. It's a never-ending challenge. But we finally agreed that we'd go ahead and have kids. And so we did. I wanted to make sure I had a house, which we didn't at the time. And go ahead and have college for me, which I didn't. So that was a kind of unsettling thing, to go from following this nice neat path to success. And here's the time to have kids. Here's the time to do this, to do that. I couldn't do that. So that kind of bothered me.

Marvin had not finished college, but he told me that not having a college degree had not been a real obstacle in his career, and he and his wife had bought a house with help from his wife's parents.

The men from Meadowview discussed their decisions about timing in terms of their "readiness" to become fathers. Leone's (1986) study of middle-class white women's childbearing decisions revealed the importance of "readiness" for women as well as for men. Both men and women spoke of readiness as a psychological state that did not necessarily coincide with the birth of the first child. Some men reported "being ready" before their wives were, and then embarking on campaigns to persuade them to become pregnant. For these men, it was not women's enthusiasm that drove the decision, but their reluctance or hesitation that put women in a position to control the realization of men's plans for fatherhood. Men may realize that they are "ready" when their first child is born, but they may also feel "not ready," causing personal anxiety and strains on their marriage. Several men told me that they became ready to be fathers only some time after the birth of their first child, usually at a point when they felt they could "relate" to their children. Conventionally, men have talked about relating to their children at the "age of reason." Those men who are actively involved with their children during infancy may feel they can relate to their children at an earlier point. Diane Ehrensaft interviewed couples who had decided before the birth of their first child to share the work of parenting: "The gap between the anticipation and the reality [of having children] was smaller" for women than it was for men (1990: 119–22). The men in Ehrensaft's study were anxious in anticipation of the parenthood, but reported "falling in love with" their children and being surprised by the intensity of their feelings after their children were born. Other researchers who have interviewed fathers who were actively involved in the daily care of their children report similar responses (Hertz 1998: 773; Levine 2000).

The men I talked to described the timing of births as if they were perfectly controlled, and difficulties getting pregnant, as well as unplanned pregnancies, as surprises. From my perspective as an observer who knows something about the variability of human biology, this sense of being in perfect control was itself surprising. But being in control was a central organizing element of their stories in all areas. Being out of control was an explanation for the bad things that happened, and a good deal of rhetorical effort was expended to create a life story characterized by control and the realization of intentions.[2]

Because of their identification of having children with being married, and because of their belief that it was appropriate as well as convenient that women should take primary responsibility for contraception and the timing of births, the men depended on women to mediate their fatherhood in the sense of facilitating their reproduction. These men also put their wives in the position to mediate their efforts to fulfill the four facets of fatherhood by placing them, physically and symbolically, at home, between them and their children.

Gendered Expectations: Parental Gender

Talking about their own childhoods, the men from Meadowview told me much more about their fathers than their mothers. Talking about their children, they very often told me more about what their wives did than about what they did themselves (cf. Lareau 2000). These imbalances in what men said reflect two dimensions of gender in fatherhood: lineal and parental. I will return to lineal gender in Chapter 7, where I consider the centrality of the relationship between father and son to men's vision of fatherhood. Here I use the concept "parental gender" to describe the gendered division of parenthood between motherhood and fatherhood.

That the men told me about their fathers more than about their mothers did not at all mean that their mothers were unimportant to them. Only a very few men had anything negative to say about their mothers, and the overwhelming majority, when they did mention them, expressed love, admiration, and respect for their mothers. It was just that they did not talk about their mothers as intensely, or as much, as they talked about their fathers. The explanation for this may be found in the very different expectations that children, as products of their culture, have of mothers and fathers.

We know that these expectations are cultural rather than innate, because they vary over time and from society to society, and we see them as expectations because they are not descriptions of uniform behavior. Mothers in the United States are expected to be active participants in their children's daily lives, to satisfy their needs and wants, to love unconditionally, and to "be there," physically and emotionally, for their children (Garey 1999; Hays 1996). When they do all these things they are seen as acting appropriately. They are taken for granted, not in the sense that they are unimportant, but rather because their central importance is assumed. Fathers, on the other hand, are expected to be less expressive emotionally, to play more physically with their children, to provide financially rather than to be day-by-day caretakers, and to be disciplinarians. Whereas a mother's love is expected to be unconditional, a father's approval is seen as conditional and as something to be earned.

The impact of these expectations on children's perceptions of their parents are enormous, for children notice and must account for their parents' departures from them. Mothers' day-by-day attention to their children becomes a background or foundation for their children's lives, whereas fathers' play, family meals, or family vacations are "special" (Contratto 1987). Indeed, that some meals are described as "family meals" and therefore "special" conceals the fact that it is the presence of *fathers* that makes them "family meals." The men I talked to remembered and appreciated their fathers' employment, while their mothers' employment was minimized or forgotten. In addition, their mothers' parenting was taken for granted, while their fathers' more occasional attention was treasured. Men's own accounts of what they do as fathers concentrate on special events and activities rather than on the daily routine. Mothers are noticed when they are not there; fathers are remembered when they are.

Despite the gendered differences between motherhood and fatherhood, the men I talked to frequently spoke about "parenting" in a way that linguistically erased gender lines. They spoke of "being parents," what "parents" should do for their children, and the "we" that mother and father constitute in relationship to their children: "We" give them a good home, "we" teach them good values, "we" think it is important for someone to be home when they get home from school. The use of "we" obscured the inequality in the division of parenting labor.[3] Using the words "parent" and "parenting" to conceal gendered activity, and gendered blame, is also a feature of public discourse (Fineman 1995; Garey and Arendell 2001). When we hear, for instance, that children are unsupervised because "parents" are not at home when they come home from school, or that "parents" are putting careers before children, the reference is clearly to mothers, since fathers are *supposed* to be working away from the home. Men's use of "we" and their talk of "parenthood" not only concealed a gendered division of labor but also acknowledged it and expressed the sense in which husband and wife were seen as a team or joint enterprise. The men I talked to saw fatherhood and motherhood as different but complementary. One of the features of this complementarity was that they saw fatherhood as essentially dependent on being part of a partnership with motherhood.

Barry Richards said he spent more time with his children than his father had with him. He described how he pitched in and cared for them, but he made it very clear that he was not the primary caregiver and that equal care of the children was not essential to his definition of good fathering. Barry had worked full time since before his marriage. His wife, Linda, who had a full-time job when they met, left it when their first child was born and resumed working part time from home selling household items when the baby was a year old. She arranged evening events at which she could display and sell her products. Like so many men who told me of their wives' employment, Barry emphasized the personal benefits, rather than the income, from his wife's activity.

> It was really good for her. She'd get out and it was her way of relieving all the stuff that she had to cope with with the children at home when they were so small. I'd come home and I'd watch the kids, and I'd play Mr. Dad and give them their bath. I would get involved with the children that way. I didn't mind. I guess the only thing that I didn't like was, if I had something I wanted to do, and she happened to have a show that night, I couldn't do it. So it was kind of "Well, OK, I guess I can't do it." And the guys would say, "Hey, we're going for a beer after work." And I'd say, "No, I can't. Linda's got to work tonight." But it wasn't anything that was going to change my life. Plus it is kind of a two-way street. Both parents have to share as much— I'm sure she does probably more than I do with the children.

Clearly, "playing Mr. Dad" was very different from being a full-time caregiver, and was something that Barry said he did for the sake of his marriage and his wife at the expense of what he saw as his entitlement to leisure time with his male friends. Barry continued:

> I don't think I could stay home all day with the children and take care of them. I love my children dearly, but you have to put up with a lot. I don't think I'd want to play Mr. Mom. I really don't think so. Especially when they were younger. Maybe at this stage it might be a little bit different, because they have set patterns. They get up, get dressed, eat breakfast, brush their teeth, off they go to school. And then there's a period of time in there where there is a little bit of serenity to yourself. But when they were both in preschool or not in school and you have them all the time, that can be very taxing on the patience, believe me. Back then I don't think I could have done it. Now I don't think it would be quite as bad. They are becoming a little more self-sufficient, sort of relying on themselves, and we give them some responsibilities. We bought my daughter an alarm clock, we set it, and her job is to get up when the alarm clock goes off and get herself dressed and get ready for school.

Although Barry believed it was important to play "Mr. Dad" with his children, he was not about to become the primary parent, or "Mr. Mom." His contrast between these two idioms concisely expressed the difference between cultural views of a father's involvement (intermittent and supplementary) and a mother's (constant and essential).

Men at Work, Women at Home: The Structural Division of Labor

Men presented their own employment as primarily oriented toward providing the material resources for them to protect their children from danger and endow them with opportunities. They felt that their employment also contributed to the emotional closeness that is an integral facet of fatherhood, because these men interpreted providing as an expression of paternal love. In some dual-earner couples, husbands who wanted to emphasize that they were the primary providers for their families explained that their wives' incomes were used for "extras" or "luxuries." Other men said their wives worked to add variety to their lives, for social contacts, or to "get away from the kids." These men were all doing cultural work to interpret their arrangements as conforming to a hegemonic picture of the structural division of labor in marriage.

For these men one of the most important contributions of employment to fatherhood was that it enabled them to provide their children with a mother who was at home for them and could be close to them almost as a surrogate for their father. Jean Potuchek (1997) studied the gendered division of labor, identity, and responsibility in dual-earner couples. She described the distinction so many of these employed husbands and wives made between working (and earning an income) and breadwinning (and providing for a family). Some employment and income, that is, was described as more essential and basic than others. It is not that the couples Potuchek interviewed denied that both were employed, but that they described the husband's breadwinning as central to their family strategy while the wife's earnings were supplemental. The decline in the family wage (the ability for one worker to be able to earn enough to support a family) has made the simple division between "father breadwinner" and "mother homemaker" harder to maintain in its pure form, but many couples maintain and reinforce the division of responsibility that accompanies it. For the men I talked to, the division of labor in which they were the primary breadwinners reinforced not only their own identities as workers and providers but also enabled them to fulfill other facets of fatherhood by ensuring that there was an available parent in the home.

In support of this division of labor in their parenting, the men I talked to made three interlocking arguments: They liked or chose the arrangement, it was best for the children, and it was natural. Gordon, the engineer with three sons who felt "more married" once he had children, expressed very clearly the structural division of labor between parents: One parent should stay home to raise the children, and it should be the mother.

> I think it's wrong to have kids and then lock them in daycare centers while you're working. That's why I'm really grateful that my wife can stay home. And although at times we were real tight for money, and I told her she might have to start looking for a job if we were going to make ends meet, I was grateful when things worked out and she didn't have to. Because this is really the place the kids need a full-time mother, to watch them.

This arrangement worked, Gordon said, because "She's not the working type." This gendered division of labor between husband and wife was a reproduction of his parents' pattern. His father had been a skilled machinist; his mother, with a college degree, had stayed home and not worked outside the home until her children were in high school. Gordon explained the arrangement he had with his wife as the result of their "choice" and in accord with his wife's personality. Although Gordon described both the division of labor and the fact that he followed his father into working on machines as "natural," he and his wife's arrangement was an instance of a social fact: In the overwhelming number of cases where one of a couple works full time, it is the husband.

Like Gordon, Marvin attributed the division of labor in his marriage to his wife's preference. She had worked off and on, he said, selling products from the home and working as a teacher's aide for the local school district, which "gives her a lot of flexibility." When I asked him if she had ever wanted to work full time, he said,

> She seems to have wanted more to be a good mother. And she was the type of person that when we got married, she had this view of herself as not "Super Mom," but "Nice Mom" that does the things that moms do and takes the kids and gets involved in things. And that was a really big thing to her.

Marvin was articulating what Garey (1999) points to as a dominant cultural image of mothers as oriented either to work or to family. Garey argues that many employed mothers downplay their aspirations to "career" or to being "Super Mom" and, rather, practice "maternal visibility" by making a point of being seen as doing "the things that moms do."

Paul went a step beyond Gordon and Marvin in his defense of a structural gendered division of labor, turning it into a timeless and natural pattern. Paul was a serious, intense man who talked quietly but displayed a fierce protectiveness of his family. He worked a night shift with lots of overtime and shift differential pay. He and his wife, who was employed full time, lived with their two sons, ages six and eight, in a townhouse near his work. His mother-in-law cared for the children during the day, but she was about to move away and Paul's plan was for his wife to reduce her hours of employment and work part time:

> I was thinking about trying to buy a [single family] house over here, but if it's going to cause me to be away from the family, or cause [my wife] to have to work all the time, I think we're gonna back out. If I can't afford a house on my pay alone, and make it, if we can't do it on my paycheck alone, we're not gonna do it. Because that's just basic. It's just the way it's been since time began. Women stay home. I'm not trying to be chauvinist by any— but if you're gonna have a family, that's the way it works best.

The gendered division of labor, then, puts women in the home as the mothers of men's children, and this division of labor is reinforced by cultural work that emphasizes men's responsibility as providers and women's involvement in their children's lives. Such a division of labor is presented as natural and equal, but it is a product of a particular economic structure and social organization of work. The gendered division of labor at the structural level also has profound implications for the daily activity of parenting.

PROTECTING, ENDOWING, AND BEING THERE: GENDERED PARENTING

In the activities of parenting and child rearing, men who devote themselves to material providing once again place women between themselves and their children. Their interactions with their children are controlled, arranged, or supervised by their wives. Women have most of the responsibility for organizing and enforcing children's activities, with men exerting their influence through their wives. Some men do put a lot of energy into their children's activities, especially into their athletics, and even more express the desire to do so, especially to do more with their children than their fathers did with them. But studies of time use continue to find differences between working husbands and wives in the total number of hours worked when paid labor, childcare, and housework are combined. Studies in the 1980s concluded that employed husbands worked between ten to twenty fewer hours per week than their employed wives (Hochschild 1989: 3–4 and 271–73). More recent studies have found that men and women spend approximately equal amounts of time on the combination of housework and paid work (Ferree 1991; Pleck 1985; Schor 1991), but certain domestic tasks continue to be overwhelmingly women's work (Coltrane 1996; Shelton 1992), and men's contribution to housework still tends to be thought of, by both husbands and wives, as "helping" (Coltrane 1989; Walzer 1998). When married couples have children, the division of domestic labor tends to become more traditionally gendered (Cowan and Cowan 2000) and women spend less time in the paid labor force and men spend more (Shelton 1992).

Not only is there a difference in the number of hours men and women spend in child rearing, but fathers and mothers approach parenting very differently. The men I talked to expressed the belief that mothers are the "default parent." They acted on this belief and by their actions made it true. Being the default parent means being the one to whom a child turns first, and being the one with the responsibility for knowing the child's needs and schedules. The default parent, ultimately, is the one who must be there, to whom parenting is in no sense optional (Walzer 1998). For example, even though fathers sometimes went to meetings at their children's schools or took their children to sports practice, it was usually mothers who kept track of the meeting and practice schedules. Lareau (2000), in her study of children's routines, reported that fathers were very vague and general in their accounts of their children's daily routine, in contrast to the detailed and specific responses of mothers. In general, the men I talked to indicated that their wives kept the mental and physical calendar. In parenting, as in so many areas, the person who keeps track of scheduling often has a great deal of control over what activities and events become scheduled.

Even in the area of discipline and punishment, where it would seem that the father's position as ultimate authority was secure, mothers are the gatekeepers or mediators. Consider the proverbial threat of mothers to their children: "Just wait until your father gets home!" A number of men used exactly this expression to show that they were deeply involved in their children's lives. It was meant to indicate that they were the source of discipline, even if they were not directly supervising most of the time. The words, however, indicate a very different relationship, for it is the mother who decides when and what the father is told, and thus when he can act. Rather than being in an immediate disciplinary relationship with his children, he is a resource to be mobilized by his wife in her dealings with the children, and thus in a relationship mediated by his wife.

The disciplinary dynamic in families could take several forms, but two were common. While they may seem very different, in both cases the wife and mother was ultimately responsible for discipline. In the first, the husband was an authority figure and disciplinarian who saw himself as supporting or backing up his wife. In the second, the husband was allowed to be the fun parent because his wife was the disciplinarian.

Both Ralph Colson and Terry Evans used the word "enforcer" to describe their role in their children's discipline. Neither of them liked this, though both accepted it as their responsibility to support their wives. Ralph told me that there had been one disciplinarian in his family when he was growing up, and that it was the same in his marriage:

> One parent seems like the disciplinarian and the other one is not. And in my family I am. And my wife doesn't understand: "Why won't the children listen to me?" Because it's always: "I'm gonna tell your father." She had to call me here [at work]. I've had to talk to them on the phone. And they straighten right up.

Ralph felt that his wife should be more consistent in her discipline so that the children would not ignore her threats and cause her to lose her temper. She, on the other hand, sometimes felt overwhelmed and told him that if she were to hit the children instead of threatening them, "I'd beat them to death. I'd be constantly hitting them."

Terry, the father of two boys, was also critical of his wife's treatment of the children, but he, too, accepted his role as enforcer:

> The thing is, you've gotta be the enforcer. The man has to be the enforcer and that's the only thing that sometimes irritates me. I come home from working a hard day and my wife right off: "Terry, he's done this, he's done that." And I get mad and I go in there and yell at him. That's where a lot of times I would like to say, "You're the mother. Handle it. If you want to restrict him, restrict him. If you want him to be whupped, do it." She's home every day. She knows exactly what's going on. I think she ought to handle it more herself.

For both Ralph and Terry, the structural division of labor, their position at work, and their wives' presence at home meant that their wives determined where the children were and what was expected of them. The women then decided what to tell their husbands and so shaped the types of interactions between the fathers and children. Terry yelled at his children and Ralph spanked his, but their wives, as the default parents, mediated the flow of information and expectation between fathers and children. Women's mediation should not be seen as deliberately manipulative. The gendered division of discipline is not simply an individual choice or decision, but part of a whole gendered system of division of labor.

Gordon's situation was a rather different manifestation of the same gendered system. In Gordon's family, he was the one who could relax and have fun with his sons because his wife was protective and strict. When it came to parenting, he said,

> My wife does a better job, although she is very protective of the kids. Like my eleven-year-old, she won't drop off at baseball practice. She'll stay and wait until it's over. And even though sitting in a car, she's always there. She won't leave the kids anywhere alone. . . . I think she's just worried about something happening to them. Not having an accident, like falling off of something, but with all the crazies out there, she's just worried about losing one of them. Which is— I mean, it's a real-life concern. I can't blame her for that, but it gets a little excessive sometimes. And she does discipline them better. They mind her better; she's more sensitive to their feelings and that kind of thing. It's the insensitive dad, sometimes. . . . I don't treat my kids the way [my father] treated us. He was a *very* heavy disciplinarian and we were afraid of him when we grew up. I don't want my kids to be afraid of me.

Partly because he did not want his children to fear him as he had feared his father, and partly because his wife was watching over them, protecting them, and disciplining them, Gordon felt he could relax and let them run a little wild: "When they're just goofing off and it's Friday night, I'm not going to crack the whip and put them to bed." He laughed: "It wouldn't work anyway."

Roy's wife, Sarah, also mediated Roy's position as a "fun dad" to his children. She had run a childcare business in her home when the youngest was a toddler and taught at the private school the children attended. Sarah was very involved in the lives of children in general and her own children in particular, and part of her involvement was in scheduling her husband's time with his children. Roy said, "When there are three there, it's tough. They're all vying for your attention." So Sarah intervened and Roy described to me what he would say to his children:

> "Your mom says it's your turn." So each time I do something I take a different child with me. And it works out two ways. It's a lot cheaper for one. And also I get that one-on-one with my kids.

Many of the things he did with his children, such as going to baseball and basketball games, were recreational activities he himself enjoyed. While Sarah was orchestrating this activity, Roy was the fun father, spending quality time with his children doing things they could enjoy together. Roy also was able to be spontaneous with the whole family. Several times he told me that he would, "on the spur of the moment," sweep the family up and drive to the beach:

> ke I get them going at seven in the morning up to Santa Cruz and I'll bring my camping stuff and we'll cook breakfast and we'll just have breakfast and when other people are coming, we're leaving and coming back home. We do stuff off the wall like that. Spur-of-the-moment-type things. On Friday afternoon I'll tell everyone to pack their suitcase and we'll go to Monterey for a night and things like that. I think that's pretty neat.

Overall, Roy emphasized the fun and spontaneity of his relations with his children: "Agewise, I'm probably considered an adult, but you talk to my kids and I'm probably the biggest kid around. I'm not kidding. I'm a big kid at heart. I love sports. I love my kids." It is important to notice that Roy's ability to be spontaneous and to have fun with his children, just like his one-on-one time with them, is dependent on the routine, day-by-day, planned, and conscientious work of his wife.

The gendered division of labor in parenting not only distributes work and fun differentially between fathers and mothers, it also distributes who gets taken for granted, and who gets the credit. Hochschild described how couples negotiate not only a material division of labor, but also an economy of gratitude (1989): People do not just want to be appreciated, they want to be appreciated for the contributions *they* think are important. Psychologists Carolyn and Philip Cowan (2000) observed that, for men, employment "counts" as childcare—both they and their wives interpret men's employment as doing something for their children. What is more, wives not only appreciate their husbands' work as something they do for their children, they also see their husbands' direct attention to their children as contributions to the marriage relationship. Husbands, on the other hand (and many wives), see women's employment as detracting from their mothering, and their husbands do not see the care mothers give their children as couple time or as building the marriage.

Mothers who are supervising and caring for their children may well know more about those children, about their hopes and insecurities, than fathers who are there to have occasional fun. This puts mothers in a position to relay or to hold back information about their children, and mothers are the ones who both fathers and children talk to about one another. Roy related a typical story of an incident between him and his daughter about which both of them had, independently, talked to his wife. Their communication about the event, and its resolution in Roy's mind, was very directly mediated by his wife:

> I just talked to my wife the other night. My oldest daughter, somehow I felt like she wasn't communicating with me lately, the last couple weeks. I was asking my wife if there was anything wrong. What particular things had happened at school? I went to pick up my son and she was gonna go somewhere else and I saw her and I know she saw me, but she didn't acknowledge me being there. So I was kind of hurt because usually they'll come up, "Hi dad!" And my wife goes, "It had nothing to do with her not wanting— " What it was, I guess, her friends were wearing makeup and she knows I'm against girls at this age wearing makeup and I guess that was why she didn't come and talk to me. So that's fine. I can see why she didn't want to talk to me.

These examples illustrate that the structural division of labor, in which men are seen as providers and women as homemakers, is connected to a gendered division of parenting.

Some people object to this assertion about the gendered division of labor between wives and husbands, between mothers and fathers. Surely, they say, the norm of breadwinning men and homemaking women is not a reality in a postfeminist world of gender equality. At the very least, they assert, this norm is outdated and both expectations and behavior are changing rapidly. Their objections, however, often are based on those familiar tendencies we examine in courses on social science methods: overgeneralization and selective observation. We tend to notice the exceptions. Women in traditionally male fields, for instance, or men who stay home with their children, stand out from their peers. They get noticed, they get remembered, and they get attention. Representations in popular culture and the news media concentrate on these exceptions, with the justification, if one is offered, that they are interesting or newsworthy. Selective observation is accompanied by overgeneralization and the assumption that what we have noticed is in fact representative of the whole.

Admittedly, in the cultural repertoire there is an attitude or image of sharing between couples, of equal participation in children's care, and of work being important to both women and men. But social and cultural institutions have an enduring persistence. In a review of the history of the family in Western Europe and North America, Martine Segalen (1986) concluded that, although norms about domestic life were fiercely debated during the 1960s and 1970s, behavior changed less than the representation of it, and marriage and parenthood remain key institutions and personal goals (cf. Modell 1985). We find a similar disjuncture between cultural attention to change and enduring patterns of behavior when we consider parental and household division of labor. Sara Harkness and Charles Super (1992) report that in a group of thirty-six middle- or professional-class fathers in intact marriages, all "committed parents," fathers spent only a little more than a quarter of their child's waking hours in the presence of their children aged one to four, and about 15 percent of their child's waking hours as primary caretaker, and were engaged in direct interaction with their children for less than half that time. The evidence for gendered parenting is overwhelming whether we look at cultural attitudes or actual behavior.

In impressive reviews of the recent literature, Coltrane (1998a: 64–74, 2000) described the basic inequality, and limited change in labor force participation, earnings, housework, and commitment to home and work between men and women in the United States. His summary picture is one in which changes have been more limited than attention to "new men" might suggest, and in which the transition to parenthood continues to be accompanied by an increase in men's hours of paid employment, a decrease in women's hours of paid employment, and a more traditional gender-based division of labor between husband and wife (cf. Cowan and Cowan 2000; LaRossa 1997; Walzer 1998).

Both structural reasons and deep cultural orientations work against the easy imposition or implementation of ideologies of equality. In *The Second Shift*, sociologist Arlie Hochschild distinguished between what she called "shallow" and "deep" gender ideologies in order to explain the contradiction between statements of belief in gender equality with very unequal divisions of domestic labor. She argued that many men and women profess an egalitarian gender ideology that is shallow because it is contradicted by their deep feelings (1989: 14–17). The behavioral reality is that only 2.5 percent of men in the labor force are the primary caregivers of a child under age fourteen (Marin 2000).

What *is* changing in the culture of the United States is the nature of the expectation of paternal closeness and involvement. It seems that mothers, children, and men themselves are less likely to assume paternal love and more likely to expect that it must be demonstrated and enabled through paternal practice. Successfully fulfilling the providing, protecting, and endowing facets of fatherhood is no longer enough to fulfill the emotional closeness facet as well. Fathers are experiencing a cultural pressure to contribute to the emotional closeness facet of fatherhood through direct action and personal interaction.

William Hughes, a married father of two children, who attributed his rise from the loading dock to a senior managerial position to the work ethic he had learned from his father, identified the change in cultural expectations of fatherhood. William also made the critical connection between changing visions of fatherhood and changing definitions of masculinity as he compared his own father with his peers. His swift transition from talking about domestic chores to talking about emotional expression indicates their close association in his mind. Changing diapers and showing affection seem to be linked as gendered activities:

> My father was lord and king of his realm and essentially he ruled the roost. And my mother accepted that and was glad for it and that's the way their relationship was set up. He handled all the money, he paid all the bills, he doled all the money out. I never saw my father wash a dish, sweep the floor, or do much of anything around the house. And my father didn't change diapers. My father was not extremely involved in all those little parts of our lives. And the men I know now, they change the diapers, they share the cooking, they help clean the house, they share in all the duties around the house. And I think relationships have really changed that way. It's more socially acceptable to be physically demonstrative and to show affection and love for your children. You're not considered weak or a pansy or anything along those lines. Or hugging and kissing your wife and children. Hugging friends. The image of a man I think has changed— What a man really is.

Despite his portrayal of an expansion in men's family activities and emotional expressiveness, William continued, as I describe in the next chapter, to identify male responsibility in terms of work and providing and to devote his time to his job. He had often worked late into the evening and on many Saturdays over the years while his wife, a college graduate, had left her job when their first child was born. His embodiment of a new masculinity rested on achieving success by the old standards, and that relied on a gendered division of parenting.

Surveys of attitudes or aspirations indicate that a high percentage of men, and especially of young men, accept the notion that they should see themselves as fathers first and workers second, agree that they should aim for work schedules that allow time for family, and say they would give up pay to spend more time with their families (Radcliffe Public Policy Center 2000). However, there is overwhelming evidence not only that men's behavior has not changed to keep pace with their aspirations, but also that basic aspects of fatherhood have endured. Men still see being involved in the daily routines of their children as optional. They may be involved, but this is not constitutive of their fatherhood in the way that such involvement is constitutive of motherhood. And providing is still seen as fathers' primary responsibility.

Three recent studies of the attitudes of college students, who are frequently proposed as the wave of the future, reveal the enduring gender asymmetry of parenthood. Spade and Reese found that both women and men in college were committed to employment, and that both valued family, but that, in spite of these similar aspirations, they did "not anticipate symmetrical relationships" because "both men and women expect that women will play a more prominent role in the family and men a stronger role in the workplace" (1991: 309). Claire Etaugh, who has conducted extensive research on the perception of employed mothers, and Denise Folger examined the perceptions of college students in the Midwest of parents who had, after the birth of a child, either reduced their hours of work or worked full time. They found that mothers who worked part time were judged to be just as professionally competent as mothers who had not reduced their work hours, but that mothers who worked full time were seen as much less nurturant. In contrast, fathers who worked full time were seen to be just as nurturant as those who reduced their hours of work, and were simultaneously seen as more professionally competent (1998). In a similar experiment on the perception of mothers and fathers who stopped working in order to stay at home with their children, Riggs found that "Approval ratings deteriorated significantly when a father sacrificed financial security for care giving; the same behavior by mothers received high approval" (1997: 565).

That the cultural attitudes expressed by the students in these studies are translated into behavior is evident from the continuing very high levels of fathers' labor force participation, mothers' tendency to leave employment or reduce their hours after the birth of a child, parents' very general agreement that mothers are the "experts" on children

(Cowan and Cowan 2000: 103), and the fact that women continue to do two-thirds of household labor (Coltrane 2000: 1223).

Mothers not only do more childcare and domestic work, they also know more about what their children are doing and feeling, they talk to them more, and they control the flow of information between fathers and children. They also schedule their children's lives and the interactions they have with their fathers. As part of this gendered system, the relationships that mothers have with their children even influence the quality of fathers' interactions. Mothers may invoke their husbands as disciplinarians and enforcers, so that the fathers are stricter or sterner than they might otherwise be. Or mothers may maintain the structure of family life, giving men the space to be spontaneous and fun.

Within this gendered system of parenting, men and women act out and reinforce gender stereotypes. Men are expected to play more actively with children than women do, and as a general rule they do so. Mothers, so I was told, control male exuberance, calming fathers and children and discouraging dangerous or overexuberant play. It is mothers, I was told, who set limits on the activity of men and children. By doing so, they constrain themselves or, rather, are constrained by an entire system of expectations from being "fun" in quite the same way that men are. Men's playfulness and men's anger, their distance and their sense of inadequacy, are reproduced in the daily interactions of family life. A crucial element of these interactions is the mediating position of women, as wives and mothers.

After Divorce: Stepmothers and Former Wives

After a divorce, the effects of men's mediated relationship with their children become most apparent. In 1980, when the men I talked to had been out of high school for eight years, 56 percent of the divorces in the United States involved children (Sweet and Bumpass 1987: 179) and in 90 percent of those, women were awarded custody of the children (Cherlin 1988: 8). In very few cases did men contest the custody award (Polikoff 1983). Only 12.5 percent of non-Hispanic White children in one-parent families lived with their fathers (Sweet and Bumpass 1987: 269).[4] Throughout the 1980s, only about half the divorced mothers who were awarded child support actually received the full amount of their award; one quarter received partial payment; and one quarter received no payment at all (United States Bureau of the Census 1992).

Divorce means not only that men almost always stop living with their children and frequently stop making any financial contribution to their upkeep, it also means that any relationship between fathers and children is attenuated or even ended altogether. This is certainly the picture that presented itself to men who were young adults in the 1970s. Discussing the experience of children aged eleven to sixteen in 1981 whose biological parents were not living together, Furstenberg and Nord concluded: "Marital disruption effectively destroys the ongoing relationship between children and the biological parents living outside the home in a majority of families" (1985: 902). Ninety-three percent of the nonresident parents were fathers, and of those fathers, 42 percent had not seen their child in the previous year, 64 percent did not see their child in a typical month, and 80 percent never had their child sleep over at their house (Furstenberg and Nord 1985: 895). Furstenberg and Nord also reported that children applied "a scale that is far more generous than objective standards might permit" (1985: 902), with three quarters of the children who were not living with their fathers responding positively to the question whether he "spends enough time with you," regardless of the amount of actual contact (1985: 898).

At the end of the 1980s, 30 percent of children whose parents were divorced did not see their father at all in the previous year, and only 25 percent saw him at least weekly (Seltzer 1991). The general pattern reported from a range of studies is one of "modest initial contact" after divorce and "a sharp drop-off over time" (Furstenberg and Cherlin 1991: 36). Hochschild (1991), pointing out that the rates of paternal contact after divorce in Sweden are much higher than in the United States, suggested that the problems of families cannot be blamed on prosperity, government aid, or feminism, but must be located in "the culture and social world of men" (p. 113).

The picture of the cultural world of men that emerged from my interviews was one in which men, because much of their contribution to the emotional closeness facet of fatherhood has been symbolic or through their wives, have neither the experience nor a clear definition of a direct interpersonal relationship with their children. For men, "wife and family" is a unitary concept—"having a family" means being married. The desire to "have a family" and to "be a family man" is strong, but it does not necessarily equip men to relate successfully to their children outside of the context of their marriages. When men remarry, they frequently find a new family, a new set of children to relate to through a woman. When the children from a previous marriage can be reintegrated into a new family, a man can more easily remain a good father to them.

It was George Peters's second wife, for example, who cemented his relationship with his children from a previous marriage. He told me repeatedly that his children had been very young when he was divorced and that he had been overseas during some of the marriage, so that he did not know the children very well:

> My current wife is very good with my ex and my ex is very good with her. In fact, my current wife here, I was surprised at how well she adjusted and how well the kids took to her. She just took charge and I guess they wanted that.

Chodorow (1978) developed a psychoanalytically based account of the creation of different dispositions toward parenting between men and women. In her account, girls can have a direct identification with their mothers, whom they see around them on a day-to-day basis. Boys, on the other hand, have an identification with their fathers, which is more idealized, less grounded in daily experience, because their fathers are emotionally and physically distant. My own analysis does not address questions of object relations or psychodynamics, but I share Chodorow's interest in and emphasis on the way in which *institutions* and social structures support men's and women's actions, however they are motivated.

The position of non-custodial parent is admittedly structurally difficult. Parental relationships are built on the repetition of actions and interactions that are intrinsically insignificant but that add up to an intimate connection. The individual events of waiting for the school bus or watching television together, of eating meals and saying "good night" are not in themselves instances of particular intimacy, but their routine repetition creates closeness. This pattern can not be duplicated in "visits" of a few hours or even a day or two. Men who are divorced speak of the difficulty of having their children with them unless they are established in a suitable home (Arendell 1995). Given the realities of the job and housing markets, of wages and rents, it is not easy for anyone, man or woman, to set up a home. But it is significant that men seem to feel that they have the time to get established and that their parental role is in some sense optional, whereas their former wives become single parents "naturally," and without choice no matter how difficult their circumstances. The non-custodial parent may "plan," "want," or "intend" to have the children once the suitable situation is established, but the custodial parent must find a place for them to sleep right away and every night, "ready" or not. Just as men may or may not feel "ready" to become fathers to their children, divorced men may or may not be set up, physically and psychologically, to maintain a parental relationship and parental responsibilities. In both cases women are the ones who face necessity, while men exercise options.

Jim was separated from his wife, Monica, and living with his brother and sister-in-law and their children when I met him. The story Jim told was complicated and sometimes contradictory, and thus typical of real life. There is no doubt that Jim's version of events was sometimes self-serving and highly selective, but his enthusiasm for his children was, I judged, genuine. Even as he presented himself as someone who always wanted children, and as an equal parent, his story illustrated the pattern of parenthood after divorce, and also illustrated several of the ways I have described in which women mediate men's reproduction and their relationships to their children.

Jim and Monica had two children, a son in the first grade and a two-year-old daughter who had been born when the couple had reconciled after a previous separation. This time, the separation seemed permanent, and they were engaged in painful negotiations about custody. Jim's story illustrated in one particular case the complicated dynamics behind the common pattern of men's diminishing contact with their children after divorce:

> I didn't get married until I was thirty, and we had kids about two or three years later, which we needed to do because my wife is only two years younger than I am. I'm thirty-seven now and she'll be thirty-five in August, so we wound up having to start about the time we did. . . . We probably would not have got married if she did not want to have kids, because that would have been an argument, I'm sure, during our marriage, if we didn't have kids. But I don't think I would want to argue with somebody about having kids. It would have to be the two wanting.

Jim had never thought about marriage without children, and when I asked him how he would have felt if Monica was unable to have children, he said, "She and I would have to have something real special." For Jim, as for the other men I talked to, having children and being married to their mother were inextricably connected. Jim claimed that he and Monica had shared the childcare when they were married:

> We shared everything with the kids. Nobody ever has to tell me to change their diaper. When I knew the child needed something, I would get it. As a matter of fact, I think I only asked Monica maybe twice during the time we were married to change a diaper. If I couldn't do it because I was in the middle of something, or wouldn't stop to do it and saw that she wasn't really doing anything. Otherwise, anything that I saw, or they said they wanted something, I stopped and gave them a glass of juice, or diaper change, you know, anything. And she did the same. I don't think she asked me more than two or three times herself if I would change a diaper when she was into something. Which was fine.

Jim said they also shared the transportation chores. Monica would take the baby to the sitter on her way to her work at seven o'clock. Jim would take the older child to school on his way to work. Whoever finished work first would pick up the children. This mutuality had continued after they first separated, when Jim had rented an apartment near to the family house where Monica had remained and had been available to be with the children when Monica had been on-call to work the night shift. Jim was enthusiastic about that arrangement, which had allowed him and Monica to divide the children's time between them:

> When I had the apartment, it was great. I could have the kids come over and they could roam freely in the house. I set the house up so the days I picked up Peter, I keep the things that he needs at the preschool. I have this wall full of his pictures and painting and cutouts and plaster things, whatever. In one of the closets I have their toys and I cooked their meals and gave them naps (for Louise) but for Peter I would continue playing. It worked out real good.

Even though Jim no longer had his own apartment, he talked as if that child-centered arrangement was still in place. For Jim, having his own apartment in which he had felt at home with the children and had enough space without worrying about the effect on roommates had been a physical expression of closeness. He told me he would like to have his children with him all the time:

> The only thing I'm not happy with right now is that until I can really get my (as they say) shit together, I'm not going to be able to have my kids as much as I want. And I know that is just myself having to do it. Nobody can do it for me. I need to establish a place of my own and have it furnished and have it very solid so when I say I want my kids half the time, everybody sees that it's all there and set and then it will happen. Because the courts are saying nowadays that as long as both parents want the kids, both parents are going to get the kids. If they don't take anything from one or the other, that will be just fine with me.

Here an explicit contradiction arose in Jim's narrative. Jim's interactions with his children appeared close and attentive, and whatever the details of the division of childcare between him and Monica had actually been, it was evident from watching them that Jim spent a lot of time with his children and knew them well. His reported conversations and concerns about his son demonstrated a level of genuine concern and thoughtfulness. However, the arrangement that Jim had following the separation, with his own apartment set up for the children and an equal division of time, had not lasted. Jim had quit his job as a skilled craftsman, an occupation in which he had worked for years, because, he said, of back pain. Although the heavy lifting he had to do at work was undoubtedly hard on his back, Jim indicated to me that quitting his job was also motivated by his reluctance to pay child support, which he saw as money paid to his wife. There was a real ambivalence in Jim's account at this point. On the one hand, he claimed, "I wish I could have kept my job, but my back was killing me. I should have continued and found something else, but it wasn't working out there. So, I just went ahead and made the change." On the other hand, he was not looking for another job, but for a way to be self-employed or paid "under the table" because, he said, "If I work with somebody else, they'll take too much taxes out, too much child support, where if I can do something on my own then I can take care of my kids my way instead of somebody telling me how to do it."

This is the sort of resistance to seeing child support as part of paternal responsibility, and the sort of backing oneself into corners by trying to avoid it, that Arendell (1995) described for divorced men, and that is apparent in sections of the "men's rights" movement. Some men do not want to pay child support, which they see as payment to their former wives, so they quit their jobs or refuse to pay, and are then in a much weaker position in the eyes of courts, and much less likely to get the sympathy or cooperation of their former wives, when it comes to determining custody or visitation.

Jim himself described how his relations with his children were affected by his current visiting relationship with them:

> At the end of the day [with the children], it sure seems like a long day. But I think that's because I get them such a short amount of time that I try to do as much as I can with them. If I had them, like for a week's time, then I don't think they would be looking to always come here doing something. If they were here full time, they would entertain themselves at times. Because when I stop in at the house and see the kids, she's [Monica] always doing something around the house and the kids are playing with each other. So she doesn't have the constant—like, little Louise, she wants to be held quite a bit by me. Peter still wants to be held by me too. And sometimes when I hold the two of them, Louise is pushing at Peter, like, "Hey, get out of here!" So they are really—when they are with me—*really* want to be with dad. Whereas, as I was saying, she can let them just play in the house or the backyard and they play with each other and play with their own things. She doesn't have to carry them, or deal with them, or think as much as I do.

Every element of the "package deal" of marriage, fatherhood, work, and home ownership was involved in Jim's picture of post-divorce fathering. His job and being a provider would, he claimed, allow him to have a stable home, and a home would allow him to have his children with him a substantial amount of the time, and having his children with him a lot of the time would allow the kind of relaxed closeness that he would like to be the dominant feature of his relationship with his children. But in the absence of a partnership with his wife, this entire chain of mutual support between the elements seemed to collapse. Jim's future as a father was dependent on his relationship with his wife, who he continued to put in the position of determining the relationship he had with his children:

> I know on her part, she wouldn't go for the six months/six months. Because right now, she doesn't even like it— at one point she said, "You know, you get the kids three straight days. That's too much time away from me." I said, "You get them the other four days, that's

> too much for me. I'll be glad to switch. If you want to go four days from you and three the next, or split them up every other day or something?" And she said: "Oh, no, no, that's OK." I said, "I thought so. I'm the one who has to suffer right now. You just wait. I'll get it together and then you're really going to be crying."

For Jim and Monica, as for many divorcing couples, the arrangements for their children were closely entwined with their personal bitterness, disappointment, and desire to hurt each other. But what was so striking about Jim's entire account was that he felt he had the option of "getting it together" as a parent, while his wife had to continue being a parent no matter what her circumstances.

The cultural norm of mother as default parent and the person at home was reinforced in Jim and Monica's case by the decision that it should be Jim who moved out of the family house. This certainly gave Monica the opportunity to be the default full-time parent after the separation, but while Jim portrayed this decision as a concession he was prepared to make to Monica's possessiveness and materialism, it also meant that he could avoid the day-to-day chores of parenting.

The question arises of whether women jealously guard their control over the family or whether men relegate women to the less prestigious area of domestic work and childcare. At the level of family life and the lives of individual men and women, clearly both are occurring (Coltrane 1989; Cowan and Cowan 2000; Garey 1999; Hertz 1986: 64–65; Hochschild 1989; Walzer 1998: 45 ff). The gendered division of labor in parenting is part of an "arrangement between the sexes" (Goffman 1977)—a constructed and continually reinforced division of being between men and women. Men often develop a learned or deliberate incompetence in certain areas. It is a running joke among both men and women that after a man has once done the laundry and mixed white and colored clothes turning everything pink, or fixed a meal and turned the kitchen into a disaster area, or looked after the children for a weekend during which they ate nothing but pizza and never bathed, it is easier for women to do these things themselves. But men also develop different ways of doing things—playing more aggressively, teasing, and challenging children to take risks or break out of routines. Both men and women live out and perform stereotypes, frequently performing them while acknowledging that, in some sense at least, they should not do so. So a woman who says, "I know I should learn how to check the oil on the car, but I let my husband do it" or a man who, like me, sheepishly excuses himself from making social arrangements because "My wife keeps track of the calendar" is perpetuating a particular gendered division of labor at the same time that he or she is criticizing it.

Gender and Power

Any analysis of gender must also be an analysis of power. Feminist analyses have always recognized that power, whether physical, ritual, social, or economic, is integral to gender relations. In 1938, Virginia Woolf made the crucial connection between issues of women's education, women's employment, and peace. In her analysis of education for peace, and her consideration of the kind of society we would need to build in order to make peace a real possibility, she added to the condemnation of war the critical recognition that the oppressive and aggressive movements of her time were headed by men, and that these men were represented as "the quintessence of virility, the perfect type of which all the others are imperfect adumbrations" (1966: 142). From this she concluded that "the public and the private worlds are inseparably connected; that the tyrannies and servilities of the one are the tyrannies and servilities of the other" (1966: 142). Woolf's realization has propelled analyses of the private and personal oppression of women by men and of the links between this private power and the public power also controlled by men. From the feminist perspective, the relationships between the personal and the political have been generally clear—and the criticisms of western feminism for ignoring both the heterogeneity of women's condition and the privilege enjoyed by white middle-class western women do not deny the relevance of feminist analysis so much as demand a reevaluation of some taken-for-granted assumptions.

In describing the men from Meadowview High School I have stressed the importance of two controlling structures in their life histories: dominant cultural values and economic change. Appreciation of these structures takes us beyond their own perception of themselves to see the ways that their life courses have been constrained. In their accounts of their own lives, however, these men did not talk a great deal about control, constraint, and power. Rather, they portrayed their marriages and family lives in terms of personal preferences and choices, and their work lives as responses to opportunities and options. Indeed, the men from Meadowview High are particularly well suited for the examination of dominant cultural values because their power relations are concealed from them. They are not men who have experienced their society as directly oppressive, nor are they men whose oppression of others is directly expressed.

Men frequently deny, or do not see, that they have power, and researchers who analyze men as gendered face an apparent paradox. Joseph Pleck, one of the pioneering scholars of men's condition in the United States and one of the founding figures in the pro-feminist men's movement, outlined this paradox in 1974: "At one level, men's social identity is defined by the power they have over women and the power they can compete for against other men. But at another level, most men have very little power over their own lives" (1995: 10).

Robert Connell (1987) subsequently provided pro-feminist men with a sustained examination and theoretical development of the connections between the experience of varied masculinities and sexualities and the social structures of economic and political power. One of Connell's central contributions was in his analysis of the disjuncture between personal and public power. Men who embody aspects of hegemonic masculinity in their physical strength and displays of virility may be economically and politically marginalized, while the men who exercise corporate and state power may, in their personal lives and their physical appearance, depart markedly from the fantasy of ideal masculinity: "The public face of hegemonic masculinity is not necessarily what powerful men are, but what sustains their power and what large numbers of men are motivated to support" (Connell 1987: 185). Connell's analysis allows us to see that elite men, who embody hegemonic masculinity, have great power over others and control over their own lives, but may be less directly oppressive to the women and children in their lives than are men who are excluded from social power and dominant norms. His point is that the men with power in mass societies do not achieve that power through physical violence or sexual conquest, but their hold on power is supported, in part, by cultural ideals of what a man should be. By separating the personal relationships from the political structures, while nevertheless maintaining a central focus on their mutual reinforcement, Connell helps us to understand how it is that powerless men may directly oppress women and other men, and how powerful men may not appear to be directly oppressive, but hold power through institutionalized dominance.

This theoretical development has allowed scholars of masculinity to explore the paradox that Pleck described. In an influential analysis of modern masculinity that, like much of Connell's work, stresses the conflicts, oppressions, and fears *between men,* Michael Kimmel identified the origin of this paradox in "the discontinuity between the social and the psychological, between the aggregate analysis that reveals how men are in power as a group and the psychological fact that they do not feel powerful as individuals" (1994: 136). Kimmel's argument, which situates men's fear of other men, and their fear of being judged failures as men, at the heart of the contradictions of masculinity, hinges on his examination of the appeal of an image frequently used to describe the position of modern men—that of the chauffeur, who appears to be in charge but is only following directions. This image resonates for men, according to Kimmel, because it allows them to deflect the external criticism of them as dominant and "in the driver's seat" with their own perception of themselves as subject to the authority of others. The task for analysts of masculinity is to transcend this simple opposition of viewpoints and to situate men in their institutional context in order to resolve the paradox of male power.

Scott Coltrane, a sociologist who has paid close attention to fatherhood as a gendered activity and to marriage as a gendered process (Coltrane 1996, 1998a, 1998b), has described men's situation in terms of "the contradictory co-existence of felt powerlessness and actual (if latent) power" (Coltrane 1998b: 201). Recognizing this contradiction between men's sense of themselves and their objective positions in families and society, Coltrane has criticized research that concentrates exclusively on marital interactions and ignores the institutional contexts that shape relations between spouses. It is that institutional context that must be the focus of research directed at understanding men and of policy that aims to alter men's relationships.

Judith Stacey (1990), a sociologist who conducted her research in the county containing Meadowview, has described the new family forms created by women after divorce. Stacey pointed out that what is often, in the United States, called the "traditional family" of breadwinner husband, homemaker wife, and their children, is historically "modern." Her picture of the "brave new families" being forged in the wreckage of the modern family is very different from the family lives of most of the men to whom I talked. In part this is because Stacey's work illuminated at the individual level the gendered impact of divorce, which has generally left custody of children to women and worsened the economic position of mothers (Cherlin 1992; Furstenberg and Cherlin 1991). But the two pictures of family life also differ because they are drawn from different perspectives. I argue that Stacey, starting from the experience and accounts of women, described the consequences for women and children of the pattern of mediated family relationships that I have dissected. Relationships with children look very different to men, seeing them through women, than they do to women, who see themselves in the middle.

My own account of family life, based as it is on the stories of men, does not accentuate the abuses of power and the selfishness of men. As an observer I was aware of the asymmetries in families and of the way that men can and do depend on them to get their own way and to maintain their privilege within families. But the men I talked to did not see it that way, and in reconstructing their worlds and their intentions I have not put this analysis in the foreground. What I have done is to examine men's stories about their lives for clues to a central paradox about fatherhood: Very many men say they want to be involved fathers, but frequently they are not involved and remain emotionally distant and unsure of their ability to connect to their children.

The accounts of the men I talked to emphasized that they had very strong feelings about wanting children and about being responsible for them. They valued children and responsibility both for their own sake and for the changes they brought about in their own sense of self-worth. They recognized the restrictions of family life, but dealt with them by inserting a period of male irresponsibility and sexual license into the life course before family formation. For these men, however, family formation was centered on a relationship with a woman, through whom they had children and through whom they related to those children and to their larger kin network.

I would explain male behavior in families not so much in terms of a conflict between commitment and selfishness but rather in terms of a unified desire to have a responsible family life that can, in men's eyes, be achieved only through the mediation of women. In this view, men's desire to have families and children, and their difficulty in maintaining these relationships after divorce, are both aspects of the way they relate to their families through their wives.

5 Employment as Fatherhood

Everybody has a purpose in life. It's the same basic, mundane thing: You get up, you go to work, you come home. Your purpose is to provide for your family. Obviously, when you have children, you have more of an incentive for that, to get up and go to work. —*Skip*

Everybody wants better for their children. I want to provide that. I don't care the cost. . . . I'll work whatever I have to work, two jobs, whatever it takes to make sure they come out [OK]. —*Paul*

In the United States, one thing that almost all men do is "work." For men in the United States, participation in the labor force dominates their lives and their identities. Men's labor force participation is long term, consistent, full time, and almost universal. In every year since 1960, more than 95 percent of married men aged twenty-five to forty-five have been in the labor force.[1] Men spend many hours daily at work or in work-related activity. Work and money are dominant topics of men's conversations. Men's prestige, their value to others, and their self-worth are measured by their identity as workers and their earnings from their work (Gini 2001; Goode 1982; Pleck 1995). Men who do not have jobs are frequently branded as unworthy, morally inferior, and failures *as men*.

In his study of African American working men, Mitchell Duneier emphasizes their sense of their own respectability and righteousness—the way that they as individuals and as a group embody a set of moral values that guide and judge their actions (1992: 173–74). Work is important to these men's sense of their own value, just as *unemployment* is central to the cultural devaluation of black men. Duneier points out that dominant cultural images of black men overemphasize unemployment and criminal activity and, whether in liberal sympathy or conservative blaming, disproportionately attribute to them membership in the "underclass." In fact, the overwhelming majority of African American men are employed, and there is great diversity of education and income among African Americans (Rose 2000).

Lillian Rubin documented working-class attitudes toward family and work and demonstrated the central importance of employment in working-class men's lives (1976) and the devastating effects of unemployment on their personal sense of self and on their families (1994). The overwhelming importance of work to men's self-worth and to others' judgments of their moral worth is general across class and racial–ethnic categories (Dudley 1994; Furstenberg 1995; Lamont 2000; Newman 1988; Sennett and Cobb 1972; Wilson 1996; Zussman 1987).

For the men I talked to, work and employment were essential to their sense of accomplishment and worth: Work was what they did and work defined who they were. Many, like William Hughes, learned to respect work through the example of their fathers. William's father had worked two manual jobs when his children were young. After high school, William had lived at home and attended community college. According to William, "If I'd had ambitions to go anywhere, my father would have paid for me. He would have mortgaged his soul to support me if I had the grades, shown the initiative." But William had been more interested in partying, and he told me how his father had confronted him about his grades:

> He said, "If you can't get a job or hold a job, you're out on your own. I'm not supporting you anymore. I don't care if you have to go live in the car. The time has come." And there was no arguing about it. I knew he was serious about it. And about a week later, I had a job working full time. Managed to show up on time and everything.

William worked his way up from the loading dock to a management position. Like many other men, he took his mother for granted, and concluded that he and his siblings had learned to work and be successful from his father: "My mother, she was Mom and things were OK, but I think that most of us turned out the way we did—strong work ethic and real feeling of responsibility for ourselves—because of him." To get where he was, William told me, he had spent many evenings and Saturdays at work. But, like so many of the men I talked to, he presented his work for pay as his way of caring for the family by providing for it and expressed the value of this in a discourse of "responsibility."

Although many of the mothers of the men I talked to had been employed, the normative or cultural picture of parenting when these men were young children was of full-time mothers who were exclusively responsible for the care of children and of fathers who were providers and little else. While adult children are well aware of their fathers' employment, their mothers' work has been made invisible to them (Garey 1999). Many men minimized the labor force participation of their mothers and their wives (Potuchek 1997). Margaret Nelson and Joan Smith (1999) described the strategies families use to survive in rural Vermont. Their wonderfully close-grained analysis divides working families into two sets: those with "good jobs" that can dependably support a family and those with "bad jobs" that do not carry benefits, security, or good wages. Comparing the two sets, they found

> no consistent difference in patterns in the attitudes expressed about women working. In both sets, some husbands minimize the importance of the work done by their wives and define themselves as the family breadwinner; in both sets, some husbands clearly acknowledge the importance of their wives' wages. Although women in both sets of households sometimes reject disparagement, in both sets women occasionally collude in this degradation of their work, defining it in the same trivial terms as do their husbands. (1999: 131)

Barry, in an instance of this trivialization, described his mother's work as a waitress as something she did "to keep herself busy" and his wife's home-based sales as an opportunity for her to "get out and socialize." Some of this minimization is cultural work done to emphasize the importance of the man's role as primary provider. Talcott Parsons, one of the most influential sociologists of the 1950s, expressed and reinforced the cultural rule of the time: "A mature woman can love, sexually, only a man who takes his full place in the masculine world, above all its occupational aspect, and who takes responsibility for a family" (Parsons and Bales 1955: 22). That is to say, according to Parsons and Bales, a woman can only love, sexually, a man who has a job.

The men from Meadowview certainly took seriously and valued their own contributions as providers, even when they agreed with a cultural norm that providing alone was not enough to make a man a good father. Christiansen and Palkovitz (2001) take issue with the negative stereotypes that have been attached to the good provider role, and they argue that providing should be recognized as an important aspect of fatherhood, one that makes contributions to children's development beyond the material. They review a wide range of research that supports the notion that providing makes other forms of paternal involvement possible, and that not being able to provide makes other paternal connections impossible. Their summary of Cazenave's (1979) study of middle-income black fathers is illuminating in comparison with my own discussion:

> The provider role was found to be a very salient part of the father's identity. When fathers were asked to rank their major roles in order of importance, out of the four possible choices of provider, husband, father, and worker, provider was ranked first (37%). When asked the most important thing fathers could do for their children, the largest specific category was to provide (25%). When asked what the idea of being a "good father" meant to fathers, out of nine categories, the highest percentage was a good provider (30%). Finally, when asked the worst aspect of raising children, of eight response categories, the largest was not being able to provide (26%). (Christiansen and Palkovitz 2001: 90)

While members of the black middle class are differently situated from the white middle class and experience a particular sense of precariousness and vulnerability (Pattillo-McCoy 1999; Williams 1988), research shows that they have similar concerns and attitudes about fatherhood.

Christiansen and Palkovitz deploy the categories of human and social capital to argue that providing includes giving children social connections and skills and "is both a salient part of being a father and a form of paternal involvement" (2001: 93). Their argument, based on survey and observational studies and arguments from sociological theory, supports my analysis of the complexities of the cultural definition of fatherhood. My analysis of what men say about the four facets of fatherhood is a cultural approach to this complexity: endowment with opportunities and character is the provision of human and social capital.

"Job" and "Career": Two Orientations and Two Trajectories

Although almost all the men I talked to were employed, committed to being providers, and convinced that they could serve their children well by working long hours for pay so that their wives could be the primary parents, there were important differences in their orientations to work. The most basic difference in orientation fell along the division between work as "job" and work as "career," which roughly paralleled the division between blue-collar wage earners and white-collar salaried employees. Blue-collar occupations of the men I talked to include the construction trades—carpenter, plumber, electrician; manufacturing—machinist, shop fabricator; transportation—bus driver, truck driver, and delivery; and service—firefighter, police officer. White-collar occupations include engineer, manager, circuit designer, system analyst. Sales work, depending on the price and volume of the goods, whether the selling is retail or wholesale, the degree of technical expertise required, and the mix of salary and commission, may fall into either "job" or "career" category. While blue- and white-collar are descriptive classifications of types of job, they also describe status differentials. The associations between blue- or white-collar work, relative status, and such objective criteria as income or qualification, are imperfect at best.

Christopher Jencks commented on the effects of our typologies of people on our view of the world:

> We use terms such as "middle class" and "underclass" because we know that occupation, income, educational credentials, cognitive skills, a criminal record, out-of-wedlock childbearing, and other personal characteristics are somewhat correlated with one another. Class labels provide a shorthand device for describing people who differ along many of these dimensions simultaneously. . . . Relatively few people fit either of these stereotypes perfectly. . . . We use class labels precisely because we want to make the world seem tidier than it is. (quoted in Duneier 1992: 173–174)

Mitchell Duneier, from whose book on working men I have borrowed Jencks's quotation, described how the incomes, backgrounds, values, educations, and expectations of the men he studied did not fit the stereotypes, and concluded, "Because of the difficulties involved in any system of classification, I am wary of making claims regarding what these men typify within the class structure of the black community" (1992: 174). Similar discussions are common from authors who describe people they have come to know well. To know people well and to try to understand who they are and how they see themselves is to come to see them in their variety and idiosyncrasy—it is to come to see them as constellations of characteristics that are not necessarily combined in accord with any formula.

My experience in talking to the men from Meadowview certainly agreed with this humanistic appreciation of diversity and individuality. The man with the college degree working in the most monotonous of blue-collar jobs, the senior administrator who had barely graduated from high school, the burly construction worker who spoke sensitively about his love of art, and many others showed me the danger of facile generalization and easy assumptions. Similarly, the great variety of family backgrounds, parental occupations, educational attainment, aspirations, and attitudes of the men make it risky to treat them as a group. On the other hand, the variety of ways of being human does not make us each unique in every aspect. Men with college-educated parents very generally share a set of expectations for their own lives that differs from that of men whose parents finished only high school. Men whose parents can help them buy houses have a different structure of opportunities than men whose parents have no financial support to offer. Men with unionized jobs have a different orientation to work than either non-unionized wage earners who are at the whim of their employers or salaried men whose career aspirations and employment pressure push them into uncompensated overtime.

To compress these crucial differences in social situation and opportunity structure into the categories of class, however, is particularly problematic in the United States. Americans, partly because they like to believe in the importance of individual effort, partly because they like to think that all people are equals, and partly because they want to deny that inequalities are human creations, are very reluctant to discuss class (DeMott 1990). When I was growing up in England in the 1960s, class was a familiar idiom for talking about people and their differences. Many people were unselfconsciously labeled as, and identified themselves as, "working class," and within the middle class such categories as "lower middle," "upper middle," and "professional" were widely used and generally agreed upon. According to a Gallup poll conducted in September 2000, 69 percent of adults in the United States considered themselves middle or upper middle class, while only 24 percent identified as being working class (Zeller 2000). Being "in the middle" is an important American cultural value, and the denial of class differences is essential for the maintenance of a whole system of cultural evaluations (DeMott 1990; Ortner 1991). Being "middle class" is essentially and necessarily a comparative and relative position. Whether the middle is defined in terms of income and status between the "upper" and the "lower" or in cultural terms between extremes, the definition cannot help but be a comparison with other class positions. In the third quarter of the twentieth century, the middle class in the United States was expanding in size and growing in cultural importance—it was not only in the middle between the upper and the lower but in the center of cultural discourse, adopting the values that became defined as normal and normative.

While the inflation of the "middle class" blurs analytic distinctions, it also reveals important attributes of life in the United States. David Halle (1984), in a study of factory workers, noted the distinction at work between blue-collar and white-collar employees. About 45 percent of employed white men are in manual occupations, but Halle reported that men with blue-collar occupations identified themselves as "workingmen" rather than as "working class." These men distinguished themselves from white-collar workers (cf. Lamont 2000), but they lived in neighborhoods that were occupied by a mixture of blue-collar and white-collar workers and that all their residents saw as being in the middle between rich and poor neighborhoods. For the blue-collar workers Halle studied, being "workingmen" and being "in the middle" were not mutually exclusive, but were different aspects of their identities and social positions. Their attitudes as a whole were the result of switching or negotiating between two perspectives.

The primary attitudinal difference between a job orientation and a career orientation is the degree of emotional investment in getting ahead: Men with "jobs" tend to compartmentalize their work lives and take them as fixed, whereas men with "careers" think and talk about them more and spend more time and energy planning their next step. Among the men I interviewed, both white-collar and blue-collar workers drew on aspects of their employment that they felt were supportive of their fatherhood. Some of the men with white-collar and professional occupations pointed to the flexibility their jobs allowed and claimed they could use that flexibility to be participant fathers. Many of the men with blue-collar jobs, on the other hand, claimed that their rejection of a careerist orientation was an indication that they rejected the materialism of the upwardly mobile in favor of a more authentic human life that puts family first (cf. Lamont 2000). Attitudes, however, do not predict practices. The flexibility supposedly offered by professional positions was not necessarily used, and the demands of an eight-to-five manual job left some men feeling too physically exhausted in the evenings to engage with their children.

In these men's lives the important distinctions between "job" and "career" were in their ultimate income level and lifetime income, the formal and informal qualifications required, the trajectory of income and promotion, and the investment of time and energy in work. For men graduating from Meadowview High School in the early 1970s, it was possible to get a good job with only a high school diploma and then to obtain whatever further qualification was necessary through apprenticeship or on-the-job training. Men who did this quickly reached a relatively high level of earnings and could be solidly established in a couple of years. Once established at the journeyman level, however, they reached a plateau in both earnings and promotion. While not all blue-collar workers remain at their original job level for the rest of their lives (an electrician may work independently in his off time and eventually set up as a contractor, or a grocery clerk may aspire to a management position), moving off the earnings plateau entailed a change of job category and usually a changed orientation to work. Mark expressed the "job" orientation succinctly:

> I would never be a contractor. Never. I'll work for somebody else. I make good enough money; let them have the headaches. Because there's a lot of headaches out there and that's just one thing I don't need. I'm not greedy. I just want to go to work, get my eight hours in.

Other men I interviewed were similar in their appreciation for a job with familiar routines and no surprises. Barry, for instance, explained,

> I'm at a level, in my position, where I really can't go any higher. I'm maintenance manager of this whole division, and there's really, in my field, no further up I can go, unless I got into the manufacturing aspect. And I really have no desire to get into that. It's a lot higher stress, more work, and the pay differential isn't that much.

While Barry felt secure in his job, the situation of blue-collar workers in general is more precarious. Fundamental shifts in the economy have removed many of the unionized, well-paying, secure jobs in manufacturing that had supported sections of the (white) working class in a middle-class cultural pattern of home ownership and aspiration for their children (Dudley 1994). The specter of downward mobility has been raised and has not been exorcised by the "boom" of a high-tech and service-oriented economy. In fact, while the boom of the third quarter of the twentieth century decreased poverty and economic inequality in the United States, the boom of the last quarter has increased inequality (Hernandez 1993; Scott 2001; Wilson 1999). The middle class is no longer comfortably expanding by incorporating both the wealthy and the working class, but finds itself suspended uneasily between an increasingly wealthy elite and an increasingly desperate and marginalized lower class.

The "career" path, on the other hand, generally requires an initial investment of several years in obtaining formal qualifications while living on a relatively low income, although men earning formal qualifications frequently have a higher standard of living than their incomes alone would suggest because of subsidies, such as health benefits, vacations, recreation, and entertainment facilities, from parents, the state, and educational institutions. Subsequently, there is often an extended probationary period during which a man must prove himself to his employer. The compensation for a long period of preparation is the potential for promotions and increases in income, which can continue throughout a man's working life and can take him to a level of status and standard of living unattainable by a blue-collar worker. The subsequent cost to these men is that, because promotions are a scarce resource, employers can successfully make demands on their time, effort, and demeanor that can absorb their lives. For those men whose upward path is not as rapid as they would like, there is the added cost of feelings of personal inadequacy, bitterness, and the sadness of potential unfulfilled. Even for men who are successful, there may be constant competition and anxiety over the next step (Newman 1988, 1993; Sennett and Cobb 1972).

From the point of view of a high school graduate, the difference between the job and career paths is in the length of time that must be spent before a man is established at the occupational and income level he considers necessary and adequate for starting a family. The respective levels may differ considerably, and the timing varies, but the connection between work situation and family formation is a common feature of both scripts.

Highly educated men not only postpone having children until their education is completed, but they also construct an age identity that is in keeping with their progress along the career path. Being highly educated equips them for professional careers in which the trajectory of rewards, prestige, and power continues to rise, so that the passage of time is not simply a process of decline. A forty-year-old male attorney, for instance, is a "young" man; an attorney in his fifties is seen as being at the height of his productivity and professional involvement. In most sports, by contrast, a forty-year-old athlete is thought to be at the end of his career, if he has not already been retired for years. To the extent that young men identify with athletics as a mark of their masculinity, and to the extent that they are on employment paths that reach a plateau relatively early, they will compare their ages more to the athlete than the attorney.

Mark and Hal, who I will take as exemplars of work and career, respectively, both came from two-parent families in which the father worked in construction and the mother stayed at home while the children were in primary school. Both told me that their parents did not pressure them to pursue any particular career; both described their fathers as distant, restrained, and with similar "old country" values (although the "old countries" in question were at opposite ends of the earth); and both had always assumed they would have "a wife and family."

When I met them in their mid-thirties, however, these men's lives and situations were markedly different. Mark, a journeyman in the building trades for fifteen years, was married to his high school sweetheart and had two children aged nine and twelve. Mark and his wife lived within fifteen miles of both their parents in what had seemed, when they had first bought a house there a dozen years before, a remote, but affordable, new area of construction. Hal, on the other hand, had spent eleven years in undergraduate, postgraduate, and professional training and had only been established in his profession for five years. He told me he felt "adult" only since finishing his postgraduate degree and beginning to make a real income of his own. During his training the only consideration he had given to starting a family was to think how hard it would be to have one. Hal met his wife at work, when both of them were over thirty. His wife had recently completed her own professional training and they had then bought a house in a comfortable neighborhood of a city one hundred and fifty miles away from Meadowview. Only then, when Hal was thirty-four, had they started to try to have children.

These outline biographies illustrate the difference between a job and a career path, with their accompanying differences in formal qualifications, geographical and social mobility, enlarged marriage pools, income, status, and the timing of marriage and children. In the next thirty years, taking Mark and Hal to retirement age, the differences will widen as Mark's adequate income stays about the same while Hal's higher one increases, and as Mark's modest social standing is maintained while Hal, at least potentially, moves into the circle of influential community leaders.

Despite their differences, these two lives share a common sequence. The differences are in the timing of events and the duration of particular stages, not in the order of those events and stages. For Hal, education was a means to an end and was pursued with single-minded purpose. His choices of graduate school and postgraduate training were based on his perception of the quality of the programs, and it was only once he was established in his career, making a good income, and able to stay in one place, that marriage and family became realistic goals. Mark, on the other hand, made decisions about training and work based on his desire to get married. He had attended the local community college for two years while living with his parents and working nights at the manufacturing plant where his mother then worked. His college experience was not directed toward any particular career or qualification; he saw it as an extension of high school, which he had enjoyed, an excuse to live cheaply and comfortably with his parents, and an opportunity to continue playing sports. At the end of that two years, his girlfriend graduated from high school and, he explained,

> Well, we knew we were going to get married and going to [four-year] college just didn't seem like the thing to do. I considered the trade as just like going to college, it gave me something to do. You know, I had a skill I could use.

Marriage, in other words, required that Mark be able to earn a living and, because the right woman was there to marry, this propelled him into a trade, where the wages for an apprentice were 70 to 80 percent of the wages for a journeyman, and the formal component of instruction did not interfere with working a full forty-hour week.

While Hal postponed family formation in order to establish himself at work, Mark accelerated his attainment of financial stability in order to start his family. These differing paths had enormous ramifications for the rest of their life courses and for their children's lives. Mark's children were growing up in a blue-collar neighborhood of mixed owner occupiers and renters similar in socioeconomic terms to the neighborhood in which Mark grew up. Hal's children will grow up in a very different upper-middle-class professional milieu and will be confronted with different opportunities and expectations.

Many of the men I talked to described how, from their perspective as young men in the early 1970s, the job and career trajectories appeared as optional alternatives. They described their decisions to go to college or to get a job as choices they made on the basis of their situations at the time and their anticipation of likely consequences. The options were not as open to them as they sometimes suggested, however, and some of them realized this as they complained about the lack of opportunities and advice they had received. But for these men born into a booming economy with a rapidly growing and well-funded public higher education system, the paths to upward mobility were more open than for most men of most preceding or succeeding generations. Looked at from an observer's vantage-point twenty years after high school graduation, it was the long-term consequences of the job and career tracks that loomed so large. But underlying the very real differences between these two orientations to employment was a shared set of assumptions about the proper sequence of a man's life, the place of work in that life, and the centrality of work in the definition of a man's responsibility to his family.

Work as Expression of Paternal Responsibility

The extreme gendered division of labor within nuclear families raises immediate and pressing contradictions for men and women. Almost universally, the men I talked to said that they wanted to spend more time with their children than their fathers spent with them. The demands of work made that very difficult. We might expect that the entry of mothers into the labor force in great numbers would, by augmenting family incomes, release men from some of their work pressures and allow them to spend more time with their children. Stable employment in the United States is, however, structured around full-time jobs that require a minimum of forty hours a week and often demand more hours in the form of extra commitment from salaried employees and compulsory overtime for wage earners (Schor 1991; Williams 1999). The direct competition for time between men's employment and families is concealed by the cultural position that providing is something that men do *as fathers*. Devotion to one's job is both a sign of commitment to fatherhood and an activity that detracts from the time a father spends with his children.

Being a worker is a central element of American masculinity.[2] A first job and a first paycheck are important rites of passage, and having a job and earning an income are vital parts of being an adult man. The centrality of work is reinforced when a man becomes a husband and father, a family man. The men I interviewed described a mutual reinforcement between the responsibilities of work and of family. Becoming "ready" for marriage and family required an initial degree of responsibility and commitment, having children brought new responsibilities to be a provider, those responsibilities induced a greater dedication to work, and being a father meant being taken more seriously as a worker by peers and employers (Deutsch 1999; Nock 1998). In terms typical of the men I interviewed, Paul described the onset of responsibility occasioned by marriage and children, and the transformation of his sense of self:

> I thought I had responsibilities until I got married; then I found out about *that*. Then I had my first son and my second son and the responsibilities are just incredible. If you've never had a child or if you've never been married, you're just a selfish individual. You just do whatever it takes to make you happy. And by having children and being married, you just *have* to share and it makes you a better individual. I mean a better person in society. It makes you a rounded person.

Similarly, Frank talked about the change in the way his supervisors and co-workers saw him, and the change in his own attitude toward work, that was attendant on his getting married and having children:

> I think I got a lot more respect from my working environment— on my job. Once you got married and had kids, they felt you were more mentally stable, as a person. They felt: "He's gonna be more settled down and he's gonna be a lot more responsible for his job and he's not gonna screw off at two A.M. and get drunk." [Which, he admitted with a rueful laugh, he had been doing.] So I think, professionally, I think I felt like people respected me for it. Maybe it's something I was reading into it. But I think I got a lot more professional respect on the job from my direct supervisors. I definitely changed my perspective on my job too, so that had a lot to do with it.

Frank's personal experience, and his personal reaction, were thoroughly in step with the policy of employers and the experience of men in general. Married men, and particularly married fathers, are seen as more committed and responsible workers who take fewer sick days and can attend work reliably.

While employment is a way of meeting the expectations of the providing facet of fatherhood, the time it claims reduces fathers' direct daily involvement with their children and the potential for emotional closeness (Crouter et al. 2001). Many men remembered their own fathers' absences at work. Marvin Middleton, for example, compared himself with his father, who, he reported, was away at work a lot: "I want to be there more because he wasn't." Marvin had worked his way up through the computer industry from production to programming. In contrast to his brother, who he described as a "workaholic," Marvin said he managed to do things besides work: "And almost exclusively I don't mix work and home. I leave work at work and I go home. I don't work a whole lot. Basically put in about a ten-hour day, but then on top of a commute, it gets to be a long day." Although he spent twelve hours a day (with, he claimed, only occasional weekend work) at work or commuting, Marvin believed:

> A good father is someone who is with his children. I think someone who just takes time and does things with them and listens to them. I don't think I do nearly enough of that, especially getting home to where maybe they're up for an hour and then it's "Goodnight." Sometimes I wish I had your basic seven to three-thirty job and blow out of here and go home. But it's not quite that kind of job. But everything is a balance. I could work for a lot less money and do that kind of stuff and be totally bored out of my head. And spend more time with them. I'm not sure I'd be all that much better for it either, for myself.

Marvin worked long hours and spent less time with his children than he would have liked, but he justified this in terms of both the quality of his own experience and the money he provided for his family. He argued that by having less money and being "bored out of my head" he would be a worse father, even if he spent more time with his children.

Paul did not talk of his work in the same terms of finding personal fulfillment as did Marvin, although he did believe that his work was useful and important and that he was good at it. He too wanted to be closer to his children than his father was to him, and to spend more time with them. But at the same time, Paul also wanted his children to be cared for by a family member, not by strangers, and he wanted to make this possible, not by doing it himself, but by earning enough so that his wife could stay home with the children.

The strategy of working overtime or working two jobs was a common one for the men I talked to, and in many couples both husband and wife felt that this was the obvious arrangement for providing their children with an at-home mother. Ralph explained how his own extra work was motivated by his wife's strong desire to stay with the children, not just by *his* preference that she do so. Ralph said that his wife wanted to be with their daughter all the time and he, "naturally," worked harder to make this possible. Spending less time with his daughter was not his inclination, but was a consequence of his contribution to family life. For Ralph and his wife, the obvious solution was for him to work two jobs while his wife stayed home with the children:

> My daughter was born and it was quite an experience that first year raising her. My wife was working and she went [out of town]. She had to fly. I stayed home with my daughter. So we decided that it would be better that— My wife just didn't like being away from us. And so when she came back we talked about it and we could afford to live on my salary if I worked on my days off in construction. So I did that and she quit her job and she stayed home and became a housewife. Which is a *very* difficult job. I felt fine [about caring for my daughter]. My wife was the one that was nervous [about being away]. I wasn't nervous a bit because I had done everything. I had changed diapers. I had done everything my wife had done basically except breast-feed and I almost simulated that when I gave her the bottle. I'd walk the floor with her when she was sick. Played with her and watched her grow, helped her grow. So it was no problem. But my wife was the one who was nervous about it. And it was just real hard to convince her I'd be OK. I know when to feed her. I know how to change her. I was perfectly comfortable with bathing her, everything else. No, it was no problem for me at all. Just my wife was nervous. Plus this gave her an excuse to quit her job.

When I asked him if he minded working two jobs, Ralph minimized the personal impact:

> Not at all. No. Because there was no way that we could work it out where my wife could work on the days I'm off. That wouldn't have been good because we couldn't have seen each other.

Being employed was one of the elements of the package deal. Earning an income enabled men to fulfill the material expectations of the providing facet of fatherhood. It also, as Paul and Ralph exemplified, enabled them to provide their children with the at-home care of their mother, which contributed, albeit in a surrogate fashion, to the facet of emotional closeness. Employment also made contributions to the protecting and endowing facets of fatherhood.

Paul emphasized the contribution his employment made to endowing his children with opportunities—opportunities he wished, in retrospect, had been provided for him:

> I got a house, a family, I'm making decent money and all I've got is a high school education and barely that. I was just a product of the public education system. They didn't do anything for me. I just showed up, occupied space, and when my time was done, I punched my card and left. Nobody ever pursued me and said, "Hey, you've gotta do this. You gotta do that. You gotta do that." Nobody ever took the effort. So like I said, I squandered a lot of education opportunities. I regret it to this day. *The only reason I regret it is probably because I could have been a better example to my sons by having an education.* And I could probably work with them a little better than I can now. When they get into math and English and stuff like that, I'm not gonna be able to help them. I'll have to get them tutors. But I'll go out and buy books. I'll buy computers and try to educate myself so I can work with them. I already bought the computer and I sit down and I taught them how to use the computer. I got a math book, which I read, and learn the math so when he has questions, I'll be able to help him. But if I can't, I'll go out and hire somebody or go to school and have them work with him. [emphasis added]

Paul expressed his caring by providing material supports—books, computers, and tutors—as well as by his own direct action. He played with his children and did things with them as part of being emotionally close, but he also saw himself as caring and close when he bought them things with his earnings.

Paul emphasized that by providing things that cost money, including a private Christian school, he was fulfilling his responsibilities as a father:

> But the way we're raising the children, I'm responsible to at least, as the Bible says, to make them accountable to God when it comes time.

> So I've got them in a Christian school. And it costs us a lot of money to put them there, but I think they didn't ask to be here and so that's my primary job. Being a good husband and a father, but it's primary to let them know about God and stuff like that. And when they become the age of accountability, at least they'll have the knowledge of what is right and what is wrong. They won't be screwing up like I did. Everybody wants better for their children. I want to provide that. I don't care the cost. Plus they're gonna get a good education out of it. I'll work whatever I have to work, two jobs, whatever it takes to make sure they come out. At least they can't say, "Well you didn't offer me the opportunity to go to the good schools, to be what I wanted." "Yes, I did. I sent you to almost the best schools. And I showed you what God is all about." So boom!

The men I talked to wrestled with the contradiction between intensive employment and involved fatherhood, frequently resolving it for themselves by expanding the meaning of "providing" to embrace paternal care. The asymmetry of parenting, combined with their feeling that one parent should be home with the children, encouraged some men to work even more hours so that their wives could work less, or not at all, when their children were young. These men saw themselves as caring fathers by providing things, including an at-home mother, for their children.

The Identification of Employment and Fatherhood

I contend that the identification of employment and fatherhood is central to the dominant cultural values about men's roles in the United States. What distinguishes the men from Meadowview High School is not the value they put on work, but the situation that has given them jobs. These men were fortunate that the economic situation they lived in made it possible for them not only to work, but also to emphasize the importance of work to their feelings of success. Had their economic position been different, had they not been faced with good employment possibilities, their lives would have been very different. Obviously, they would have had less income, but perhaps as importantly, though less obviously, they would not have been able to base their self-esteem and their self-confidence as men and fathers on the foundation of their success as workers and providers. The cultural work they do to emphasize the centrality of work to what they do and who they are would have to be redirected. And it is possible that no amount of cultural work could persuade others that a man who cannot find work can be a successful father.

Nearly all the men I talked to spoke about work as something that enabled them to provide for their families. Phil explained forcefully how important it was for him to be a good father:

> I shouldn't say this, but it's the most important thing in my life to be a good father, a good parent. I *should* probably say I should try to be the best husband I can be to my wife, but to be real honest with you, if I had one wish it would be that I was a good parent to my kids. That's the most important thing in my life. It's real, real important. Better than having a good job. Better than being happy. Better than anything is to be a real good parent and help my kids develop.

Phil went on to explain some of the material implications of being a good father. While he said that being a good father was more important than "having a good job," his subsequent comments undermined the distinction between the two. For him to do the things he wanted to do as a good father, he had to have a good job:

> I just want to be there for them, and share with them the things I didn't get when I was growing up so they can fulfill their life the way they want it. That's just the most important thing. It's real evident that that's my most important objective in life. I talk to people all the time about, "I want to be able to help my kids when they need a house or when they need to go to school." I say, "Well I'd love to be able to, if my kids got married and they couldn't afford a down payment on a house, being able to do that for them." To me that's real important. So I have some savings accounts that I've had since I was twenty years old. This is how important it was. When I was twenty years old I wasn't even thinking about marriage. I started this savings account so that I could help my kids through school. And I was thinking about it way back then, so obviously it's real important to me. So I think about it now and say, "Well, yeah, maybe I should use it for us instead of worrying about ten or twenty years down the road." But I don't think I will. Because I had to do everything on my own. I paid my own rent, bought my own house, and did everything myself. I didn't get a cent from anybody. And I think that's OK. But if I can help my kids, that's all the better. I mean, I'm not gonna do it

> if it's gonna make me suffer and eat beans. That would be a different situation. Although I don't know, if it came right down to it, I might rather them have steak and me have beans or whatever. I don't know. We'd have to deal with that at the time, but that's important to me.

Phil's income allowed his wife to be the parent at home, and it provided security, opportunities, and a start in life for his children. His sense of the primacy of being "a real good parent" had a clear and specific material side to it. His discussion was anchored in his attitude toward money. Phil used money and material things—help with education, the down payment on a house, long-planned savings accounts, and even a hypothetical steak—as symbols of paternal affection. He said repeatedly that caring for his children was important, but his examples were all founded on his being a worker, an earner, and a good provider.

Phil's identification of being a good father and being a good provider worked for him because he had been fortunate in his employment. Entering the workforce at a major electronics manufacturer with only a high school diploma, he had been promoted through the ranks of a rapidly expanding company in a booming economy to managerial and engineering positions: "So it turned out real good for somebody without a degree. They don't hire *stockroom* people without a degree nowadays." Phil had been fortunate in the real estate market also. As the company expanded, he relocated to a new site a hundred miles from the San Francisco Bay Area: "We paid a hundred and fifteen thousand for a three bedroom, two bath, on a quarter of an acre, something that would have cost us three hundred thousand in the Bay Area."

The combination of circumstances that has allowed Phil, and men like him, to be good fathers by being good providers illuminates the situation of men who cannot be good providers and therefore are castigated for not being good fathers. The concentration on the provider role is historically specific but has dominated the lives of men in the United States. The grandparents of the men I talked to had been adults during the Great Depression of the 1930s, and many of the men's own parents had childhood memories of very hard times. Their dedication to work was motivated by the immediate memory of the consequences of failure as well as by the lure of success.

I opened this chapter with a review of studies of the United States that emphasized the importance of employment to *masculine* identity. The same studies also support my contention that employment, as a critical element of the package deal, is also central to *paternal* identity. In the 1960s, Elliot Liebow (1967) described how men who depended on casual labor or had jobs that paid only a minimum wage felt they had nothing to offer the mothers of their children and, because they felt they could not satisfy their own expectations, did not become involved fathers. Wilson (1996), discussing the disappearance of work from inner-city neighborhoods, demonstrated the contribution of unemployment and low earnings to the absence of fathers from many families. At higher income levels, Newman's (1988) studies of downward mobility in the middle class vividly depict the negative impact of job loss on men's feelings of self-worth and roles in family life. Hewlett and West (1998) dissect the absence of family support policy in the United States and argue that the erosion of working conditions and wages has had dire effects on parents' ability to care for their children as they would want to. While Phil and his peers could use the cultural identification of good fathering and well-paying employment to present their long hours of work as a contribution to their children's well-being, these studies all demonstrate the negative consequences of this cultural identification when men's employment position is compromised.

The men I talked to shared the position that work was what they did for their families and their families were what justified their commitment to work. Most of them insisted that the purpose of work and of earning was to provide things for their children. Some of the things they provided, like clothes and food, are obvious and immediate contributions to the providing facet of fatherhood. Others, like security and safety, are less tangible but contribute to fatherhood as protection. Some of the things that these men wanted to buy for their children, like extracurricular activities, trips, and the possibility of attending college, were endowments that contributed to the overall quality of their lives. For some men, and on some occasions, purchases were seen as giving their children the best that they themselves had, but more often men talked about giving their children opportunities they themselves had not had.

In all these ways, men described their work and financial providing as motivated by concern for the safety, well-being, and life chances of their children; by the desire to provide the material underpinnings of family life; and by the need to present themselves (to themselves as well as to others) as morally worthwhile family men. They did not see work as a separation from family, but as a manifestation of family commitment.

There were, however, serious conflicts and contradictions within this position. Centrally, their vision of themselves as providing the material conditions for their wives to care for children founders on the rocks of men's declining real incomes, rising expectations about standard of living, and women's increasing labor force participation. Similarly, their desire to spend more time with their children than their fathers did with them conflicted with employers' ever-increasing demands for total commitment to work and with the time workers spend commuting to work from areas with affordable housing.

Attention to men's expressions of care through work, of the role that employment plays in their self-definitions as good fathers, illuminates the cultural foundations of men's actions in families. Locating men in specific historical circumstances illuminates the role of economic structures in magnifying the effects of cultural patterns. The structure of employment and rewards and the provision of benefits cause employers to extract more hours of work from each employee rather than to expand their workforce. Very unequal public education contributes to men's moves to what they see as good neighborhoods. Inflated real estate prices, partly the result of planning policy, push families to more remote residential areas. Both factors increase the physical separation of work and home, and the resulting commutes absorb even more of workers' time. Cultural and structural factors thus work together to prevent the close and involved paternal involvement that is a conspicuous feature of discussions of fatherhood and caring. It is a tragic irony of men's stories that they want to be better fathers and closer to their children than their fathers were to them, but the things they do to be good fathers perpetuate the physical separation of men and their children.

6 Home Ownership

Housing the Family

> Home ownership has helped my wife and my family and I understand the meaning of family and commitment. It is a unifying event in a person's life. Marriages and families cannot survive without it. They may get by without a house, but they never get the most out of the loving bonds a family can find. —*Computer consultant, married with two children*

> Until housing becomes either lower priced or easier financing and less greedy people, nobody can afford a new home. —*Engineer, married with four children*

HOME OWNERSHIP is the defining aspiration and sign of membership for the middle class in the United States. Home ownership is also one of the four elements of the package deal. Homes are worked for and worked on—they are both valuable and valued—but home ownership also ties people into a system of employment and consumption that has profound contradictions. Homes, the sites of class reproduction as well as individual reproduction, are the places where aspirations and desires come face to face with circumstances. The tensions and complexities of family life are there revealed.

If the four elements of the package deal were smoothly integrated, employment would mark full independent manhood and thus eligibility for marriage, provide the family income to support marriage and children, and enable the married couple to become home owners. This cultural ideal, however, has never been a general reality. Even in the heyday of the family wage, subsidies from government programs, differential access to economic opportunities, and class privileges concealed or made invisible the external material supports to this ideal of the package deal and the self-sufficient nuclear family. The tensions between the elements of the package deal result in contradictions between ideal and reality. These contradictions are concealed through cultural work that aims to create the appearance of having achieved a seamlessly integrated package of marriage, employment, home ownership, and fatherhood.

Over time, the relationships between the elements of the package deal, and particularly between employment and home ownership, have changed in ways that make the tensions greater and the cultural work harder. Home ownership has become a more essential element at the same time that the relationship between house prices and earnings has changed. Most men's employment is not adequate to ensure home ownership. Increasingly expensive and culturally valued home ownership puts great and increasing pressure on men's earnings. Men deal with this increased tension with four strategies: turning to kin, increasing their hours of employment, commuting farther, and relying on their wives' income. Each of these strategies creates new contradictions and requires further cultural work. In this chapter, men's discussions about home ownership reveal the cultural work they were doing to address tensions between the four elements of the package deal. As they described how they tried to balance their preferences for housing, their standards for neighborhoods, the length of their commutes, and their concern to support their families on one income, these men were also describing how they constructed a satisfactory image of themselves as fathers.

Homes as Symbols and Commodities

The single-family, owner-occupied house on its own lot is both symbolically and materially central to the family life of most Americans. Most people in the United States now live in owner-occupied homes. Although it is often represented as a middle-class marker, home ownership is not restricted to members of the middle class, and its symbolic importance is widespread throughout the United States. The African American owners of urban row houses in Washington, D.C., and blue-collar factory workers who identify themselves as workingmen also express the crucial value of ownership for self-worth and respectability (Halle 1984; Williams 1988). The importance of home ownership as an element of personal and social identity and the devastating effect on that identity of losing a home has been described in ethnographies of the downwardly mobile middle class (Dudley 1994; Newman 1988).

In 1920, less than half of all housing units were owner occupied; in the 1990s, the figure had increased to two-thirds. Married people are more likely to own their own houses than are others. The incidence of home ownership among married couples has increased steadily since World War II. In 1960, when the men reported on here were about five years old, 46 percent of white married couples who had been married for five years were home owners. By 1980, when these men had been out of high school for seven years, 66 percent of such couples were home owners (Sweet and Bumpass 1987: 159–60). Home ownership for married couples had become so common as to be a norm, increasing the pressure on young couples to buy a home just at the time that economic conditions made it very difficult to do so.

In home ownership, as in so many areas of life, there is a racial chasm in the United States (Krivo 1986; Massey and Denton 1993). In 1990, 68 percent of housing units occupied by whites were owner occupied, for "blacks and others" the figure was less than 44 percent, below the white level of seventy years before (United States Bureau of the Census 1996: table 1190). African Americans were excluded from government programs promoting home ownership, including New Deal policies and the creation of the Federal Housing Administration in the 1930s (Gotham 2000) and of the Veteran's Administration mortgage program after World War II (Brodkin 1998). Brodkin points out:

> The GI Bill and FHA and VA mortgages, even though they were advertised as open to all, functioned as a set of racial privileges. They were privileges because they were extended to white GIs but not to black GIs. Such privileges were forms of affirmative action that allowed Jews and other Euro-American men to become suburban homeowners and to get the training that allowed them—but much less so women vets or war workers—to become professionals, technicians, salesmen, and managers in a growing economy. Jews and other white ethnics' upward mobility was due to programs that allowed us to float on a rising economic tide. To African Americans, the government offered the cement boots of segregation, redlining, urban renewal, and discrimination. (1998: 50–51)

President Kennedy proclaimed that "a rising tide raises all ships," but the government subsidies that raised so many Americans into the middle class in the 1950s were not universal. Discrimination against African Americans in mortgage lending continues into the present (Turner and Skidmore 1999).

Home ownership is a sign not only of social position and economic success, but also of moral superiority. Home owners who emphasize the order, quiet, safety, and cleanliness of their neighborhoods are describing not only a physical difference from what they see as the confusion, noise, danger, and dirt of poor urban neighborhoods, but also a sense that they embody the moral qualities of self-control and industry that they see as so conspicuously absent from the poor and the unsuccessful. It is the sense that financial failure is moral failure that gives such an edge of desperation to the precariousness of a middle-class position that is separated from poverty only by a job.

Providing a house for his family not only establishes a man's moral worth and financial success but is also an element of the package deal that contributes to all four facets of fatherhood. Besides the manifest provision of shelter, to own a home is to live in a neighborhood of owner-occupied homes inhabited by families of similar income and background. Home ownership separates families and children from members of other social groups who are seen as directly dangerous and the source of harmful influences and thus contributes to paternal protection. The homogeneous neighborhood that is seen as safe and protecting is also seen as contributing to the endowment of children with opportunities by giving them access to the amenities of good schools and recreational facilities and by associating them with peer and reference groups that have "good values" and appropriate aspirations. Home ownership also makes a symbolic contribution to fathers' emotional closeness by linking fatherhood with all the values of warmth and intimacy associated with "home."

The family home is the focus of security and the site of family rituals and gatherings. It is the container for status-expressing and status-enhancing material possessions. The structure of the home provides age- and gender-specific spaces and is the setting for a gendered division of labor (Bourdieu 1977; Moore 1986). Home ownership is culturally and symbolically elaborated, with all the values of "home"—security, affection, pride, memory—embodied in the physical structure.

The single-family, detached house is often represented as separate and bounded, and it functions as such in our imaginings of it as a safe haven or domestic enclosure. Single-family houses are, however, integral parts of neighborhoods, and home ownership is part of a system of consumption and of a way of life. To live in a neighborhood of middle-class single-family homes generally requires being an owner occupier, since few of these houses are rentals. Developers often strategically position some townhouses and apartment buildings to benefit from the higher rents that can be charged for access to the amenities of owner-occupied neighborhoods. They limit the scale of these rental developments to prevent diluting the qualities that attract the owner occupiers in the first place. More than providing oneself with suitable shelter, owning a home in a neighborhood of owner-occupied homes is expressive of social location.

The archetypal habitat of the American family is the single-family home in the suburbs. The lives of suburban home owners have often been characterized as boring, complacent, mediocre, alienated, and frightened. The suburbs themselves, often named after the "oaks," "meadows," "orchards," and "woods" that were destroyed in their construction, have been attacked as sprawling, ugly, environmentally disastrous, rows and rows of "little boxes made of ticky-tacky."[1] But suburban communities are not simply denials of the urban and destroyers of the rural; they are distinct types of communities in their own right. This new type of community has been noticed, criticized, and taken as the base for improvement since its inception by such diverse figures as Ebenezer Howard (founder of the "garden city" movement; Buder 1990; Evans 1972), Lewis Mumford (1961), and Herbert Gans (1967). An anthropological position recognizes that the intersection of home with class and family deserves serious analytic attention and that the values of millions of Americans should be approached with empathy and attention rather than derision.

Since the 1950s, suburbs have been built around the automobile in the same way that an earlier generation of suburbs and new towns had been built around the street car and the railroad. They mark a sharp geographic separation of work and home that is made manifest in the particularly middle-class institution of the commute. Although many service workers are too poorly paid to live near their employment and so spend long hours traveling to and from work, the combination of suburban home ownership and commuting comes out of a more deliberate separation of work and home—a separation that is moral as well as physical.

To live in the suburbs is to use physical distance to express moral difference from the city, which was described to me by the men I talked to as full of crime, violence, dirt, rudeness, and laziness. These men valued what they referred to as "good" suburban neighborhoods for their schools, safety, and separation from polluting contact. Their valuation of neighborhoods had changed since they had been children, and most no longer wanted to live in areas like the ones in which they had grown up. Looking back on his childhood, Mike remembered Meadowview fondly, but he also recognized that he no longer saw that environment so benignly: "Growing up here was interesting. It was lower income, but I didn't know any better. I thought it was just fine. And back in those days, the families were nice, neat and clean. It was almost just like *The Wonder Years*, growing up there."

Some of the changed perception of the neighborhoods of their youth was a result of the cycling of neighborhoods and housing stock as inhabitants aged and were replaced. These men expressed a fear, shared by many members of the middle class, of the contagion of poverty, especially for their children. Their own upward mobility was recent enough, and they were sufficiently aware of its precariousness, that its physical manifestation in home and neighborhood was symbolically crucial. Living in a homogeneous neighborhood of "people like us" both shows who "we" are and distinguishes "us" from "them." It also makes sure that children are protected from "them" and turn out "like us." Margery Austin Turner, a researcher at the Urban Institute and editor of a major recent report on mortgage discrimination, put her finger on the link made by many white residents: "When minorities move into a traditionally white neighborhoods, it's visible right away. Many fears and prejudices materialize on the basis of race even though the concerns articulated are about crime and behavior" (Otto 2000). The association of racial difference with poverty, laziness, violence, and vice contributes to the racial segregation of neighborhoods in the United States (Hacker 1992; Massey and Denton 1993).

Material decline in U.S. cities has been accompanied by changes in the meanings and use of public spaces. The men I talked to, for instance, described their own childhood experience of public parks as safe places for unsupervised play, but they described parks today as dangerous for their children, who were escorted to the park and watched while there. For these men, ownership of one's own home meant living in a particular kind of neighborhood and leading a particular kind of life.

OWNERSHIP AND OBLIGATION

Home ownership is widely represented as a symbol of the core American cultural values of independence and self-sufficiency. Despite the image of self-sufficiency, most people do not "own" their homes, and buying a house entails being tied to a particular level of earnings and depending on help from others. Almost all home owners actually owe more than they own. In 1995, U.S. owner-occupiers owed four trillion dollars on their homes ($3.75 trillion were owed on mortgages and an additional $250 billion in home equity loans and lines of credit). In 2000 the percentage of disposable income committed to monthly mortgage and equity loan payments was at a record level (Uchitelle 2001). Rather than giving people freedom to confront their circumstances, owing large amounts of money for something that is so culturally valued, and so meaningful as a marker of position and individual worth, makes them hostages to the demands of their employers. Those who owe money on a mortgage are committed to selling their time and labor in a situation where not having a job means losing not only income, but home, social position, and individual identity. When the national, regional, or local economy declines because jobs are exported or speculative bubbles burst, home ownership rapidly becomes a liability as payments take up more of smaller incomes, values decline, and families sell at a loss or have their homes foreclosed.

Owner-occupied housing has not only become more expensive over the last two generations, it has also increased in price faster than real earnings. One consequence has been an increasing desperation in the housing market. While rapid inflation of housing prices has brought unprecedented wealth to some sectors of the middle class, it has put most people in a financial, moral, and time squeeze. The median price of a single-family house in the San Francisco Bay Area was $34,500 in 1972. This price doubled in the next five years, and doubled again by 1982. By 1989 the price had again doubled and, at $282,000, was more than eight times the 1972 level (Goldman, Powelson, and Lehrman 1990: 84). In Meadowview, the median value of an owner-occupied home in 1960 was 2.2 times the median annual family income, and this ratio was the same in 1970. By 1980, home value was 5.2 times annual family income; by 1988 it was 7.4 times as much. In addition, the flood of veterans with

Veterans Administration guaranteed, low-interest, low-down-payment mortgages that fueled the housing boom of the 1950s had greatly diminished. First-time home buyers looked instead to help from kin (Henretta 1984). In 1990, the chief economist of Wells Fargo Bank in San Francisco estimated that 80 percent of current first-time buyers received help from their families (Goldman, Powelson, and Lehrman 1990: 85).

It is easy to castigate Americans' materialism and consumerism, of which there is abundant evidence (Schor 1998). Some of the increase in housing costs is the result of increasing cultural expectations—for instance, for separate bedrooms for each child and private yards for children's play—but some is the result of improvements in housing that hardly anyone in the United States would think of as excessive. In 1950, more than 33 percent of occupied housing units lacked complete plumbing; by 1990 only 1 percent did so (United States Bureau of the Census 1996: table 1189). Especially in the case of housing, it is not easy for an individual family to reverse the trend toward larger houses with more amenities. Living in a cheaper, smaller house or apartment almost always means living in a different kind of neighborhood with inferior public services. And when enough people move to inexpensive neighborhoods, they drive up the prices of real estate.

This constellation of social, cultural, and economic processes leads to a physical separation of work and home, to commuting, to time spent away from home, to less time with family. Men are urged to step out of the rat race in order to be close and nurturing fathers at the same time as the circumstances of their lives and the insecurity of a global economy demand ever greater devotion to their jobs. For men, a norm of home ownership increases the pressure to fill the good-provider role, but also increases the tensions between the four facets of fatherhood: providing, protecting, endowing, and being emotionally close. Employment and home ownership contribute directly to providing, protecting, and endowing. But working more hours and commuting longer distances cut into the time men have available to be with their children and establish direct emotional connections. Men addressed this tension by redefining home ownership, employment, and maternal care as direct expressions of paternal love and emotional closeness, a redefinition that simultaneously rationalized increased hours of work and decreased time with children (Crouter et al. 2001).

SELF-SUFFICIENCY AND DEPENDENCE ON KIN

Because housing was so deeply symbolic, and because buying a home was a crucial variable in assembling a particular realization of the package deal, men's conversations frequently revolved around real estate. The stories I was told about buying houses, home improvement, and real estate price inflation were also stories about hard work, perseverance, and taking advantage of opportunities. Jack's account was typical in the way it conflated home ownership, marriage, and personal achievement. Jack, with his wife, Samantha, and their two sons (aged four and eight), lived in the neighborhood of Meadowview where he had grown up. Their three-bedroom, one-bath house was similar to the other houses in the neighborhood, which was one of the original developments of the 1950s. His five years in college had earned him a degree and a teaching credential but had not opened the way to the teaching job he wanted, and when I met him, he had been working in an unskilled, but unionized, public-service job for more than ten years. He had the seniority to get the shifts he wanted and as much overtime as he cared to work and had no intention of taking any promotion or supervisory position. Jack seemed morosely resigned to his situation. He was matter-of-fact when he talked to me, inserting parenthetical comments and acknowledging my lack of familiarity with his life. Jack talked a great deal about his house, which he treasured as a solid achievement, a contribution to secure family life, and a refuge against an uncertain future. His plans for the future of his children incorporated, or were incorporated within, his plans for his house:

> That was one of my goals in life: to get a house before I got married because once you got married it's pretty tough to get a house. When I got out of college, I started saving money. I wanted to get it before I got married. It's a big goal, to get married and have a house. In fact, years before I got married (we first met in 1980), I thought, "Well maybe this— She's the one for me. And if this is so, better start putting something, doing something about getting a house." I started working six days a week, ten hours a day for three years 'til I got married. Saving money then. Bought it before we got married, this house. Had enough money. Worked out all right.

The cultural value of self-sufficiency dominated Jack's account, and he described himself as "an independent-type person," but Jack's life chances had depended on a variety of kin as well as on his own efforts.

Although, like Jack, they described their lives in terms of personal choices and individual achievements, many of the men I talked to had received various sorts of material help from their families in making the transition to adulthood. Jack himself, despite his protestations, had received a hidden subsidy from his family. His father's mother had bought a mobile home in Meadowview but was still living on her farm when Jack graduated from high school. For their first two years of college, Jack and a friend from high school lived in the mobile home together, splitting the low costs. Jack then moved to an apartment for the next three years and subsequently moved in with his grandmother for the following five years. This living arrangement with kin made it easier for Jack to both go to college and save money for his marital home.

Jack's family was further involved in his home buying. His emphasis as he told me the story, however, was on his ability to be self-sufficient. I asked him if there was anyone who could have helped him when he was buying his house, and he replied with a detailed narrative:

> Well, what happened was, I did not buy this house totally by myself. *I could have.* I put down the whole down payment myself for this house. I have a sister two years younger than me, and I think she was living in an apartment. So I said, "Why don't I help her? We'll buy the house together. She'll pay me back later, half the down payment." It made it easier on me, of course, too, because I only had half the monthly payment. I could have made the payment myself. I said, "Why don't I help my sister?" We had a plan to keep the house for five years and I would buy her half of the equity out. She could buy herself a condominium or whatever. *She'd still be in an apartment if I didn't help her.* So she says, "OK." My parents actually paid me back her half of the down payment on the house, which was fine. I just put that money in the bank. And I bought her out four years later, not five. Then she went and got her condominium just like I told her she would be able to, and she has a nice condominium with the equity.

Jack was clearly proud of his ability to make this plan and of his success in establishing his sister in her own home. But what emerged from Jack's story was that his parents had managed to use their limited resources to help two of their children to home ownership, which is something they would have found much more difficult, if not impossible, without that help.

Family help combined with fortunate timing to permit Jack to realize his dream of home ownership:

> *Now* I would never be able to afford a house. If I was to walk in today, there'd be no way. Not even close. This was seven years ago. I could probably get a condominium with just one, me, working. If me and my wife were working, I don't know if I could afford this house at what they're going for now, I'm not sure. It'd be pretty tough. 'Cause we'd have to pay for a baby-sitter, care, and things like that.

Buying the house before marriage allowed Jack to put together another element of his package deal, for he could support his family and make his mortgage payments on his income, with overtime, alone.

When I asked Jack whether he thought his children would find life easier or harder than he had, Jack explained that it was his house that was going to provide his children with a chance in life. The house did not simply shelter his children but was also a material endowment. Jack was enthusiastic as he gestured around the house to illustrate the plans for expansion that he had created in his mind's eye:

> I want to say "easier," but I don't really believe that. I think things will be harder, especially when it comes to houses. What I plan on doing, I don't know if it's going to work out or not, to make it easier on them, is get a whole other house. 'Course that depends on how we're getting along. That's just things that I think about now: Where are my kids going to be living when they get older? Are they going to be living down the street in an apartment? Are they going to be able to afford their own house, which is possible, depending on what they do with their lives? Or are they just going to go out and get a normal, everyday job, you know, making seven, eight bucks an hour. They're not going to be able to afford a house on that. So if we got along really well, I thought maybe, like all these other people are doing, building another story. You know, by the time this one's twenty [his youngest], I'm going to be fifty-five, so they can take over this one [this house]. That just may sound silly, talking so far in the future, but that's just a possibility. If we got along very well, I wouldn't mind them being near. I know my parents would not ever let me build another story on their house like I'm considering doing here. I mean, I'm talking about a whole different house. I'm talking

> about a completely— like a duplex. Double except for the garage. Two or three bedrooms, and a bathroom, two, a kitchen, the whole works, stairs up— I already had it planned. Twenty-five years and see what happens.

Jack's discussion of his house illustrated the multiple significance of home ownership as a contribution to marriage, a motivator of employment, and a way to contribute to all four facets of fatherhood. Jack's story also illustrated how negotiations over real estate provide material expression for enduring ties between kin, as well as the cultural work that must be done to reconcile help from others with the norm of self-sufficiency.

For many adult men, help from kin in buying a first home was critical in achieving the package deal. But both the moral success of home ownership and the moral disaster of downward mobility hinge on a fundamental attribution of success and failure to individual character and effort. So the help men had received from their parents and other kin had to be downplayed in the interests of their presentation of self as independent, just as their wives' earnings had to be downplayed in the interests of their presentation of self as breadwinners and providers. The cultural stress on self-reliance was a theme throughout the accounts men gave of their lives. They represented their marriages, jobs, and education as the result of their own choices; they emphasized their self-sufficiency in supporting themselves through school; and they insisted that the decisions they made about having children were theirs and theirs alone.

I was struck, during my research, by the contradiction between culturally important claims that individual adults must be independent from their parents, and the continuing importance of family ties to achieving and maintaining the package deal. The tension between a cultural narrative that emphasizes self-reliance and a social context that shapes options and opportunities is particularly acute in discussions of home ownership. Men's insistence that they could afford to buy houses themselves and that they did so as a result of their (and their wives') industry and thrift coexisted with a variety of stories about arrangements that men had made with relatives in order to buy their first home. About three-quarters of the home owners I questioned mentioned at least one form of help, and many mentioned more than one (Townsend 1996).[2] Some of these were straightforward financial transactions, while others were more diffuse relations of solidarity. Even the most cut-and-dried financial arrangements between kin are, however, qualitatively different from those in the open market, having different standards of credit worthiness, propensities to foreclose, and obligations to repay.[3] Repeatedly, men who had just described to me how they could only have bought their first house because of a father's mortgage, a loan from their parents, a gift of the down payment, subsidized rent, or some other crucial assistance, immediately afterward insisted that they "made all the payments," "did it all ourselves," "handled everything ourselves," or "didn't need help." Their emphasis was not really a denial of the help they had received, for which many men were extremely grateful, but was an index of the cultural importance of making one's own way.

Providing, Protecting, and Endowing through Home Ownership

For the men I talked to, where to live, the kind of house they would live in, and the division of labor in the family were closely linked issues. In balancing housing quality, location, schools, commuting, the domestic division of labor, and commitment to work, while taking into account their resources and situations, the men from Meadowview High School have arrived at different configurations of the elements of the package deal. Jack, for instance, had used his family's help to buy a house that, while adequate, was not what his peers aspired to. By working overtime he could support the family on his income alone. He had minimized his commute time, maximized his work time, compromised on the location and size of his house, and ensured that his wife could be home with his children. In the examples that follow, other men have struck different balances between location, commuting, hours of work, and their wives' employment. Some had stayed in the neighborhood, either buying early or compromising on house quality; others had moved in order to be able to buy a house on one income; and yet others had had to combine commuting with employment for both husband and wife. For all of them, however, home ownership motivated employment, and home ownership contributed to providing for, protecting, and endowing their children.

Matthew told me that the biggest difference between himself and his father was that "I'm loyal to my family. They're the most important thing in my life." For Matthew, loyalty to his family took the form of working hard to provide his children with a home. He had worked two jobs to save money for the down payment and eventually bought a house from someone he knew who gave him a third loan in addition to the first and second mortgages he had from a bank. The house was smaller, on a smaller lot, and in a worse neighborhood than he wanted, but even so, he felt it was worth all the sacrifices he had made:

> It was very tough buying my first home. At times I thought it was impossible to own my own home. I think God has a lot to do with it. I think it would have been easier had I better educated myself. Hopefully by better educating my children and being their friend and father their life will be better.

For Matthew, educating his children (endowing them with opportunities) and being their friend (emotional closeness) were intimately connected as aspects of what he, as their father, could do to improve their life chances. Buying a home provided the material site for his fatherhood and also represented, for him, his commitment and loyalty to his family.

Frank and Carol Smedley lived in Meadowview with their three young children and, when I met them, were thinking of buying a bigger house. They were very explicit about the trade-off they faced between getting "a lot more house for the money the farther east you go" and "the amount of time you spend on the road." They also liked the area in which they were living and liked being close to family. Frank's comments reflected the tension that he and Carol experienced between their different criteria for a good place to live:

> We prefer to stay in the general vicinity. I was born and raised in Meadowview, so I like it here. And Carol was born and raised in San Francisco. She's lived down here for about eight or nine years and she likes the area. She'd like to stay in Meadowview. I think it's much different from when I grew up. But I don't think it's any worse than any other area in the Bay Area here. I think as far as opportunity-wise, schooling-wise, they have some top-notch schools and I think the education is pretty good. The only thing I don't like is the amount of traffic in the area. Everybody is concerned about water quality and radiation in the area and everybody is scared of this and that. I'm not quite sure. We've looked at the area. We love Meadowview, but we'd like to get a bigger place, more acreage. We're not

> quite sure what we're gonna do. We'd like to get out into a more country atmosphere, but Carol kind of likes having people around her and being close to the relatives. It's a hard decision. Weighing the differences before we settle somewhere, we're taking it slow.

As Frank and Carol compared their linked criteria of closeness and congestion against distance and space they were in the position of choosing between desirable alternatives. Since they had accumulated equity in a house they found acceptable they did not have to move out to afford a good enough house. They would do so only to improve their housing. Other couples, while they weighed the same set of linked criteria, were more constrained in their choices.

Barry Richards, who was so adamant about having his wife stay home with the children so that they would not be in a "baby-sitter environment" all their waking hours, devoted himself to his work so that the family could live on one income. It was Barry who told me, "I try not to work too many hours" but put in ten- or eleven-hour days, plus commute, on a regular basis. When Barry and Linda first met, he had been buying a house in a neighboring town and Linda had been buying another in the area where they now live. After several years of living together in her house, they sold it and bought their present house when their children were aged three and one. Price was important to them as they looked for a family home, because they knew couples whose "mortgage payment is so high that both parents *have* to work [and] you have these poor children who have to get up at five in the morning to make it to the baby-sitter. That's really rough on them." Location was also important because they were choosing the place to raise their children. Barry explained that when they decided on a house,

> We picked it, basically, because of the school district. Where we lived before, the immediate area was very nice, but the surrounding areas were a little rougher. The school that they would have had to go to, there had been a lot of child beatings and older kids beating up on younger kids. And we had two alternatives: either send them to a private school or move somewhere else that we felt more comfortable with and liked the school district. So we looked around and looked around. This was farther away from work. So we liked the area, we checked out the school district, and we're extremely happy. The school is really good. It's a very small school, and the kids get a lot of attention. But that's why we moved here.

The alternatives that Barry presented were also described by many parents who saw themselves facing a choice between living in a house and location they liked but where they would feel they should send their children to private schools and moving to a good school district. For many, moving to good public schools for their children meant moving away from familiar neighborhoods and extended networks of kin (Hansen 2001).

Frank and Carol were making the decision about where to live by balancing commuting time, price, and their desire to be close to their extended families and the communities in which they had grown up. Barry and Linda were less attached to place, wanted to live on one income, traded Barry's long hours at work for his wife's ability to be with the children all day and volunteer at their school, and made their decision based on their judgment of what was good for their nuclear family as a unit and their children's own futures. For all these couples, buying and owning a home was an integral part of their parenting and of their relationships with their extended families, who influenced their choice of location and helped them buy a house.

The housing market in the San Francisco Bay Area was a particularly difficult one for young couples. The area was already built up, the number of jobs grew much more rapidly than the supply of housing, and immigrants flooded to Northern California from other parts of the country. But for some, the inflated housing market had been a boon. John, the son of a warehouseman and a cannery worker, had gone to work right after high school graduation, returned to college part time after a few years, and earned a master's degree that qualified him for his professional occupation. John explained how economic changes had enabled him to own his current house:

> In 1974 we bought a two-bedroom, one-bath home three blocks from where I live now. We both had good jobs, worked at [a communications company]. We sold our first house and put down half on the new house. We made a large amount on our first house to be able to afford the one we're living in today. A two thousand square foot, four-bedroom, three-bath trilevel, hardwood floors, etc. My kids would not be able to buy a house this easy. But inheritance might play an important factor for them.

His own ability to buy in the first place came from the fortunate coincidence of a booming job market, his wife's employment, and low real estate prices; and his subsequent upgrade in housing was powered by rising housing prices. His children, however, will be more dependent on help from kin to buy their first house. Today's family house becomes a material provision for children when they become adults.

A Thousand Dollars a Mile: The Separation of Work and Family

While all the couples described in the previous section still lived in the area around Meadowview, others had moved away in pursuit of jobs and affordable housing. The social significance of geographic mobility in the United States can be easily exaggerated and wrongly identified. In 1980, for example, in the county to which Meadowview belonged, only 44 percent of the 1.2 million people over five years old were living in the same house as they had been in five years before. The image of a society in random flux suggested by this statistic is modified when we revise it to say that 75 percent of the county's population had been in the county for at least five years. Over five years, only 9 percent of the original population left for another state and only 9 percent of the final population came from out of the state during the period. Since most movement within the state was to and from other counties in the greater San Francisco Bay Area, and since interstate moving is heavily concentrated in certain age groups, the general impression of adult movement is of moves within a quite circumscribed region.

Sociologist Claude Fischer (2000) demonstrated that the common assumption of increasing mobility is false. Citing historical evidence that "Mobility has *decreased*, both in [the] long run, since the mid-nineteenth century, and in the short run, since the mid-twentieth century" (Fischer 2000: 1), Fischer made an observation and comment that is applicable not only to mobility but also to other assumptions about contemporary society:

> The long-term decline in residential mobility is well-known to historians. The annual declines are annually publicized by the Census Bureau . . . and often reported in the press. Articles on the decline have appeared before. . . . Then, why do off-hand references to "rootlessness" and increasing mobility appear so often, not just in popular publications, but also in sociological articles? One possibility is that increasing rootlessness fits too well the "grand narrative" of modernization latent in sociology and much other social science—that modernity is socially disorganizing and

> psychologically alienating—to be abandoned. When a fact . . . clashes with a grand narrative, the fact is soon forgotten and the narrative chatters on. (Fischer 2000: 12)

In a detailed analysis of the annual migration question included in the Current Population Survey, Fischer concluded, "Not only have Americans as a whole become more settled, so have . . . 'typical' middle-class families and American children" (2000: 2). Fischer also pointed out, as I have argued for the county and region including Meadowview, that "most moves are relatively short, making changes in social ties and life habits less wrenching" (2000: 2).

Many of the men I talked to had made a number of moves—at first out of their parents' home to an apartment of their own; then to a first home around the time of marriage; and perhaps to second and third homes in pursuit of affordable living space for their children, to get equity out of centrally located houses to pay for the expenses of children, to be nearer their jobs, or to move to neighborhoods, which, for a variety of reasons, they prefer. But this movement within a local area contributed to a situation that has been described as "ever more rooted" (Fischer 2000).

Luke, the son of a machinist and a housewife, went to college right after graduating from high school. He found work as a technician with a computer manufacturing company, but, he said,

> By the time I finished school, housing in the [San Francisco] Bay Area had skyrocketed. I had the opportunity to move out of state with [a computer manufacturer]. The price of houses was almost a fourth or less of Silicon Valley, yet my income was the same. Pure luck. For the fifteen years or so that we've had it [the house], we've not been able to afford anything else. In fact if things keep getting worse, we could lose it.

Luke was unusual in moving away in pursuit of work and housing, for the job market in Silicon Valley was so strong that most men I talked to had found good jobs there. For them, the problem was buying a house. This problem was particularly acute for those who did not have the support of kin, or who, like Luke, were trying to buy after the housing boom was in full swing. For them, the separation of work and family was associated with commuting.

George Peters talked a lot about how he and his wife, Cindy, were always pressed for time and about the rigors of their commute. George and Cindy worked within five miles of Meadowview High School, but were living in a four-bedroom, three-bath house with deck and above-ground pool in a development of hundreds of similar houses carved out of the orchards eighty miles away. They commuted to work and back at least an hour and a half each way every day. George identified time as the greatest obstacle to being the kind of father he wanted to be. He was a good-humored man whose conversation sprang from point to point, peppered with shorthand references and allusions. Whether he was describing his mother's dedication to work, his own time pressure, the baby-sitter's routine, or sleeping during his commute, his story was punctuated by rueful, ironic, conspiratorial, and just plain amused laughter.

George and Jack had very different houses, in very different locations, but housing loomed large in both their conversations with me. They both faced constrained choices when trying to house their families. Both, in their different styles, were trapped by their circumstances. Jack was stuck with a twenty-year sentence to a job that was just putting in time while George was tied to a schedule that left him and his children rushed all the time and that he did not think he could maintain.

George and his first wife bought a condominium, which they sold when they separated: "We sold that and we didn't know the boom was coming. If we had just waited a little bit longer we could probably have got double what we got." In his second marriage, George and Cindy had to start over, much as a young couple would have to do. The "clock" of George's life restarted with his second marriage, so that he referred to Cindy and himself as a "young couple" and they associated with other young couples with young children even though George himself was ten years older than many of the other fathers and had teenage daughters of his own:

> You know, I was like trying to save some money. But it's hard to put money away when you got a lot of kids. Cindy and I had to work our way up, you know. She talks about it all the time, because we're kind of up in years now, we're both over thirty-five. We set out a goal that we were going to start out in a mobile home and we did and we got it and we went from the mobile home to a condo in San Jose. Not a condo, a townhouse, same thing really, and got tired of paying those, whatever you call it, "club fees" or whatever, extra for all these things. And then we went from that townhouse to this one. There will

> be a time when we might be able to afford more, really. I mean we're not, you know, starving right now. But we do have a tough— We've come a long way from the Bay Area to find something that's nice.

Entering the real estate market later than Jack, and after prices had started to escalate, George and Cindy could not afford to buy the house they wanted in the Bay Area, even with two incomes, the trade-in of their condominium, and George's Veterans Administration mortgage. The trade-off they made was not in the size of the house they bought, or in their neighborhood, but in the distance they had to travel:

> Prices drop the farther you have to drive. What it is exactly is a thousand dollars a mile. It's a thousand dollars a mile; that's what they told us. Came right out and told us when we got this house. We tried in Patterson and you could see, you could just see it. And right now that big project in Turlock they're still around a hundred thousand. We got this for a hundred thirteen last year. We've, we just got our taxes and they just redid our assessment. After we put everything in, it's worth a hundred and seventy-five right now. And we've had it less than a year.

George and Cindy, like David and Mary, whom I described in Chapter 1, lived in California's Central Valley over the hills and almost a hundred miles east of Meadowview. The two couples had both moved to buy better housing than they could afford in the immediate San Francisco Bay Area, but they had moved at different stages in their families' development and had different combinations of housing and work. David and Mary had moved out to get a bigger house with the equity that had built up from earlier houses. With a big down payment, their monthly mortgage payments were reduced and David could support the family on the wages of the job he found near his new home. George and Cindy, on the other hand, bought their house in the valley because they could not afford to buy what they wanted any closer to their work. With no capital, two young children, and George's child-support payments, they needed two incomes.

George wanted to live in and own a house that he considered suitable for a family, which meant a detached house with a yard and a separate bedroom for each child. The imbalance between wages and real estate prices, however, meant that he could not afford to own the kind of house he thought appropriate near his workplace. There was cheaper housing close to his work, but it was unacceptable to him, both because of the size of the houses and because of the quality of the neighborhoods, and finding work in the area where he could afford to live was not a realistic option for him.

George had thirteen years of seniority with a large corporation. He had good benefits and wages, and he said it would be hard to find another job like that because manufacturing companies were hiring only at entry-level positions, and he did not have the qualifications to enter a new field or to bring specialized skills to a new employer. In fact, he was narrowly specialized in the procedures of his company. So his work, his income, his sense of responsibility, and the way he paid child support and contributed to his new family were all linked to spending eight hours a day in a particular manufacturing plant in San Jose.

George laughed at the discrepancy between what money could buy in the Bay Area and in the Central Valley and about the process through which he and Cindy had come to terms with the options they had:

> We tried down there [in the San Jose area], and they were showing us some shacks for [the same price as] what we could get here. Some friends of ours moved out here first, and then when we heard about it, we came out and visited them and checked model homes that they had. Those were the model homes right there. And we said, "Yeah, we want one of these." And we practiced the commute, right? And it took us three hours one time. We said, "Forget it." So we backed out. No, we hadn't really signed the papers or anything, but we said, "Forget it." And then we tried about three weeks, a month later, and said, "We got to do it, you know." Because we looked around some more, we had some realtors looking for us, and it was like, they were just showing us some real crap for the same price. Because we had a range and that was it, you know. Fortunately, I had the VA, so that helped us get in there, but otherwise we couldn't have.

George and Cindy were not at all unusual in the pressure they faced or in the choices they made.

In the Central Valley, a construction boom has been underway since the late 1970s. Visiting George and Cindy, I would turn off the highway and pass the flags and the elaborate sign at the entrance to the development, the carefully landscaped and displayed "model homes," and the sales office. Then I liked to take a drive through the development that I thought of as a time machine. The first houses I came to were the first built and had been occupied for several years, with established trees, fences, landscaping, and a generally lived-in appearance. After a couple of blocks, the houses were complete, and occupied, but some had fresh sod or grass seed coming in, while some still had bare earth in the yards, and the swing-sets, sheds, and decks of owner-occupying improvement had not yet been built. Farther along, completed houses were for sale as workers did the clean-up and final detail work, painting and laying carpet. After that, my drive would take me past houses that were progressively less complete, so that the impression was of deconstruction as windows, roofs, siding, framing, and foundation disappeared until the street ran between graded empty lots with the stubs of plumbing and conduits sticking up. Eventually, the paving stopped and the landscape was one of trenches and grade cuts as graders and backhoes shaped the dirt and crews installed the sewers and storm drains. Beyond this belt of activity, bulldozers tore out the plum trees and piled the whole trees into enormous piles to be burned. Farther out, the orchards and farmland of the Central Valley stretched away, mile after mile of some of the most fertile alluvial soil in the world.

This enormous activity and transformation of the region was fueled by the housing needs and dreams of the workers of the San Francisco Bay Area. As George explained,

> In fact, this neighborhood, this whole tract, *this whole town works in the Bay Area*, believe it or not. I haven't met one person in all these neighbors right here that does not work in the Bay Area. Bay Area people just kind of gradually moved out and, hopefully, we're hoping for some industry coming out this way, so we'll see.

Industrial developments are being built in the Central Valley, following the cheaper land that lured George and Cindy and their neighbors and the lower wages that can be paid there. But at the time I was talking to them, there was very little employment locally. George described the daily routine:

> A lot of our friends that work with us, we travel and we all have minivans. So we all have minivans and there's about six of us now, and so you only have to drive once, twice a week at the most. Four o'clock, all those garage doors go open and right down the highway. Four-fifteen you kind of beat most of the crazies out there, so it takes about an hour and fifteen minutes, an hour and a half, depending on

> no accidents. If there's a bad accident where they got the lanes closed, everybody just turns around: "We're not gonna make it." You would have to take a ride at 4:15 in the morning to believe it. I thought there would be nobody out there when I first came out there. And there was a line of headlights, because it's one lane this way and one lane this way. That's one thing that we all talk about, is it's so easy to wipe out there, because everybody's doing seventy and there's just no way that you're going to stop if you ever have to stop. And then we have the Tule fog.
>
> And I know I can't do this [commute] for the next twenty years. My body will not take sitting in a car, even though we sleep.

The long commute, and their routine of leaving the house at 4:00 in the morning and returning, on a good day, at 5:00 in the afternoon, both limits and constrains the time George and Cindy can spend with their children:

> Our baby-sitter laid down the law. We took our vacation when she says we take our vacation, because she gets up at 4:00 in the morning. You don't find too many baby-sitters who do that. Of course, our kids are carried in like this [in his arms]. Laid on the bed that she has and she goes back to bed. But still, she has to get up and let us in. And she does a lot. She walks our kids [to the bus]. Bus comes right here, but we take them over there, so she's got to walk them to the bus stop, put her in, and off they go.

The schedule imposed on family life by the effort to meet the demands of the package deal reduces the time together that is a precondition of emotional closeness. Pressure on time becomes pressure on parenting:

> You know what really bothers me? I feel like I say, "Hurry up!" all the time, you know. "Hurry up. We gotta do this. We gotta do that." And now they use that a lot in their speech: "Hurry up." When I hear them doing it to each other, I feel like— I'm talking about a two-and-a-half year old! She's telling her sister to hurry up, and I could hear the other one saying, "Hurry up! Hurry up!" And I'm going, "Hurry up and clean that room. Hurry up and do this. Hurry up and do that." You know, I use that too much. That bothers me because I don't remember that when I was a kid. And I don't remember my mother saying, "Hurry up! Hurry up!" 'Cause it didn't seem like they were in that much of a hurry. And now this. And I see it in all

> my friends here that I commute with: "Come on! Come on!" Getting those kids rounded up, you know, and it's like— it *really* bothers me.

Because the family needed two incomes, George did not even have the possibility of justifying his own absence at work by providing his children with a mother at home. He did what he could to make the time he had with his children special. When this involved spending money, of course, it committed Cindy and George even more deeply to their distant jobs:

> We get them lots of stuff that we can do, but it's not enough. Especially since we moved out here. It's not enough and that really bothers me. So we try and— weekends, we try and really make it worth their while, because it seems like all the other times we're dumping them off at some baby-sitter and going to bed, and it's like you only have so many hours when you're home, especially during the week. Weekends we try and have everything they could possibly have to have fun.

Nevertheless, George and Cindy saw the sacrifices they were making as contributions to their children's current happiness and future life chances.

Location and Life Course

Mike, who devoted himself to his work more completely than any other man I talked to, faced the same choices as George. But Mike had only one child, and while he spent even less time at home than George did, his wife had stopped working to stay with their son. Mike had bought a townhouse near Meadowview. It was not what he wanted for his family, but he saw it as a temporary measure only. He compared his townhouse with housing near where George lived:

> This is the first house that I've bought. And the next home we buy is going to be a house with property. I will move soon. I could have bought a house near George for what I paid for this and got myself a four-bedroom executive home, or five bedrooms. But I needed a little place here. It was our choice to sacrifice the size and the quality of the house to be close than to move far away. I don't want to commute. The way I looked at it, I'm not giving up the battle yet. I'm not going to leave this area. I'm going to fit myself into this area. Hous-

> ing is cheap everywhere, and that's fine and dandy. But I need to make it in this area.

Mike was one of many people in Silicon Valley devoted to making a lot of money, which drove real estate prices up and, as an unintended consequence, forced out wage earners like George and Cindy.

Jack had also stayed in the neighborhood of his youth. He described the changes in the residence patterns of his neighborhood, which he attributed to the cultural values of the new immigrants there, as an alternative response to high prices. The neighborhood, Jack said, was "a lot more mixed" than when he was growing up:

> There's lots of Asians coming in, with the multiple families because they can't afford the house. You see very few single-family dwellings now. There's still quite a few older people like my parents. Most of my parents' friends (parents of people that I grew up with) still own their houses, still live here. But when those type of people are selling, people that you're finding that are coming in are multiple-family-type thing. They add a deck on or add a couple of rooms. Three or four, in some cases four generations in these houses. And most of the ones that are coming in are Asian. So it's changing. . . . Numerous houses around here that used to all be single-family homes when I grew up are no longer like that. In this area, when people do move out or sell, houses are bought by a number of families. Two or even three. People moving in my age, couple brothers and sisters with their parents and full of smaller kids.

Jack's neighborhood was going through a typical transition as many of the original owners, who had bought the houses thirty years or so earlier as young married couples, were retiring and moving out. For new immigrants to live at higher densities than the previous inhabitants of their neighborhoods is neither a new nor a particularly Asian phenomenon. The same pattern has occurred with Irish, Italian, and Jewish immigrants to the cities of the East Coast, with African American migrants to Chicago and Oakland from the South, and with immigrants from Central America to any number of cities in the United States. The same is true of South Asian immigrants in England, North Africans in France, Turks in Germany, and of a long catalog of migrants to cities around the world. Migrants, without the social connections, political organization, and cultural capital to get the good jobs, find themselves economically worse off than the members of the population they are joining. Higher densities are a response to their economic situation. They are better off than they were in their place of origin but poor by the standards of their new communities. What is significant about Jack's account, and of so much of the response of settled populations to new arrivals, is that very general responses to economic situations are attributed to specific cultural differences.

Having achieved the elements of stable employment, marriage, children, and home ownership, Jack was looking forward to and planning his retirement. He was matter-of-fact in talking about his work and more interested in describing the minutiae of shift assignments and jockeying for overtime and holiday pay than in talking about what he actually did all day. Quite explicitly, his job was something to which he gave time and from which he got money. It was not the job he had wanted, but he felt lucky to have it. As he said, "I think I could get a job tomorrow if I needed to. Now whether I could get a job that could make the *house payment* is another story." His voice, which was full of conviction and emphasis when he was recounting his house purchase or expansion plans, fell to a quiet monotone when he talked about his future at work. The house he was so proud of had locked him into his job:

> I have at least twenty more years to go. Fifty-five [years old] 'til I get a decent retirement, but I'll probably go to sixty-two, 'cause then you get social security. Kind of hard. My house isn't paid off. At fifty-five it wouldn't be paid off quite yet. So, it'd be hard to live on that, making payments.

I asked him if he planned to stay in the house. He laughed, and some of his animation returned:

> To the day they cart me away. Yeah. I've no vision of moving to a bigger house. I know people who bought houses here or other areas. Just put up a little equity, take that money, and start all over again. Another thirty-year mortgage, usually a higher-interest-rate-type thing. No, I'm not going nowhere.

For Jack, as for the other men I talked to, owning a house enabled him to feel that, as a father, he had something to contribute to his children's life chances.

7 Fathers of Fathers
Kinship and Gender

> I very seldom saw my parents before I got married. And now we see them a lot more often. We get together all the time. —*Frank*

> I had three older sisters. So basically, it was just me and my dad, somebody to play ball with. —*Barry*

THE MEN I talked to tried to achieve the package deal by assembling the elements of marriage, fatherhood, employment, and home ownership. They talked about success in achieving the package deal as an accomplishment for which they could take credit as individuals or as part of an autonomous married couple. I have, as a counterweight to their individualist ethos, stressed the importance of social situation and circumstances to understanding the pattern and variation of these men's lives. The time and place of their coming of age, patterns of economic change, and accidents of birth have all been crucial.

Achieving the package deal was not just a goal that men had for themselves, it was the goal that many others had for them. Their personal goals were in accord with the goals of the dominant culture, and their efforts to achieve their goals contributed to cultural continuity. Just as their own fathers had tried to raise their sons to be good fathers and husbands—financially successful, with good jobs, and able to buy their own homes—they directed their own efforts toward making it possible for their sons to achieve this composite goal. The approval and collaboration of other people in men's attempts to realize the package deal are markers of the ways that the cultural system of fatherhood articulates with other systems of cultural values, especially the cultural systems of kinship and gender.

Fatherhood in the Kinship System

Becoming fathers creates new relationships for many men, pulling them back from the relative autonomy of single adulthood into a web of social relations and kinship connections. When a couple has children, their sisters and brothers become those children's aunts and uncles, and their parents become grandparents. Other people have a new interest in the couple and their children, and the new parents reinforce family connections. Parents become more closely integrated into kinship networks larger than their own nuclear families. Family gatherings, joint vacations, play dates among cousins, shared chauffeuring and childcare, sharing tools and collaborating in home improvement, and help from family members in finding and changing jobs were all examples of connections with kin that I observed or that were described to me.

Anthropologists originally described kinship relationships in terms of reciprocal *rights* and *responsibilities,* stressing the ways in which people were defined by their social positions and the ways in which social organization was maintained by their mutual dependence. As we have come to see that kinship relations, like all human interactions, are arenas for contestation and negotiation rather than for the strict following of rules, we have tended to describe people in different kinship positions as making more or less acknowledged *claims* on one another. A language of claims and negotiation certainly accords better with the view of the men I interviewed. In accord with their very general valuation of self-reliance and free choice, they tended to talk about all relationships as chosen and voluntary. Faced with the tension between their valuation of self-sufficiency and their actual interconnection with and dependence on others, they adopted two rhetorical strategies. One was to insist that they wanted and chose to do things that might appear to be expected or required of them. The other was to normalize the help and material support they received, so that, for instance, the expectation that parents would leave their property to their children (rather than to their own siblings or to non-kin) was seen not as an obligation of the kinship relationship but as part of the natural order of events.

Although their discussions attempted to redefine or conceal the mutual interdependence of kin with an image of individual self-sufficiency, the material manifestations of support between kin were crucial for determining their life chances. Many men's parents and other kin have contributed to their achieving the elements of the package deal by helping them find jobs and buy houses, by giving them advice and other kinds of help, and by endowing them with opportunities and abilities. Other men felt the lack of support from their parents when they were adults or the inadequacy of the endowment they had been given as children. In either case, as these men reflected on their own efforts, they also reflected on the contributions their parents, and particularly their fathers, had made and continued to make.

The men I talked to frequently reported that family members gave financial help and assistance with home repairs and improvements, but they also reported that kin had bought furniture, appliances, and cars for them; had loaned them cabins and recreational vehicles for vacations; had bought their children clothes and paid for their extracurricular activities; and had provided occasional or regular childcare. The couple's parents were typically most closely connected to the nuclear family and were the sources of the most significant material support. And that support was frequently conditional on, or at least connected to, being married, having children, and making coordinated decisions about location. Parents generally help adult children in the context of their position as grandparents. Data from the National Survey of Families and Households on giving and receiving between households indicate that aid for first home purchases is most likely to go to married couples, then to cohabiting couples, then to single parents, and is least likely to go to single people with no children. The results show that aid for home purchases goes from older to younger, overwhelmingly from parents to children, most frequently to people in their prime childbearing ages, and much more frequently to married than to single children. In other words, help between generations supports the reproduction of families made up of married couples with children (Townsend 1996).

Kin, in general, and parents, in particular, help and support children in both material and nonmaterial ways. Advice, encouragement, and the emotional support of "being there" may all be very powerful forms of help. Research on relationships between the generations reveals that the same people generally provide material and nonmaterial assistance (Hogan, Eggebeen, and Clogg 1993). The interview excerpts in this book are full of references to the nonmaterial provision and endowment that parents contribute to their children, and to the material assistance that often accompanies emotional support. In the previous chapter I described the help given by kin with buying a house and I have mentioned various other forms of help. This support both expresses and reinforces the relationships of kinship. Those forms of help that are directed particularly toward children, such as providing childcare, helping with schooling, and making coordinated moves, reinforce the centrality of parenthood in the kinship system.

Kin are seen as providing a safe and acceptable form of childcare, for they are linked to the children by ties of blood and emotion that paid childcare workers do not share, and they function symbolically as extensions of the parents. Relatives are "family," and leaving children "at relatives" is placing them within the larger family. I discerned a hierarchy of values about childcare arrangements. Parents found some reasons more acceptable than others for leaving children with paid baby-sitters, relatives, or daycare workers at younger ages and for longer periods of time. Parents were more likely to see work, rather than "time for ourselves," as a legitimate reason for leaving young children with someone else. But their reasons were not additive. If parents (particularly mothers) were away from their children because of work, they were likely to resist being away from them more for other reasons. So these parents included their children in their leisure activities, did not go out in the evenings, and socialized with other parents. When children were in care during the day, "couple time" became "family time." This brief account from my own research of parents' perceptions of a hierarchy of care and of the relationship between family care and paid care is borne out in general and explored in rich detail by Garey (1999), Hays (1996: 119), Macdonald (1996), and Uttal (1997).

Barry Richards's discussion of childcare conveyed both the preference for relatives as childcare providers and how this support from kin contributed to the quality of his marriage: "The kids are at the point now where they can be left at relatives and we can go out and have time to ourselves. When they were smaller, that wasn't really possible because we didn't have a lot of relatives that lived close." Barry and Linda had moved away from their kin in order to buy a house they could afford on one income in a "good" school district. Barry's in-laws redressed this separation from kin when they moved to a house just down the street from Barry and Linda, and Barry commented that his children now had "a live-in baby-sitter down there."

The coordinated moves of family members who wanted to maintain an appropriate proximity was a striking feature of the accounts I was given of housing decisions. Barry and his relatives had made a number of moves as they reconfigured their relationships with one another and their own positions within a system of kinship. Many other couples included closeness to one or both sets of parents, and frequently also to siblings, as one of the reasons for living where they did. In addition, I was told that a considerable number of grandparents had, when they retired or moved out of the family home, chosen to move closer to their adult children and grandchildren.

The ideal of self-sufficiency conceals many forms of relationship between generations. Grandparents ease some of the time pressure on parents by providing regular or occasional childcare. They also provide their grandchildren with material goods and benefits, role models, moral instruction, and cultural capital, and they make other contributions to their children's successful parenthood, such as convenience addresses and safety nets. In spite of an ethic of individual and nuclear family autonomy, kinship is a vital element in the perpetuation of class status in the United States.[1]

Because public education in California is funded by local property taxes, and because attending particular schools is restricted to children who live in the school district, a child's address has a significant impact on the resources that are expended on his or her schooling. This link contributes to differentials in housing prices, for parents are buying not only a house but also a school district. While the solution for most couples was to try to strike a balance between the cost of housing and the quality of the local schools, another strategy was to use a convenience address. A convenience address cannot be bought on the market, but it can be arranged through kin connections. One couple explained to me in detail how they had used the wife's parents' address when they registered their children for school. Her parents lived in a relatively expensive neighborhood in an adjoining town with a reputation for good public schools. Because they could use her parents' address to get their children into good schools, this couple had been able to look for a house to live in without having to be concerned about the quality of the local schools. They were able to afford a house in a neighborhood of inexpensive but adequate houses while continuing to send their children to the good schools in the wife's parents' town. In this way, the support of kin allowed the couple to circumvent the strong association between "good" school districts and expensive neighborhoods and to achieve both home ownership and a quality education for their children.

Similarly, the financial resources of parents provide an insurance or "cushion" for couples whose own resources are stretched thin. Only one man, who had been unemployed when his first child was an infant, told me that his parents had actually made a considerable number of his mortgage payments. Their help had made an enormous difference to his subsequent life and to his children's life chances, but that kind of assistance from parents was uncommon. Only eight of the 77 men I surveyed who had bought houses reported receiving some help with the monthly payments, and only two of them reported that they had received such help "often." Overall, this level of actual help made only a modest contribution to men's ability to buy houses, though it may have been vital for the few who did get help with their payments. What *was* common was the *expectation* that a man's parents would help if accident or emergency made such help necessary. Many of the men I talked to saw their parents particularly, and kin more generally, as providing an insurance against difficulties in buying a house. Eighty percent of the men I surveyed said that they were confident that they could have turned to their parents if they had had to (Townsend 1996). Interestingly, even though actual financial gifts and loans to help with the down payment were reported equally from husband's and wife's parents, only 40 percent of these men thought they might have been helped with monthly payments by their wife's parents. This discrepancy reflects men's sense of the order in which they would turn to people for help, with their own parents heading the list. The violation of an expectation could be traumatic. Ten years after the event, one man in particular was still deeply aggrieved that his own parents did not lend him money for a down payment while his wife's parents had willingly done so.

The anticipation of inheritance is another example of the importance of potential transfers between generations even when no money changes hands. Couples who expected an inheritance, eventually from their parents or more immediately from grandparents, said that they were prepared to stretch their current resources to the limit in ways they would have been unwilling to do if they had had no such anticipation. Potential support from one's kin is an important aspect of social position and does not have to be mobilized in order to operate; what counts is the perception that it could be.

The examples of such hidden forms of support could be multiplied, and more instances and kinds of support are revealed as we learn more about people's lives. It is precisely through a web of connections that people manage to achieve their goals (Fischer 1982; Wellman 1999). No one particular connection will be important for every person, and no connection will be important in every instance, but the existence of a web of potentialities is crucial to achieving and maintaining the package deal. Conversely, of course, if a man's kin or parents do not have access to resources, if they do not have savings, credit, collateral, or connections, then his chance of achieving success in the terms of the dominant culture is much reduced.

The rights and responsibilities of kinship are frequently reciprocal. Adults feel obligations to their own parents as well as make claims on them. Roy's account expressed the complexity of kinship connection. His own housing choices had been entwined with his parents' support, and his plans for the future involved discussions with his parents, their concerns, and his own sense of responsibility. About five years before I spoke to him, Roy and his wife had moved back to Roy's childhood home when his parents moved out of it and into a smaller house. His parents, his younger brother, and his sister all lived close by. He, his parents, and his brother all lived in houses owned by his father, who was still working in construction. Roy talked to me as if thinking out loud, and his fragmentary sentences conveyed the complexity of his preoccupation and the tentative nature of the conversations he had had with his father. He moved from talking about his father's houses to talking about his father's concerns about retirement, his mother's health, his sense of responsibility for his parents, and his own place in the family. His siblings, he felt, were not unwilling to help care for their parents, but they were at different stages of their own lives and family growth. In Roy's account, housing became a material manifestation of relations between the generations, a physical necessity, a marker of social position, a pathway to opportunities, a way to meet family obligations, a financial asset and investment, and a symbol of responsibility and affection:

> So we've been talking to my father about wanting to go ahead and tie some loose ends together. Eventually I was gonna buy the house from him. And he's talking to me and I guess he's thinking about my mom. She's retired; he's about ready to retire. They're thinking about their future too. And he's thinking of the future as to who is gonna take care of them. So he says, "Don't worry about the homes." I think eventually— Because I'm downright determined to take care of my parents until the day they die. So, we need to sit down and talk. Because I think eventually— Because my Mom has arthritis and such, her health isn't that good. So I think eventually we'll move in with them and he wants to maybe expand that house or do something to this house or what. I think eventually what will happen is my parents will move somewhere so I can take care of them. And it's still a long way off. My mom has a little arthritis here and there, but they're in pretty good health. My younger brother, he's got a brand new family and he's just starting off, and my sister is pretty well established in [her town]. My other brother is still away in the service. And me being the oldest son and everything, I sort of inherited the responsibility I guess. But I was always a big advocate anyway. I couldn't understand how people— I guess I could understand, but it just didn't sit right with me, how people could put parents into homes and such. I couldn't imagine my parents in a home. It's a pretty big responsibility. Kind of overwhelms me.

Roy conveyed the complex interactions between elements of the package deal, the strong sense of responsibility expressed by so many of the men I talked to, the common lack of explicit communication to accompany strong emotions, the importance of material provision as an expression of family love, and the web of relationships within which men live their lives and try to be good fathers.

For adults who are the age of the men from Meadowview High, the obligations to their own parents are more often a matter of anticipation than of current reality. Common images of the parents of adults as dependent on their children are largely misplaced. Researchers who conducted a large-scale and detailed study of the relations between parents and their adult children in the Albany, New York, metropolitan area found that the flows of support continued to be, on balance, from parents to children until the parents were seventy-five (Logan and Spitze 1996; cf. Ingersoll-Dayton, Neal, and Hammer 2001). They also found that agreement with the sentiment that parents should help their children increased with the age of the parents. Nevertheless, anticipation is a potent motivator of thought and action, and many of the men I talked to were trying to come to terms with their growing recognition of their parents' impending old age. With remarkable uniformity, they claimed, like Roy, that they would, of course, be there to help their parents if they needed them. But with equal uniformity they denied that this was because they were under any obligation to do so. Just as they had children because they chose to, and did things for their children because they loved them, all those who said they would help their parents insisted that they would do so because they wanted to. Their position was, by and large, in accord with their voluntaristic approach to obligations and in agreement with their peers in the United States (Logan and Spitze 1996). As a rule, they said they would help their own children and their own parents because they chose to do so, they denied that their children or their parents were under an obligation to help them, and they intended to be self-sufficient in their own old age. In spite of men's efforts to present all their relationships as chosen and their commitments as voluntary, it is clear from what they said that they experienced multiple obligations because of their positions in the kinship system (Stack and Burton 1993; Weston 1997).

When men have children, they move from the social position of "son" to that of "father," and their fathers move into the position of "grandfather." Fatherhood is an integral role in the kinship system. The kinship positions men move through are specifically male statuses that mark the fact that the kinship system is essentially gendered: "son," "father," and "grandfather" (Schneider and Smith 1973; Yanagisako and Collier 1987). While it is true that "children" become "parents," at the level of identification and experience it is "daughters" and "sons" who become "mothers" and "fathers." Fatherhood is gendered in two dimensions, parental and lineal. Between fathers and mothers, fatherhood is part of the gendered division of parental labor, and between fathers and sons, fatherhood is the link between succeeding generations of men. Men as fathers see themselves moving into the position they have associated with their own fathers, and they see the changes in fathers as they become grandfathers. When they turn in the other direction, away from the man who they are replacing to the child who has taken their own place, men's focus remains on the male line. It is their sons who will replace them.

Reevaluating Their Fathers

As the men I talked to described the changes that fatherhood had wrought in their lives, they also described the changes it had made in their perceptions of their own fathers. Accepting what one has achieved and what one has become as satisfactory, adequate, or "OK" often leads to recognizing that one's upbringing was, in at least some respects, also "OK."[2] As men grow older they reach a point when they can remember their own fathers being the same age. A man whose father was twenty-five when he was born, for instance, obviously has no memory or direct experience of his father as a child, adolescent, or young man. For at least the first twenty-five years of his life he cannot make direct comparisons between his own experience and feelings and his father's. But when that man is thirty he has memories of his own thirty-year-old father. When they become fathers themselves, men are forced to reconsider and reevaluate their own fathers.

The accounts men gave me of their new perspectives on their fathers were so consistently phrased that they became almost proverbial. There were two basic versions: The first was a realization that a man had become like his father; the second was a reaction against his father and a refusal to follow in his footsteps.

In the first version, often given with wry but fond humor, men recounted the things their fathers said or did that, to them as children or teenagers, were exasperating, but that they now found themselves saying and doing in their interaction with their own children, including such predictable examples as not understanding their children's taste in music and clothes ("How can you listen to that garbage?"), disapproving of their use of time, insisting that they do their chores and homework, and urging children to be quiet. Hearing themselves say to their children, sometimes with exactly the same tone and words, what their fathers had said to them, was an experience that brought home to them their own transformation from child to parent. While they grimaced at the thought of repeating what their fathers had said to them, they also often felt that it was the right thing to say. And finding it appropriate gave these men a sense of identification with their fathers. Feeling like their fathers gave men the opportunity to reinterpret their fathers' (now their own) behavior. What they once saw as nagging, criticism, and unnecessary worry by their fathers became, when *they* did it, encouragement, setting standards, and realistic concern for the future. Men sympathetically reinterpreted not only their fathers' behavior, but also their fathers' motivation. Because they were sure that they themselves were motivated by the best interests of their children and found themselves acting as their fathers had, it followed, for them, that their fathers must also have been motivated by *their* children's best interests. Men who accepted the similarities between themselves and their fathers concluded almost universally that their fathers had done a good enough job and that they themselves were also better-than-adequate fathers.

Men who offered the second version of coming to terms with their own fathers denied the direct identification that came from doing the same things and stressed the ways that they struggled to avoid repeating their fathers' mistakes. But in this version, too, the sons often came to an understanding of why their fathers did the things they did even while they rejected it as a model. Jim's experience of his father's "wrong way" of encouraging him by putting him down, which I described in Chapter 4, led Jim to want to encourage his own son very differently: "There are a lot of things I do different from my dad. A lot. Almost everything." But even when they rejected the kind of fathering they had received and resolved to do better themselves, being fathers themselves seemed to bring men a level of understanding of their own fathers. Jim was still angry that he had not been supported or given opportunities, but he looked back on his childhood with the benefit of his own experience of being a father and having someone to worry about and be responsible for. According to Jim, "Now that I can understand [my father] and what happened in my life, I think I got the *wrong kind* of encouragement." As a father himself, Jim reevaluated his father's behavior as encouragement, in the sense that it was intended to motivate him, but as the wrong kind of encouragement. His father was thus mistaken, but not malevolent.

Having achieved this profound reinterpretation of his father, Jim said he was also able to appreciate his father's good qualities. Although Jim felt that his father had not been there to talk to, he acknowledged that "he was always there to get ice cream, to buy a new glove or bat, or for affection." In concluding his discussion of his father, he was able to stress this affection: "The only thing I haven't changed is the love that he gave to us. He was the one who always picked us up, always would sit us on his lap, always would hold us all night long. Rubbed us and pat[ted] us."

Jim's comments illustrate the complexity of many men's emotions about their fathers, the tension between resentment and respect, and the contradictory attitudes they held. William, who valued the work ethic and responsibility his father had taught him, described the connection between his father's approach to parenting and his own resentment of him as a young man:

> My father worked two jobs most of the time when I was growing up just to keep the bills paid. And there were times when he worked three. And so I didn't see him a lot. He was a very responsible person. But I didn't get to see a lot of him. He wasn't around a lot and when he was around, dad was there to lay the law down. When he was around, it was time to answer to him. And he was not real understanding that way. Either it was right or it was wrong. There was no gray area. There was no argument about it. And I think that that's real necessary. Kids really need to know their boundaries. And there were times in my life I didn't really care for my father a lot, but as I've gotten older, I've seen the wisdom of a lot of the things he did. I realized just what a special guy he is.

Williams' swift transition from complaining about his father's strictness to recognizing its necessity expressed his reevaluation of his father as he experienced fatherhood himself.

Roy, who contrasted his father's distance and sternness with his own spontaneity with his children, the importance he attached to doing things with them, and the fun he had with them, also talked about how he had come to appreciate his father. He remembered his parents' reaction when he and his siblings were children: "Whenever we'd get in trouble, one of their things would be: 'We're doing all this for you kids! We're working these hours.' Put the burden on us." But as an adult he also realized what their lives had been like: "My parents really amaze me. My father has about a fifth or sixth grade education; that's about as far as he went. And my mother is about the same. But it's incredible what they have done and how they made it." Roy talked about how hard his parents worked and the pressures they faced and the strength they showed. He now reevaluated why his father did not do things like taking the family on vacations and why his father did not think that "just having fun" was a good enough use of a summer and therefore found Roy a job at a gas station:

> Dad was working. His priorities were different. And that doesn't mean to say they were any better or worse than what my priorities are, but his priority was to build a financially stable foundation for his family. And way back then when I was so young and ignorant, I didn't really realize what they went through, how they were brought up, what they had to do. Incredible. *Now* I can imagine what they went through.

Roy, like Jim, had resented the fact that he had never been encouraged to even think about going to college. This motivated him to make college a goal and a realistic possibility for his own children. But while he began by contrasting his father's priorities with his own, he also came to recognize the differences in their situations. Roy did not go to college, but he did graduate from high school, whereas his father had left school after five or six years to help support the family. Perhaps most importantly, Roy could provide financial security for his family without working three jobs.

It was not only memory and comparison that caused these men to reevaluate their fathers, but also the relationships they actually observed between their fathers and their own children. Becoming a father makes men's fathers into grandfathers for their children, creates links between generations, and frequently binds men more closely to family and kin. As the father of young children, Greg anticipated his future and identified the enduring social connections that are created by having children:

> I think that's silly not to have children because of your career. It may be fine and dandy for now, but later on when they get older and their career isn't there, they're going to be awfully lonely. I mean, what do you do when you don't have your job to keep you occupied? At least you can have some children you can talk to; you don't have to be alone. You can have grandkids and all this kind of stuff when you get older. So, yeah, I look forward to having my grandchildren. It's almost like having another set of kids.

Grandparents who do not bear the ultimate responsibility for their grandchildren and who do not have to live with their grandchildren on a daily basis are in a position to be indulgent rather than strict. The impact of this structural change on their fathers' personalities was, however, a source of surprise to the men I talked to. They said repeatedly that their fathers acted with affection, spontaneity, fun, and generosity toward their grandchildren and that they enjoyed the company of their grandchildren. "He never acted that way toward me" was the refrain of their reports. Some of their perceptions are undoubtedly the result of the age differences of the children in question; men may remember their adolescent conflicts with their fathers and compare them with the observed interactions with their own younger children. Some of their perceptions are the result of changed norms for male demonstrativeness; men compare their own behavior toward their children with the more rigid patterns of their fathers. But a great deal is attributable to the different role expectations attached to the structural positions of father and grandfather.[3] Whatever the reasons, the transformation of their fathers into grandfathers helped these men come to terms with their fathers and helped them become fathers themselves.

Many men described in similar terms the changes in themselves that they saw as the consequence of fatherhood: their new sense of stability and responsibility, a greater sensitivity and capacity for growth, anxieties they had not shared before, and a capacity for anger and the abuse of power that they did not always control. They described fatherhood as a transformation of the kind of person they were, a transformation that continued as they grew older.

The men described in this book were under forty when I talked to them, and the oldest children any of them had were teenagers. We must remember, though, that fatherhood is a status that continues throughout a man's life. Discussion of fatherhood as the care of young children, while important, leaves out of the picture the relationships fathers have with older and adult children. As men age, their concerns, their situations, their expectations, and their hopes change appropriately. Being a new father just starting out in work and home ownership is different from being established, or stuck, in job, neighborhood, and marriage as the father of teenagers. Fatherhood endures as a life-long status.

Becoming older is not simply a uniform movement through time, but also changes the context in which men compare themselves with other men, with their own fathers, and with their expectations of themselves. The high school graduating class, which ages together, is also a reference group for many, as indicated by the frequent comparisons to classmates in the men's accounts. When they graduated from high school their aspirations were often either unrealistic (to be a rock star or a major-league pitcher, for instance) or vague and indefinite, but by the time I talked to them almost twenty years later they had a clearer sense of what they had done, what they were likely to do, and what their peers had done. Several men mentioned other classmates from high school who had been killed, or had overdosed, or had ended up in prison or on the streets. So when Frank, looking back on his upbringing and his youth, said, "I didn't end up brain dead somewhere, so I think I did OK," he was not just making a joke or being ironic, but was expressing his very real sense that to survive to adulthood, to be married, steadily employed, a home owner, and able to provide for your children, is, while unexceptional, nevertheless an achievement.

LINEAL GENDER: FATHERS OF SONS

Putting together the package deal is an achievement not only as a parent and as an adult, but as a father, which is to say, as a *man*. This achievement of a specific version of masculinity depends on being situated within two families: the nuclear family created by marriage and the family of descent. Just as the position of father is embedded in a system of kinship, so also is it embedded in a gender system. Within the nuclear family fatherhood and motherhood are gendered forms of parenthood, with their different expectations, activities, and identities (parental gender). Within the extended family, fatherhood is defined by its place in the line of descent between men (lineal gender). Parental gender was the central topic of Chapter 4, and has been a recurrent theme in my subsequent descriptions of employment and home ownership. That fatherhood is also a gendered relationship can be seen in men's expressed preference for sons, their differential identification with sons and daughters, and the ways in which they treat their sons and daughters differently.

The primary experience that men bring to fatherhood is their own experience of being fathered. They think about the relationship they had with their own fathers, whether they were there or not. Their image is not of the generalized relationship between parent and child, but rather of the specific relationship between father and son. When they think of themselves as fathers, they think of themselves as the fathers of sons. The men I talked to spoke openly about how, before their children were born, they anticipated and expected having sons.

Barry's expression of a preference for a son, and his sense of the naturalness of the relationship between fathers and sons, was an instance of a pervasive theme in the accounts men gave me of their lives:

> My wife wanted a girl first and I of course wanted a boy, so that way I'd know I had my son. And when my daughter was born it wasn't really a disappointment, but it was kind of a little letdown. But then when my son was born, it was a lot of jubilation. Like I said, every man wants a son to be able to carry on the family name, take to the ball game. I'm not saying you couldn't take your daughter, but it's just really not the same.

Many of the men I talked to expressed their preference for children as "one of each" or "a boy for me and a girl for my wife" and assumed that women would want daughters in the same way that men want sons—because they would value the sense of similarity with their same-sex children. The preference for sons is part of a cultural system of gender preference, not simply an expression of individual tastes. In surveys of sex preference for children in Europe and North America, there is a consistent preference for at least one child of each sex, generally with a slight preference for sons as the first born and among people who would like an uneven number of children (Hank and Kohler 2000). In the United States, male college students reported a strong preference for a boy if they were to have an only child, while female students expressed moderate preference for a girl (Pooler 1991).

Culturally determined preferences are reflected in cultural representations. Armin Brott's (1999) guide for the single father, for example, which contains a great deal of sage advice, useful information, and suggestions of other sources, is illustrated with forty-five cartoons from newspapers and popular magazines. Two of these show a father with three children, in each case two boys and a girl. Thirty of the cartoons depict a father alone with one child. Of these, twenty-four, or four out of five, depict a father and a son. Only six depict a father and his daughter.[4]

Not one of the men I talked to said he would have had more children than he planned in order to have a daughter. But, in response to hypothetical questions, almost every man said he would have pushed to try again if he had had two daughters, and that if he had had two sons the choice about having more would have been up to his wife. David and Mary, despite all they had been through, and even though Mary told David: "I don't want to have another child with you," agreed that they would have had more than one child if their first had been a daughter. Frank and Carol, with two daughters and a son, also shared the feeling that men wanted sons.

Men's identification of fatherhood with having sons does not mean that they are all successful fathers of sons or better at fathering sons than daughters. Many men, in fact, are very successful fathers of daughters. All of them, however, talked about being fathers in terms of the relationship between fathers and sons. Men with both sons and daughters talked more about their sons and reported more activities with them. In this they are typical of the national pattern. In families where both mother and father are present, mothers in general report participating in outings, playing, reading, and talking with their children more frequently than do fathers; fathers of daughters report less of these activities than do fathers of sons (Lye 1990).

Paul Watson, the transport worker who was so concerned about his two sons' safety, was, as usual, unselfconscious and to the point when he commented on his feelings about sons and daughters:

> I used to rub my wife's stomach when she was pregnant, like it was a crystal ball, and I'd say, "Boy! Boy! Boy!" I'd tell everybody I wasn't capable of fathering females. And if I had one, I'd do like the Eskimos do, I'd set them adrift on an ice floe. Yeah, I wanted to have boys so I could take them out and do all the things that I never had done with me and do with them. And that's what we're gonna do this summer. They're eight and six, pretty much the age where we can go out and do things. Got a bunch of camping equipment. I got a pickup truck. We just throw it in the back and blow town and have a good time.

In a few words, Paul conveyed his preference for sons, the age at which children can "do things" with their fathers, the active and spontaneous behavior appropriate for fathers with their children, and the centrality of masculine objects like pickup trucks and male activities like camping to the relationship of fathers and sons.

Mark Baxter, a journeyman in one of the construction trades, had both a son and a daughter, but talked more about his son, noticed he was doing so, commented on it, and continued to do so. Although he denied that he "cared" more about his son, he was aware that he gave him pride of place in his account: "This may sound one-sided," he said, "I always bring him up first." Mark had married his high school sweetheart two years after his high school graduation, was still married to her, and had two children, a twelve-year-old boy and a nine-year-old girl. He described them as "The typical Joe American family." When we talked about the decisions his wife and he had made about having children, he said,

> We knew we wanted two. And with the boy the first that made it a lot easier. You know, chances are if we had had two girls we might have gone for three. Because I'm the only child. I'm the last one to carry the name on in the West half of the States. So the boy was great. And when [my daughter] was born that was, you know, that's perfect.

When their daughter was five, Mark and his wife had a serious discussion of the possibility of having a third child but decided against it. Mark's reproductive decisions were made sequentially in the context of a general normative goal of two children, a boy and a girl. While Mark wanted two children, having a son first was "easier" *for him* because it took the pressure off. Having a daughter second then made it "perfect," but, as many men indicated, would not have been essential.

Barry shared Mark's normative picture of the family. He and his wife had both been married and divorced when they met. They both knew they wanted a family and "figured it was about time" (he was 28 and she 26). His daughter was born first, and he and his wife had faced the decision about having another child. Barry said that their decision to do so was based on "Male ego, so to speak, that wants to have a son to carry on the family name." Although not sure if they would have tried a third time if they had had two girls, he knew that "I still would have had that feeling, well, jeez, I would really like to have a son." Fortunately, he said, he had a boy and did not have to go further.

Like most of the men with both sons and daughters, Barry moved easily from talking about his "children" to giving examples of his "son" in a way that privileged their relationship and the male activities they engaged in together:

> It's a real good feeling when your children learn to talk and they say "daddy" and "mommy," or like my son, playing T-ball and he hits a

> home run, he comes over and is real proud of himself. That's kind of self-rewarding. That's something that we work for. If we go out and play catch and stuff and he does something good, something I try to teach him, that's kind of a self-rewarding thing that he's done, or that we've done together. It's kind of a payback for the effort that I had put with him. And it's paid off. That is a certain kind of love.

Barry also emphasized the link between fathers and sons when he talked about his own childhood:

> I had three older sisters. So basically, it was just me and my dad, somebody to play ball with. . . . My biggest disappointment is that my father, and even my mother [who died when his daughter was three months old], weren't able to see my children. No kids are perfect, but I think my kids are fairly well behaved. My dad would have just loved my son. He's a lot like him.

Like David, who in Chapter 1 represented himself as an only child even though he had an older sister, Barry saw his sisters as irrelevant to his picture of his relationship with his father. The relationship that counted, for Barry, was the one between fathers and sons, and the grandparental connection he mourned was the one between his father and his son.

For many of these men the excitement, joy, and relief they felt at the birth of their daughters could overshadow their gender preferences. As Barrie Thorne (1993) pointed out, a social and cultural system of gender differentiation can encompass a great deal of variation in the degree of gender salience in different situations. Sometimes gender is very salient and dominates the definition of a situation; sometimes the salience of gender is diminished or overwhelmed by other considerations. In the case of childbirth, particularly after a difficult pregnancy or delivery, or when the health of the mother or child is potentially at greater risk than normal, the health and survival of the baby is crucial to the experience of the situation, and the baby's gender is less salient. Phil Marwick described his experience of situational gender salience as he told me about his emotions at the time of his first son's birth. Phil had lived with his wife for five years before they married when he was twenty-seven. He worked as a production supervisor, and his wife stayed at home with their two young sons. His story of his son's birth expressed both his secret longings for a son and his dawning realization that the experience of fatherhood did not depend on having a son:

> I always wanted to have a son. It's funny. When my wife was pregnant, I went to Lamaze and the whole thing and cutting the cord and the whole thing. And I remember thinking all night, "Gosh, I want to have a boy." But I would never tell anybody that. People would ask me, "What do you want to have, boy or girl?" And I would always say, "Oh, I don't care as long as it's healthy" The standard routine. But in fact I'm just praying, "Gosh, I hope it's a boy. What am I gonna do if it's a girl?" And then we were in the room and the baby came out and the doctor said, "You want to cut the cord?" And I said, "Yeah." And I was so excited. It was so neat and I didn't even know it was a boy. Took me five minutes or so after the baby was out to realize it was a boy. So then I don't remember how I felt. I don't think it was, "Oh great! It was a boy." I was just excited the baby was OK. But I was proud. I was a proud daddy. I had my boy. Made me feel real good. I always thought it would be a good thing to have a boy, so it was definitely a good thing. I never thought before I got married, "Gosh, what am I going to do if I don't have a daughter?" That never came to mind. I think it would have been nice to have one. But I'm just as content not having one.

In these last few sentences, Phil captured the gendered asymmetry between the fatherhood of daughters and sons. It was not that he would not have wanted, loved, or looked after a daughter, but that as he had anticipated fatherhood his image had not included a daughter.

Accepting Daughters

Phil realized that his longing and praying for a son should be concealed behind the "standard routine" of "I don't care as long as it's healthy." He recognized, too, that his praying was motivated not only by his wanting a son, but also by his anxiety about having a daughter. In the event, the safe birth of a healthy baby eclipsed his concern about sons and daughters, but since the baby in question was a boy he did not have to maintain the position that he did not care about its sex. Men who had sons were pleased and relieved and, since they had what they had wanted, did not have to do cultural work to redefine either their preferences or their situations. Men who had daughters only, on the other hand, did have to do such cultural work. These men were able to mobilize cultural norms about equality and the priority of having healthy and happy children to reconcile themselves to not having sons. While the fathers of daughters were sometimes anxious about them, not one of them ever said to me that he did not want them.

George Peters, whose commute I described in Chapter 6, was a production supervisor for a large manufacturing company that also employed his current wife and many of their neighbors in their new subdivision. George had been married before and had two daughters with his first wife. Like Phil, he had hoped for a son but had come to recognize that other things were important. But while Phil's indifference to his son's sex had been a five-minute experience of excitement in the delivery room, George had had to adjust his vision permanently to incorporate having two daughters and no son:

> In the back of my mind I always wanted a boy so that the family name could go on and this and that. So I wound up with the two girls and after we decided that was all we wanted, it just didn't mean as much as I thought it did to me. I mean if I had a boy it would have been great, but I didn't and the family name just didn't really mean anything to me. It's like it was really important before, but then after I had two girls and we decided we're not having anymore children then it didn't bother me.

When George remarried and he and his second wife decided to have children together, they were under great pressure from his family to have a son: "My parents, my dad, God, from my cousins to my aunts and uncles and everybody was on us." However, George and his second wife also had two daughters. George recounted several conversations in which he had been put on the spot and had had to defend his own masculinity and the decision he and his second wife had made not to have more children.

George's achieved family was a marked departure from his personal preference, from a cultural norm, and from the urgings of his extended family, but he had arrived at an acceptance of the turn of events:

> I always just wanted to have two. I wanted to have a boy and a girl like my parents did. I thought that worked out OK. Although I kind of missed having a brother, I guess. But I thought that was perfect, having a boy and a girl. When I married my second wife, she wasn't supposed to have any children. And I thought it was safe [laughing]. But I could see her get excited about it, and talk about it all the time, so I said, "OK, we'll have, you know, we'll probably have one. Hopefully we'll have a boy!" But, you know, I was never really disap-

> pointed. I mean, even though I knew the pressure was on. And as athletic as I've been, I really am not that disappointed. I was in there counting fingers, toes: "Healthy, is she healthy?" And the last one, we almost lost also because she was a preemie. Tiny [laughs]. And we battled with that one and she was a battler. So, she made it and I wasn't thinking about son or daughter or anything. I was thinking about a baby that's fighting for her life. And it was like, "Hey, no problem." You know, I'm glad they're healthy and that's all there is. That's all there is.

When I saw him with his younger daughters, George was affectionate and seemed at ease with them, but he told me that he sometimes did not know what they wanted in the way that he assumed he would have known with sons. Even though he had four daughters and lots of experience as a father of girls, he said,

> I have a hard time, even though they're— You know, they're girls. I still try and do everything they like, but sometimes it's hard because you don't know what they really like. They don't like a lot of stuff that you'd like to do. But I try and play ball with them, and you know, take them to ball games. I'm a baseball freak [laughs]. And the two older ones are into baseball, but the two little ones aren't.

All the men I talked to who were fathers of daughters shared some of this sense of distance. They all claimed that the disappointment they had anticipated about not having a son had evaporated or was dissipated by the relief they felt at a safe birth and the joy they found in their relationships with their daughters. But the reduced salience of gender at some moments of fatherhood does not mean that gender disappears from the relationships between fathers and their children.

George, for instance, interpreted his daughters' likes and dislikes in terms of gendered activities. He took particular pleasure in sharing with them the masculine ball games and roughhousing he would have shared with a son. It was particularly in his youngest, who had been born prematurely and who had "battled" to survive, that he saw the qualities he would have wanted in a son and that he interpreted as masculine. He chuckled as he told me:

> I wouldn't give her up for the world either, that one. Even though she's the wildest one. I'm telling you, my little one, out of all four, is the wildest. I think she was supposed to be a boy.

George did not see his youngest daughter's "wildness" as simply child behavior, or as within the range of girls' typical behavior, or as non-gendered youngest-child behavior, but as "boylike."

George not only described his youngest daughter's characteristics as masculine, but he also described her as performing some of the functions he expected a son would have performed in his extended family and in his relationship with his own father. George said that when he and Cindy had not had a son, his father was disappointed. He was the one telling Cindy, "'Oh, you got to try one more.' And we said, 'No. We can't have no more.' And until this day he still gets us about that." George, however, presented his wild youngest daughter as the functional equivalent of a son in the way that she established a link across the generations: "I'll tell you what. The littlest one, she looks just like him. And they have some kind of bond, because I've never seen her react that way to anyone." What was significant in George's telling was that his daughter could not *as a girl* do all that he and her grandfather wanted from a child. She had to be constructed, to some degree, as "supposed to be a boy" to do what a son should have done.

The fathers I talked to had many shared concerns about their children, whether they were boys or girls. In addition, men with sons worried about violence, delinquency, risk-taking, and the other dangers they saw threatening boys, while men with daughters expressed anxiety over their daughters' greater vulnerability. In general, they did not attribute agency to their daughters. Boys get into trouble by *doing* something; girls get into trouble by having something *done to* them. They frequently expressed this anxiety in comparison with the way that they, as teenagers, had thought about and treated girls. Mark, anticipating his nine-year-old daughter's teenage years, commented,

> I think you tend to be more protective over your daughter, at least the man does, than his son. You know what you did as a teenager, and you don't want that happening to your daughter. Not that I did anything all that bad, but there were times when you went out, you had a one-night stand with a chick after a football game or something. Do you want your daughter in that situation? No!

That fathers were concerned about their teenaged daughters' sexuality was not surprising, given the sexual focus of their own attitudes about young women when they were adolescents.[5] Just as their worries about their sons were reactions to their own experience as teenagers, their worries about their daughters were reactions to their own juvenile behavior toward girls. This gendered worry reflected and contributed to their perception of their daughters as very different from themselves. It was a common theme in my interviews that a father, as a man, could understand what his son was going through, could "be there" for him, and could offer appropriate advice, whereas parts of his daughter's experience would be insurmountably alien to him, although comprehensible to his wife.

Fathering Gendered Children

Indeed fundamental tensions remain in men's fathering of girls that distinguish it from their fathering of boys. Frank, father of two daughters and a son, dissected this tension as he described his own attempts to live with the contradiction between a preference for sons and a norm of equal treatment:

> I'm fortunate enough to have both. I'm very close to my girls, but it's a different feeling I guess I have. I like to treat them all equally. I love them all the same. It's a different feeling. It's more of a one-on-one relationship because you feel you can relate more to the boys than the girls. And I think I have a tendency to be harder on the girls than I do on [my son] for some reason. I don't know what the reason is. Maybe it's just that cosmetic difference between male and female, but I have a tendency to be harder on the girls, even though I try to be equal discipline-wise. I don't know what it is. I can't explain it. I try not to do it, but it still just mentally happens.

One indication of the generality of these feelings and these tensions is the finding that, at the national level, fathers are more involved with the care of their sons than of their daughters and that couples who are parents of daughters are more likely to divorce than are couples who are parents of sons (Morgan, Lye, and Condran 1988). Another indication of these tensions lies in the perpetuation of stereotypical gender roles for children. There is a basic cultural formula that equal love and different treatment are compatible, and that different treatment of boys and girls can be justified through appeals to their essential differences.

Jim summarized the appeal to essential sex-linked differences in his description of his children. He told me first about the physical similarities and differences between his five-year-old-son and fourteen-month-old daughter; then he turned to their behavioral differences:

> What is really neat is the way they handle themselves. He never stops, never stops motion, never stops being rambunctious and all boy, and she is the little girl. Everybody says, "He's the little boy that everybody says is rambunctious and all boy and she's the little girl, all girl." She likes to put bracelets and necklaces on.

His daughter, he said, was quieter, more passive, and more interested in pretty things. Jim expressed his surprise at the differences between his children: "Even though they have the same parents, a lot of the same genes. We don't know where my son came from."

The gendered differences Jim described are typical for boys and girls in the United States: Boys are seen as more exploratory and physically active, girls as quieter and more concerned with personal adornment (Vogel et al. 1991). When fathers have both sons and daughters, their description of, and attribution of qualities to, their children are predictably gendered. In the 1970s a classic study found that new parents described their male and female infants very differently, seeing daughters as softer, prettier, more delicate, and smaller than sons even though independent observers saw no differences (Rubin, Provenzano, and Luria 1974). More than twenty years later, change had been only modest, and parents still saw their newborns in stereotyped ways (Karraker, Vogel, and Lake 1995).

What is noteworthy in Jim's account of gender differences is the invisibility of the processes through which they are perpetuated. A fourteen-month-old baby, boy or girl, likes to wear jewelry only because it has had it put on by adults and has then been praised for looking pretty. There is a great deal of evidence that parents treat girls quite differently than they do boys (Beal 1994). Typically, fathers play more physically with, and spend more time with, their sons than their daughters (Karraker, Vogel, and Lake 1995: 688; Lindsey, Mize, and Pettit 1997). Research done in the 1990s on the differential perception, description, and treatment of male and female infants and children still replicated earlier findings (Coltrane 1998a: 124–27; Howard and Hollander 1997).

In Jim's case, the gender construction of his son as "all boy" was a pervasive feature of the relationship between father and son. Jim's five-year-old son was well stocked with sports equipment, masculine toys, and a three-foot-long car with an electric motor that he would drive wildly around the yard, banging into trees, fences, and buildings while his father encouraged him. Many of Jim's interactions with his son were exuberantly physical; he and his brother would throw their children back and forth between them in the house, and when his son was three Jim used to throw him as far as he could above his head. (Jim was a large man who had done physical work and played sports for many years; he could throw a three-year-old a good number of feet in the air.) Jim was proud of his son's adventurous approach: "Anything I do he wants to do too, which is neat. And I let him." So, for example, Jim's son helped him push the lawn mower and used hedge clippers and pruning shears. He even held the wedge when his father was splitting firewood and stood with him holding the chain saw. Jim's wife and sister-in-law would remonstrate with him. Both women, he said, had seen too many children with broken bones and dislocated joints from such roughhousing to find it amusing.

Jim's interactions with his son encouraged physical activity, exploration of new activities, manipulation of the physical environment, being with and emulating his father, and ignoring, or at least discounting, his mother's "feminine" concerns and reservations. With all this, it is hardly difficult to see where Jim's son got his "rambunctiousness," but it is important to notice that Jim explicitly denied the causation and wrapped the process in mystery. He attributed the outcome to essential differences between males and females.

Jim was more than usually involved with the care of his children, partly because of the relation between his wife's and his own work schedules, partly because he and Monica were separated when I talked to him, and partly because his aspiration to be a family man outweighed his interest in having a career. As an artisan, he had been able to adjust his schedule to his wife's shift and on-call work, taking sole responsibility for the children for long periods of the day. He was also unusual in the extent to which he talked about including his son in his second job as a self-employed handyman. In most jobs, whether on assembly lines, at construction sites, or in offices, men cannot bring their children with them, whereas Jim could take his son along when he went to clear a gutter or prune a tree.

Jim was not unusual, however, in the gender distinctions he made between his children, or in the emphasis on physical activity, particularly sports, as the most important area of contact between father and son. Sports were very important to many of the men I talked to, and they had been even more important to them in their teenage years. Anthropologists and sociologists have commented on the cultural significance of sports in the adolescence and growth to maturity of men in the United States (Burnett 1975; Fine 1987; Fiske 1975; Messner 1992). Many of the men from Meadowview High School continued to be involved in sports, as participants as well as spectators. They reported playing golf, tennis, and racquetball; swimming, jogging, and running; weight lifting at home and at the gym; and playing in softball leagues. Besides the manifest functions of pleasure in physical activity and the maintenance of health, all of these activities serve the more or less latent function of maintaining social relations. Sports also serve as important markers of masculinity, as activities into which to socialize sons, and as experiences for fathers and sons to share. Both in response to my questions about what they would like to teach their children, and as spontaneous contributions from men regarding their roles as fathers, the most frequently mentioned subject was not morals, or vocation, or even schoolwork, but "playing ball." The picture of father and son playing ball together was, for these men, the image that defined the relationship.

As domestic life and industrial life have become increasingly separated, socialization of sons to the world of work has been increasingly removed from families. The state and the marketplace have taken over the education and vocational training that were traditionally provided by apprenticeships and families. At the same time, particularly in cultural images, the amount of physical labor in men's work, and hence the essentialist support for a sexual division of labor, has diminished. The stereotype of family life in the decades after World War II was one of strict division between the provider role of the husband and the domestic and childcare responsibilities of the mother. But it was also a picture in which the work fathers went off to was in offices. The work they did there did not require any of the "masculine" qualities of physical strength, speed, and coordination that ostensibly justified the division of labor in the first place.[6] In these circumstances, sports (and recreational hunting and fishing) became a bastion and marker of traditional masculinity.

David Brown and I had been talking about martial arts classes, and I had, rather naively but earnestly, said how much one of my sons had gained from the respect, responsibility, and discipline taught in them. In response, David expressed the complex interconnections between character-building, competitiveness, and self-discipline that are enshrined in sports, and also the very close identification between father and son, as he shifted back and forth between describing his own reactions and the feelings he ascribed to his son:

> It just builds character for him you know, and I'm all for that. It's not that I want him to beat up on somebody. It's just for his own character and stuff, it's good. And now he's getting a lot of contact. He's already got the respect. And the other part he's been through, he got bored with it. You know I was too. I was bored going to the same things, hearing the same thing. And I'm paying sixty bucks a month and I said, "Well, we gotta hit something once in awhile, you know." I mean he's getting bigger. It's OK when he was a little kid: "Kick left! Kick right!" But over here if you can kick left and kick right and get through your basics they let you do a lot of stuff. Sparring with the full head gear and the whole bit and it's good. I enjoy it. I enjoy it now. He likes to go now. More than he did. Then I think it was more us. Now it's him. Now he knows he's gotta start training harder.

David found closeness with his son through his identification with him and his efforts in martial arts. It is, of course, also quite possible that David was pushing his son in directions that he did not want to go. David's best memories were of his sports achievements and his father's support, and he was certainly doing for his son what his father did for him. Sports also provided the idiom for talking about fathering in a variety of situations. Playing catch, playing ball, and going to the ball game often came up as markers of fatherhood, and were often problematic for the fathers of daughters.

Paul Watson shed an interesting light on sports and paternal closeness in his comments on his sons, who had minor physical conditions that made playing catch inappropriate. For Paul, cultural norms did not simply direct activity, but had the flexibility to compensate for the unexpected:

> I think God— I know He does. He's got a hand in this because I'm a natural athlete and everything sports-wise came easy to me. Where with my guys, they're not natural athletes at this point in the game. So I've got to work with them more. And I think it's a blessing because had they been natural athletes, I wouldn't have had to work

> with them. So they would have taken it for their own and gone on their own and done their own thing. This way I have to work with them and keep close touch with them. So I'll have the opportunity to be with them more.

Fatherhood as both institution and experience incorporates gendered expectations of fathers and mothers, of husbands and wives, and of sons and daughters.[7] As a social position and social institution fatherhood is part of a system of gendered roles and norms that accompanies a gendered division of labor and responsibility as well as different treatment of boys and girls. Fatherhood is also a gendered experience, a gendered identity, and a gendered sense of self in relation to others. Within the dominant culture of the United States, a man's experience and expectation of himself as a father hinges on the gendered experience he has of his own father and mother and on the gendered expectations he brings to his experience with his sons and daughters.

8 Implications

THE IMPORTANCE of fathers for children has been both minimized (Stephenson 1991) and exaggerated (Blankenhorn 1995; Popenoe 1999). Research reveals a more nuanced picture (Amato 1998; Belsky 1998; Furstenberg 1998; Harris, Furstenberg, and Marmer 1998; Marsiglio et al. 2000), but the debate over the importance or irrelevance of fathers will not be decided by research, no matter how careful and controlled. This debate taps into fundamental cultural notions of what life is about. The family is one of our basic moral metaphors, and the appropriate place of the father in the family is a key marker of moral positions (Lakoff 1996).

By describing the dominant cultural values that simultaneously constrained the men I talked to and provided them with the vocabulary for justifying and explaining the patterns of their lives, I have unpacked and disassembled a particular version of masculinity and fatherhood. The men from Meadowview accepted and embodied the dominant cultural image of fatherhood, and their lives were shaped by the working out of this image in the face of circumstances both changing and not of their own choosing. The variety of their life situations did not imply a variety of ideals but a variety of outcomes reflecting the impact of varied circumstances described and justified in the same terms.

The group of men described in this book have a culturally and historically specific vision of successful male adulthood as a package deal of interconnected elements. The four crucial elements of this package deal are fatherhood, marriage, employment, and home ownership. Focusing on fatherhood, I have considered how each of the other three elements contributes to the four facets of fatherhood: emotional closeness, provision, protection, and endowment.

Whole Lives in Social Contexts

Two features of this picture of fatherhood and men's lives stand out in contrast to much discussion of men and masculinity. First, the different activities and relationships in men's lives are not separate and isolated but integral parts of wholes. And second, men's options and actions occur in a social context. These two features are not, of course, restricted to the lives of men from Meadowview High School—they are, in fact, virtually axiomatic to anthropologists. But they are so frequently ignored in studies and discussions of particular aspects of men's lives that they bear repeated emphasis. Studies or policies that focus on a specific aspect of men's behavior, whether it is condom use or nonuse, sexual behavior, recourse to vasectomy, child support, commitment to work or refusal of responsibility, inevitably fall short when they ignore the interconnections between the selected aspect and the rest of men's lives.

The implications for research are that the specific focus of every research question must be complemented by a broader vision of the way that people's aspirations and activities in one domain are related to their aspirations and actions in others. The study of men must include the cultural constellations that define various masculinities. The implications for policy are twofold: Policies must take account of men's complex aspirations, and individual change occurs within an institutional and economic context.

The dilemmas, burdens, and oppressions of masculinity are not just private problems, but are also public issues (cf. Mills 1959). Blaming individual men or attributing their shortcomings to some version of an essential masculinity ignores the contexts within which men act. Awareness of the structure of the package deal and the facets of fatherhood helps us to understand features of men's lives and actions that appear to be contradictory or self-defeating. Recognizing the mediating position of women between fathers and children in intact families, for example, contributes to our understanding of the distance between men and their children when divorce disrupts that mediating role. Similarly, understanding that men see being a good worker, a responsible employee, and a reliable provider as an expression of their paternal affection helps make comprehensible so many men's devotion to paid work at the expense of time with their children even as they express a heartfelt desire for emotional closeness with them. And understanding the centrality of home ownership as a symbol of successful providing, class position, moral value, and autonomous adulthood indicates that suburban spread and very long commutes, even as they separate workers from their families, are expressions of the value of family.

The structure of the package deal is such that strains on the structure do not lead to straightforward adjustments, but often to increased tensions as existing contradictions are sharpened rather than dissolved. Mothers' increasing labor force participation, measured both by the increasing number of mothers who are employed and the increasing number of hours that employed mothers work, does not necessarily result in a sigh of relief from fathers that they can therefore work less and be more involved with family life. Instead, men frequently redouble their efforts at work, experience greater insecurity about their roles, and do cultural work to belittle the importance of their wives' employment.

In a fascinating history of the fifty-five-year experience with the six-hour work day at the Kellogg plant in Battle Creek, Michigan, Benjamin Hunnicutt chronicles how the six-hour day was introduced and welcomed in 1930 as a way to ensure full employment and to give workers time for leisure, family, and community. Hunnicutt then describes how the six-hour day was replaced with the arbitrarily defined "full-time" shift of eight hours a day as part of a management strategy "reaffirming work as life's center" (Hunnicutt 1996: 110). Significantly for my argument, Hunnicutt details how the six-hour day was redefined as something for women and for men who could not, or would not, measure up. Men's anxieties about their ability to construct male identities outside of work led most of the male workers at the plant to go along with a public relations campaign that trivialized and feminized leisure and family time (1996: 142–46). Work was reestablished as the all-consuming center of men's lives, where it remains as the cornerstone of the package deal. In a change that has been described as a "stalled revolution" (Hochschild 1989: 12), women have entered the labor force and taken on essential providing roles, but men have not taken on the "second shift" of domestic work, childcare, and emotional identification with the nurturance of children. Men's identification of masculinity and successful fatherhood with employment and provision helps explain why the revolution in family life has stalled.

Politics and the Package Deal

Any piece of research is subject to misinterpretation and to being used as support or ammunition in debates or struggles about policy. This is particularly true of research on an issue as controversial as fatherhood. My analysis of the package deal does not fit easily into contemporary gender politics. Seeing men's lives and experiences as wholes avoids seeing men as either villains (patriarchal; using their physical, social, and economic power for their own interests; selfish; afraid of commitment; and socially irresponsible) or victims (hard working; abused by exponents of political correctness; unappreciated for the sacrifices they make in terms of hours of work and shortened life span; taken advantage of in divorce courts; and expected to support a variety of disadvantaged groups). While I have tried to present sympathetically the men I talked to and to portray the package deal as they see it working in an ideal world, I have also tried to point out the inconsistencies in their accounts and the contradictions in their goals.

My readers should not take away the idea that the package deal is a functioning reality and that policy should be directed at helping as many men as possible to achieve it. Certainly, there are policies and cultural changes that are proposed to do this. Campaigns for the "family wage" that focus on making men's earnings adequate to support a family, for instance, address a central contradiction within the package deal by reinforcing the importance of men's employment and by stressing the providing facet of fatherhood. They find support from men's willingness to see their wives' being at home with their children as a surrogate for their own closeness. But they do nothing to address the gender inequity within the "father breadwinner, mother homemaker" family, or the expressed desire for emotional closeness between fathers and children. Similarly, suggestions that American families turn their backs on galloping consumption and live on one income by cutting expenditures, which come from a variety of points on the political spectrum, have the potential for perpetuating and reinforcing gender inequity.

Understanding the package deal helps us to examine the likely, though often unintended, consequences of these proposals. The lack of involvement between non-custodial fathers and their children after divorce, for instance, is very generally seen as causing social problems by depriving children of paternal role models, plunging women and children into poverty, and imposing a burden on public resources that should be borne by individual fathers. These problems are frequently misidentified, but they nevertheless drive a variety of proposals for social change. Joint custody, for instance, is proposed as a fair adjustment in exchange for child support. The argument is that if a father is expected to provide for his children, he should have an equal say in the conduct of their lives. Whatever the justice of this argument, it ignores the ways in which marriage and having children are intimately linked in men's cultural view, as well as the identification of both with coresidence. The cultural resources for men to make sense of a situation in which they are equal parents of children with whom they do not live, and to whose mother they are not married, are lacking.

A similar argument may be directed at less controversial policies intended to stimulate men's involvement with children. Expressed desires for men to be closer to their infants and to share in the care of children, combined with straightforward arguments for equity between working women and men, have driven campaigns for paternity leave. When paternity leave has been made available, we find that it is used infrequently and that men expect to be criticized if they avail themselves of it. The very limited participation of fathers in the (very limited) benefits provided by the Family and Medical Leave Act, for instance, indicates that fatherhood is inextricably bound up with cultural constructions of masculinity and social expectations of men as workers (Levine 2000; Wisensale 2001). Again, understanding the dynamics of the package deal helps us to understand this behavior. Within the package deal, men are finding their primary valuation as fathers in providing for their children, and they are defining their wives' presence with their children as their own emotional connection with their children. Given this cultural position, staying home with their children does not contribute to their valuation of themselves as men or as fathers and, in fact, appears as a diminution of their primary responsibility.

The linked emphases on employment as constitutive of masculinity and on providing as constitutive of fatherhood are at odds with direct contact and emotional closeness between fathers and children. The problem of involving fathers more with their children turns on this central contradiction within the package deal. The cultural work that is done to address this contradiction manages to both conceal it and to reinforce it. Because the interactions of institutional arrangements and cultural values are so strong and manifold, attempts to redress the imbalance between family and employment frequently end up reinforcing it.

The cultural and institutional context reinforces the pursuit of the package deal and its attendant emphasis on the providing facet of fatherhood. The structure of work is such that high pay, benefits, and prospects for promotion are almost entirely restricted to positions that demand full-time or greater commitment, essentially forcing families to depend on a primary breadwinner. Men's power and privilege as a group means that they have greater access to those full-time jobs and are, in the negotiation about the division of labor between spouses, at a competitive advantage to be selected as that family's breadwinner. This division of labor ensures that men maintain their economic advantage, for they are not only earning more money than their wives, they are also accumulating retirement benefits and increasing their future earning power. Cultural definitions of masculinity reinforce both the division of labor and men's material advantage by validating their employment, their commitment to hard work, and their specialization in providing.

Caring for children, in contrast to employment, does not bring material rewards. Full-time parents are not paid, they do not receive benefits, they do not acquire marketable skills, and they do not accumulate retirement credit (Crittenden 2001; Folbre 2001). Institutional arrangements privilege commitment to employment, male power gives differential access, and cultural values reinforce this arrangement. What is needed are changes in both the structure of employment and the cultural definition of masculinity.

Possibilities for Change

Discussion of changing fatherhood is in the air. The surge of research on fatherhood and the proliferation of advice books, websites, newsgroups, and newsletters all indicate a great deal of interest in what fathers do and, especially, in what they should do. Much of the advice in this literature consists of helpful hints to fathers on how to structure time and activities with their children, how to talk to and play with them, and what to expect as children grow (Brott 1999; Wolgemuth and Blanchard 1999). This advice, in general, makes suggestions about what fathers can do as individuals to change their own behavior, attitudes, and relationships, but does not address the institutional and cultural contexts in which they live.

My analysis, which points out that the package deal is culturally valued as a whole, not as a set of disconnected bits, makes it clear that there are definite limits to what individuals can do in a piecemeal way to change. Seeing how success in achieving the package deal is connected to circumstances beyond individual control makes us recognize additional limits to individual action. Recognizing the limits to individual action, however, is not the same as despairing of change. Many of the men I talked to, for example, told me how unusual it was for them to talk about fatherhood and family, but that did not mean that they did not care. Rather, it meant that they did not find or create situations in their everyday lives to talk about shared issues and recognize shared situations. Almost all of these men said they wanted to be close to their children, and as individuals, many of them *were* more involved in their children's lives than their fathers had been in theirs. Many of them had changed diapers, cooked meals, and attended their children's events on a routine basis, and several were the primary caretakers of their children when their wives were working. Many of them also made very real efforts to talk to and listen to their children as well as play sports with them. In their more involved fathering, they were participants in a cultural change that, while "stalled," is not stopped. It is stalled, however, by institutional arrangements as much as by individual unwillingness.

While celebrating what change has occurred, it is possible to exaggerate the scope of change and the difference between past and present. Ralph LaRossa, in a historical examination of the emergence of "modern fatherhood" in the United States during the 1920s and 1930s, points out that neither the physical involvement of fathers in their children's lives nor the ideal that fathers should be emotionally close to their children is a complete novelty (1997). He comments wryly, "While it may be gratifying for men in the late twentieth century to believe that they are the first generation to change a diaper or give a baby a bath, the simple truth is that they are not" (1997: 3). In general, LaRossa concludes, "Some of the features that we have come to identify with fatherhood today were part of American fatherhood long before now" (1997: 3). Not only can change be exaggerated, but, as I discussed in Chapter 4, the extent of cultural persistence can be underestimated.

We must restructure the world of employment so that paid labor neither defines our personal and social identities nor consumes the bulk of our time and energy. We live in a structure that perpetuates a particularly rigid and dehumanizing gendered division of economic and emotional labor. In such a system, we can hardly avoid feeling inadequate, or that our success is fragile and needs to be vigilantly guarded. A few of us may be able to negotiate work situations that are flexible and fulfilling, but most of us confront an organized structure of jobs and employment that dictates where and when we work and that pits us one against the other as competitors and potential replacements. There are things we can do as individuals, but they are limited without the participation of many of us. For example, any one of us may stop admiring the workaholic at our place of work and refuse to work excessive hours, but as long as cultural values respect and employers reward devotion to employment at the expense of personal and family life, and as long as our co-workers continue to put in unpaid or compulsory overtime, those of us who do this will be marginalized in the vital world of work.

Concerned observers of American families make frequent proposals for the introduction or expansion of "family friendly" policies such as parental leave and adequate funding for childcare programs (Folbre 2001; Hewlett and West 1998; Heymann 2000; Parke and Brott 1999). Many of the sources of advice or comment on involved fatherhood also recognize the importance of the social and policy context of fathers' lives and recommend changes in the orientation and organization of social institutions. Some of this work, particularly James Levine's Fatherhood Project, also addresses the need for changes in employment practices and the organization of the workplace (Levine and Pitt 1995; Levine and Pittinsky 1998). Suzanne Braun Levine (2000) describes the obstacles that men who want to be more involved in parenting encounter from women, employers, and other men. She asserts that for involved fatherhood to become widespread, a "revolution" will be required in political support for families and in the workplace.

Labor organizations are increasingly recognizing that family benefits and a work structure compatible with family life are critical issues for working Americans. In the 1990s, compulsory overtime was a key issue in many labor disputes, including contract negotiations at General Motors, United Parcel Service, CP&I Steel, US West, and Bell Atlantic (Galvin 1998; Goldman 2000). The campaign for Jobs with Justice addresses the connection between employment conditions and family life for members of the working class. Their issues need to be addressed in tandem with the issues of white-collar fathers emphasized by the Fatherhood Project.

In the concluding chapter of *The Time Bind*, a study of the organization of time in working families and of the tendency for work to colonize time at the expense of family, Arlie Hochschild calls for a "time movement." Recognizing that company executives "are likely to exacerbate, not relieve, the time bind of their workers" and that "many working families are both prisoners and architects of the time bind in which they find themselves," Hochschild argues that a successful time movement "will not succeed without change in many of the underlying social conditions that make it necessary" and must "challenge the premises of that work culture" (1997: 248–58). Many analysts from a range of disciplines endorse this position and some go much further. Lawyer Nancy Dowd (2000) analyzes the links between fatherhood and power that exist in common law, the model of family economic dependence on the father, the privileging of marriage, and beliefs about masculinity and biology. Her policy recommendations are for universal economic support for children and caregivers and for a reformulation of legal and cultural definitions away from those based on marriage, biology, and common law and toward those based on social fatherhood. Joan Williams (1999), another legal scholar, argues that the entire structure of work and of family policy is predicated on what she calls the "ideal-worker norm" of the employee who works full time and overtime when needed and does not take time off for childbearing or child rearing. She proposes to eliminate this norm from the organization of work and from family entitlements, arguing, for instance, "Economic entitlements upon divorce should be redefined to eliminate the unstated principle that the ideal worker owns 'his' wage" (1999: 5). Family assets, Williams argues, including the earning power of family members, are created through joint activity and should be jointly owned.

In spite of overwhelming evidence that relying on isolated and unassisted young adults to raise children on their own is not the optimum solution for adults or children, the institutions of marriage and the autonomous nuclear family are fundamental to our cultural patterns and social structure. Suggestions about sharing the responsibility for children more broadly or for separating the identification between marriage and child rearing are met with furious opposition and are, on the face of it, impractical in the United States. I refrain from making any such suggestions, but I would argue that any policy, whether modest or far reaching, be judged by its exclusions and implications. Dominant cultural values do not operate only through expectations and valuations, but also by providing the cultural legitimation for structures of exclusion. Cultural values about what is appropriate for men to be doing are used first to exclude whole categories of men from access to jobs, credit, and housing, and then to explain or justify those men's unemployment, poverty, or homelessness. Some policies, although they address the real and expressed needs of children and parents, are tied to the heterosexual married couple as the only focus of child rearing. Other policies, while they help married parents, do not disadvantage children with single parents, with two parents of the same sex, or with three or more involved adults in parental situations. The actual involvement in children's lives of grandparents and other non-parental kin, as well as of step-parents and non-custodial or non-coresident parents, is already great. Every indication is that this involvement will increase over time. Family policies must not continue to conceal this involvement, but should facilitate it by removing current obstacles.

Restructuring employment to make it compatible with family life and the care of children is an enormous undertaking. Altering the cultural definition of masculinity to validate men for being emotionally involved with their children is equally daunting. One starting point in this double task of cultural and institutional change is to consider the structure of rewards. I have described how men are both culturally and materially rewarded for stressing employment as the key element of the package deal and provision as the essential facet of fatherhood. Men in general deploy whatever power they have to avoid assuming identities and tasks that, while intrinsically rewarding, confer neither material benefit nor cultural validation. Rewarding care by ensuring that care work carries with it entitlement to income, to health insurance, and to retirement benefits, would directly and immediately improve the situation of people who care for others. It might also encourage men to reorient the package deal toward greater involvement and emotional closeness with their children.

Redefining Masculinity

My analysis of the package deal and its contribution to the four facets of fatherhood suggests that effort directed at individual change will make progress only to the extent that it is accompanied by changes in the definition of successful masculinity.

What we learn from the accounts of the men from Meadowview High School is how the cultural ideas of separate spheres and a gendered division of labor and attention are integral parts of a cultural model of adulthood and fatherhood that responds to changes in circumstances and values in unanticipated ways. The institutional context of the organization of work, the structure of schools, and the expectations of men and women provide the situation within which men find social and personal validation for concentration on employment. The cultural model provides men with a justification for committing time and attention to providing and for placing the ultimate responsibility for children on mothers as default parents.

Feminist scholarship has created the space within which to study men as well as women as gendered, and to see masculinity as well as femininity as socially constructed and variable. Gender studies document the varieties of masculinities and femininities and how different gender definitions are socially ordered so that some carry prestige and power while others are denigrated and oppressed. In *The Package Deal* I have built on these analytic developments to analyze a widely accepted and powerful cultural construction of adult masculinity. I have pointed out how this culturally dominant image excludes and oppresses many men, both those whose circumstances do not allow them to fulfill it and those who find themselves trapped in a struggle to attain an unattainable position. My central concern has been to dissect this particular cultural image and to analyze its internal contradictions. Dominant cultural values hang together in constellations, bundles, or packages, but they do not form seamless wholes. Rather, they are in constant tension, forcing people into courses of action that, while they are intended to address conflicts of values, at the same time raise new contradictions.

The package deal is integral to dominant cultural values about fatherhood and masculinity in the United States. The lives and life stories of the men from Meadowview High School illustrate how the structure of the package deal influences the life courses and choices of men who accept its definition of success. Men who are not heterosexual or who do not want to get married or do not want to have children, men who want to pursue a vocation that does not provide for a family, men who cannot find employment that will pay even an approximation of a family wage, men without the family connections and credit to buy into an inflated housing market, are judged by, and either judge themselves by or must come to terms with, the values embedded in and expressed through the package deal.

Being close to one's children and earning a living are not necessarily incompatible, for women or for men. Understanding the contradictions within the package deal is a first step towards reassembling it into a humane vision of fatherhood.

Appendix 1

The Men from Meadowview High School

THESE TWENTY men, listed in the alphabetical order of the first names by which I refer to them, are those who I quote or discuss in detail or on more than one occasion. Their names are pseudonyms, and I have altered or omitted identifying details. These brief descriptions provide comparable information about each man and are intended to help readers to connect the remarks of particular men, which, in the text, are arranged by topic. Two of these men were Hispanic American, three were Asian American, and fifteen were European American. Each of these twenty men is included in the index under his first name.

BARRY RICHARDS and his second wife, Linda, lived with their two children, a son and a daughter. Barry's first marriage had lasted only two years when he had been in his early twenties. Barry and Linda had lived together for several years before deciding to get married and have children. Barry had not attended college. He was a maintenance supervisor and worked ten or more hours a day in order to be able to support his family on his income. Linda had worked full time until the children were born, and then worked part time from home. They bought a house almost an hour away from Barry's work because of the school district. Linda's parents had since moved close to them.

DAVID BROWN and his wife, Mary, had one son. David had not attended college. A manager in a retail store, he owned a house near his work, about one hundred miles from Meadowview. David and Mary had started dating one year after he graduated from high school, and they had married soon after. They had moved away from the San Francisco Bay Area when their son was eight to be able to afford the house they wanted on one income. Mary had worked full time on an electronics assembly line until they moved; she then started working part time for the local school district. Their discussion of why they had only one child is in Chapter 1.

Frank Smedley and his wife, Carol, had three children, two girls and a boy. Frank had found a well-paying job while he was attending college and had never graduated. He had worked as a design engineer and had been promoted to a management position in the same company. He owned his house in Meadowview and was deciding whether to move away from work to more space and better schools. Carol had been employed full time before the birth of their first child, but had quit to stay at home with the children.

George Peters lived with his second wife, Cindy, and their two young children in a new house in a new subdivision in California's Central Valley. George's education since high school had all been vocational. Both George and Cindy worked full time for a large manufacturing company. They had an hour and a half commute each way to their jobs in the San Francisco Bay Area. George had two teen-aged daughters from his first marriage, which ended in divorce when the children were young. Both these daughters lived with their mother.

Gordon Mackenzie was married with three sons. The son of a skilled machinist and of a college-educated mother who stayed at home to raise her children, Gordon himself had a college degree and worked as a mechanical engineer. He and his wife had met, married, and had their first child when he was in college. Since then, his wife had been employed part time.

Greg Turner and his wife, Maggie, had been married for eight years, having lived together for a year before that. They had two preschool-age daughters. Greg had no education beyond high school and had worked in quality control before stopping work eight months ago to stay home with the children while Maggie, a resource manager, went to college to get her bachelor's degree. Neither Greg's nor Maggie's parents had a college degree. Greg's father worked as a skilled operative, and after Greg had left primary school his mother had worked full time in electronics manufacturing. Greg and Maggie owned a home near Meadowview.

HAL LONG had married for the first time when he was over thirty. He and his wife were trying to have their first child at the time I talked to him. Hal had graduated from college and had then obtained a professional graduate degree. He had met his wife, who also had a professional career, at work. They had bought their first house after they married.

HOWARD GARBETT was married to Margie, who he had dated in high school, and had two children. He had not attended college, and he worked long hours as foreman for a small but busy construction company. Margie stayed at home with the children in their house near Meadowview. Howard was tormented by his inability to be the kind of father he wanted to be, which he attributed to the lack of examples in his life and the time pressure of his work.

JACK COOPER had been married for eight years and had two children, a boy and girl. He had graduated from college but could not get the kind of job he wanted with his degree and worked in a non-skilled but unionized job. His wife, Samantha, stayed home with the children in the house in Meadowview that Jack had bought in cooperation with his parents and his sister.

JIM MITCHELL was separated from his wife, Monica, who was living with their son and daughter in the house they were buying in a community near Meadowview. After briefly attending community college, Jim had worked full time for years as a skilled craftsman, but he wanted to be self-employed (partly to avoid having his wages attached for child support) and was working as a handyman. Monica was employed full time in a professional position.

MARK BAXTER was married to his girlfriend from high school. They had a son and a daughter. Mark had attended community college for a while, and had then entered an apprenticeship program in one of the building trades, in which he had since worked as a journeyman. A few years after he graduated from high school, Mark and his wife had bought the house in which they still lived in a new subdivision near Meadowview. Their children were aged nine and twelve, and Mark's wife was working full time in the office of a small business.

MARVIN MIDDLETON was married with two children. His college-educated parents had assumed he would go to college and he had planned to finish college and buy a house before having children. He and his wife had children before he completed college, however, and his wife has worked sporadically and part time since then. Marvin worked in purchasing, putting in ten or more hours a day in a job he found interesting and fulfilling. He said that not having a degree had not been an obstacle to his career. He and his wife bought a house with help from her parents.

MIKE MARTIN, married with one son, had not attended college. He ran his own business and owned a townhouse near Meadowview. The son of immigrants, he had married in his late twenties and worked very long hours at his business. His wife had left her job when their son was about three years old. They were living in a smaller house than Mike would have liked, because he was determined to remain in the area and make a success of his business.

PAUL WATSON married at age thirty and had two sons in primary school. Paul worked the night shift and overtime in a unionized transport job in Meadowview and lived in a townhouse there. His wife worked full time in purchasing and their children were cared for by her mother, who lived with them. As a teenager and young man, he had been part of a "rough crowd," but he now felt very responsible and protective of his wife and sons.

PHIL MARWICK, married for seven years, had two sons. He and his wife had dated for five years before getting married. Phil had started working for a large electronics company when he graduated from high school and had stayed with that company ever since, rising through the ranks to a supervisory managerial position. When the company reorganized, he had accepted a job three hours away and had moved his family. His move made it possible for him to buy a house and for his wife to stay home with the children.

RALPH COLSON, married with two children, was the safety coordinator for a large corporation. His only college experience was the courses he had taken to advance in his job. His wife, who had had a professional position in business, had left her job when their first child was an infant. Ralph had taken a second job to make this possible. His adolescence had not been easy, but his former classmates all spoke of him with admiration.

ROY WARNER and his wife, Sarah, had three children: two daughters from Sarah's previous marriage and a son. Roy had no education beyond high school, but he was determined his children should go to college. He worked in an electronics manufacturing plant, where he had met Sarah. She left her job when they got married in order to care for the children. She had done childcare at home and then worked part time at the children's school. Roy and Sarah lived in the house in which he had grown up, from which his parents had moved when their children were grown and they wanted a smaller place.

SKIP BARNES was married with two children. He had a college degree and worked as an engineer. He and his wife had met at the electronics company where they both worked. When their first child was born, Skip's wife had left her job to stay at home with the children.

TOM DOUGLAS, married with a son and daughter, had not gone to college. He worked as a construction foreman and his wife stayed home and home-schooled their children. He owned a home in a community about fifty miles from Meadowview, where he had moved for a previous job. Tom and his wife were committed evangelical Christians.

WILLIAM HUGHES had been married for fifteen years and had two children. He had attended community college briefly but had left and taken a job on the loading dock of an electronics company when his father refused to support his failing grades. He had worked his way up to a responsible managerial position in the fast-growing company. His wife was a college graduate. She had worked for the first three years of their marriage, until she had their first child.

Appendix 2
Bibliographic Essay

THE PURPOSE of this essay is threefold. First, it acknowledges more general intellectual debts than are specified in the citations to the text. Second, for readers who are familiar with the literature, it situates my work. And third, for readers who are unfamiliar with existing debates, it points the way to classic, contemporary, and review sources.

The contributions of feminist anthropologists have been vital to work on gender in general. The collections edited by Rayna Reiter (1975) and by Michelle Rosaldo and Louise Lamphere (1974) had an enormous impact when they were published, many of the essays have continued to reverberate over the subsequent twenty-five years, and many of their authors have been influential researchers and theorists. Louise Lamphere (2001) has neatly summarized the contributions and limitations of the early formulations of the dichotomy between private and public spheres and examined the impact of feminist anthropology (1987). In an examination of the daily activities of women and men in antebellum New England, Karen Hansen (1994) described the social as a distinct sphere of interaction that cuts across the distinction between private and public. The introductions by Micaela di Leonardo (1991) to *Gender at the Crossroads of Knowledge* and by Sylvia Yanagisako and Jane Collier (1987) to *Gender and Kinship* make important theoretical contributions while surveying the historical development of the field. *Gender in Cross-Cultural Perspective*, a collection edited by Caroline Brettell and Carolyn Sargent (2001) includes both classic and contemporary work and provides an overview of anthropological work on gender.

Basic insights and theoretical positions that have informed subsequent thinking about motherhood and fatherhood were developed in Nancy Chodorow's *The Reproduction of Mothering* (1978), Patricia Hill Collins's *Black Feminist Thought* (1990: 115–37), Adrienne Rich's *Of Woman Born* (1976), Barbara Katz Rothman's *Recreating Motherhood* (1989), and Sara Ruddick's *Maternal Thinking* (1989). Among the important recent studies are Anita Garey's *Weaving Work and Motherhood* (1999), Sharon Hays's *The Cultural Contradictions of Motherhood* (1996), and Martha McMahon's *Engendering Motherhood* (1995). The diversity of mothers' experiences within the context of a hegemonic cultural view of motherhood is captured in the essays in *Mothering against the Odds* (Garcia Coll, Surrey, and Weingarten 1998) and *Mothering: Ideology, Experience, and Agency* (Glenn, Chang, and Forcey 1994).

Studies of fatherhood that have recognized the importance of these gendered formulations of motherhood include Terry Arendell's *Fathers and Divorce* (1995), which investigated fatherhood and the "masculinist discourse" of rights through the ruptures created by divorce; Scott Coltrane's *Family Man* (1996), which focused on new fathers and gender equity in the United States; Kathleen Gerson's *No Man's Land* (1993); and Matthew Gutmann's *The Meanings of Macho* (1996), which examined the variety and complexity of men's fatherhood in Mexico City. Coltrane's *Gender and Families* (1998a) provides a thorough and accessible introduction and review of a wide range of the literature.

A great deal of the recent research on fathers, particularly the contributions from psychology and sociology, is reviewed in the chapters in Alan Booth and Ann Crouter's collection *Men in Families* (1998), William Marsiglio's *Fatherhood* (1995), and in Tamis-LeMonda and Cabrera's *Handbook of Father Involvement* (forthcoming). The overwhelming orientation of this literature is on the impact fathers have on children through their presence or absence and through the nature of their involvement in children's lives. Barry Hewlett's *Intimate Fathers* (1991) is a detailed description of fatherhood in a small-scale society, and Hewlett's volume on father–child interactions surveys the biosocial approach within anthropology (1992).

Research on the history of fatherhood has been particularly important to a recognition that the meaning of fatherhood to fathers and their societies changes and is constructed in the context of changing social and economic circumstances and changing definitions of gender. Several influential overviews and theoretical models have proposed mechanisms driving change and have sketched a series of stages in the history of fatherhood in the United States (Demos 1986; Lamb 1986; Mintz 1998; Pleck 1987; Rotundo 1985; Stearns 1991). These have been elaborated and modified in fuller histories of masculinity (Kimmel 1996; Rotundo 1993) and fatherhood (Griswold 1993) and supplemented by historical studies of particular stages and transitions (Carnes 1989; LaRossa 1997).

Attention to fatherhood as a gendered activity has proceeded as one aspect of a research and political project to examine men and masculinity as gendered. Erving Goffman (1977) recognized that symbolic interactionism as a theoretical position had to address gender and was ideally suited to do so. The interactionist perspective on gender has been elegantly developed by Barrie Thorne in *Gender Play* (1993), which weaves theoretical sophistication into close observation of the interactions of boys and girls. Joseph Pleck, in his book *The Myth of Masculinity* (1981) and in collections edited with Elizabeth Pleck (Pleck and Pleck 1980) and Jack Sawyer (Pleck and Sawyer 1974), did a great deal to establish a pro-feminist study of men. A pioneering article by Tim Carrigan, Bob Connell, and John Lee (1987) set out a theoretical agenda. In 1987 four key works were published that developed the theoretical perspectives of the field: Robert Connell's *Gender and Power* (1987), Jeff Hearn's *The Gender of Oppression* (1987), and two volumes with coherent editorial positions: Michael Kimmel's *Changing Men* (1987) and Harry Brod's *The Making of Masculinities* (1987). Subsequent work in the field is voluminous, with major contributions by Brod and Kaufman (1994), Connell (1995), Kimmel (1996), Messner (1992, 1997), and an accessible collection edited by Kimmel and Messner (2001).

Specifically anthropological contributions to the literature on masculinity include Stanley Brandes's analysis of the symbolic representation of conflicting cultural values in *Metaphors of Masculinity* (1980), David Gilmore's cross-cultural argument that masculinity must be made (1990), Gilbert Herdt's ethnography of Sambia male initiation (1981), Roger Lancaster's analysis of the intersections of politics and masculinity in Nicaragua (1992), and Richard Parker's depiction of varieties of sexual cultures and meanings in Brazil (1991). The collection edited by Roger Lancaster and Micaela di Leonardo (1997) provides an introduction to the field of gender and sexuality studies in general, and Matthew Gutmann (1997) has written a review article specifically on the anthropology of masculinity.

Feminist research on men as gendered and the profeminist men's movement are distinct from the positions of neotraditionalism, "men's rights," and the mythopoetic men's movement. The distinction has been made most effectively by commentators who are sympathetic to men's experience but critical of imposed political agendas (Kimmel 1995; Kimmel and Messner 1995; Kimmel and Mosmiller 1992). In his book *The Gender Knot*, Allan Johnson (1997: 181–208) dissects the antiwoman, patriarchal position represented by the most cited ideologues of the men's rights movement, Robert Bly (1990) and Sam Keen (1991). The neotraditionalist position is most forcefully presented by David Blankenhorn (1995) and David Popenoe (1988), who inveigh against the decline of the nuclear family and what they see as the consequent moral decay and social problems. Although colored and distorted by a relentless and blinkered polemic, Blankenhorn's *Fatherless America* (1995), is an impressive review of a mass of research on families and fathers.

A great variety of voices offer advice to men on how to be fathers. Allan Johnson (Johnson 1997: 255–64) provides an extensive list of organizations, publications, and resources directed to changing gender relations from a feminist perspective. Armin Brott (1997, 1998, 1999) is among the most popular writers of advice to new fathers and his books describe a range of organizations and resources promoting involved fatherhood. James Levine is a tireless advocate for paternal involvement, whose work is directed at changing workplaces as well as the attitudes and behaviors of fathers (Levine 1976; Levine and Pitt 1995; Levine and Pittinsky 1998).

Notes

Chapter 1

1. Most discussions start from Gramsci's (1971) development of the concept of hegemony as an extension of Marx's theory of ideology. Contemporary development of the ideas is clearly and forcefully laid out in the work of Dorothy Holland and her colleagues (1998; Holland and Skinner 1987), and is expressed in a different vocabulary by students of cultural "schemas" (D'Andrade and Strauss 1992).

2. Throughout this book, I present what people said to me in enough detail to bring out the complexities of their stories and positions. I have chosen to present people's words in a way that emphasizes their meaning and content and that does not undermine their articulateness and expressivity. I have not, therefore, recorded every "um," "er," and "you know." Unless otherwise indicated, italics within quotations mark the speaker's own emphases. Omissions are noted with ellipses. When I have added a word or phrase to clarify the meaning it is enclosed in square brackets. Parentheses indicate parenthetical comments by the speaker. A dash following a word indicates that the speaker did not complete the sentence or thought, or changed the direction of what he or she was saying.

3. Norms are culturally specific. Having two children is normatively appropriate in the contemporary United States and needs no explanation. In many other times and places, having only two children would attract attention and require extensive explanation.

4. The way that attention to others is gendered is discussed in Sara Ruddick's (1989) *Maternal Thinking* and in Arlie Hochschild's (1989) discussions of care.

5. The great racial–ethnic division in the United States has been the color line between white and black, rooted in history (Du Bois 1999; Hacker 1992; Massey and Denton 1993). Race is a socially constructed set of categories, reflecting social and historical processes, not essential biological differences (American Anthropological Association 2000; Gregory and Sanjek 1994; Montagu 1964). Historical and ethnographic studies have revealed the changing definition and treatment of minority ethnic groups as they confront and negotiate this division (Brodkin 1998; Delgado and Stefanic 1997; di Leonardo 1984; Frankenberg 1993; Waters 2000). Micaela di Leonardo (1998) brilliantly dissects the changing patterns of depiction of race and gender difference during the twentieth century and the role of anthropologists in challenging and contributing to these depictions.

6. A "good neighborhood" is considered to be one with a high percentage of owner occupiers, as expensive as could be afforded by people with stable jobs, accessible to stores and services, with amenities such as parks, and attentive public safety service. Schools with high test results, small classes, and equipped facilities are considered to be "good schools." For both neighborhoods and schools, "goodness" and "whiteness" are highly correlated.

7. Nationally, in 1977, 85 percent of whites aged twenty to twenty-four (the age group centered on the high school class of 1972) had completed high school; the figure for Hispanics was 57 percent (Center for Education Statistics 1984: 26). In 1980, of those aged over twenty-five in the county including Meadowview, 83 percent of the white population were high school graduates, compared with 53 percent of the Hispanic population (United States Bureau of the Census 1983).

8. Nationally, of men aged thirty-five to forty-four in 1995, 11.6 percent had not graduated from high school, while 26.6 percent had a bachelor's or other advanced degree. An additional 28.4 percent had some college or an associate's degree, and 33.3 percent had graduated from high school but had not attended college. Sixty-one percent had graduated from high school, but not from college (United States Bureau of the Census 1996: table 243). Years of schooling for the population have been rising steadily, although differentials by racial–ethnic category remain.

9. Goodell (2000) has written a first-person account of growing up and coming to adulthood in the south part of the San Francisco Bay Area during this period. His story of finding meaning and seeking redemption begs for a cultural analysis of its narrative structure and sense of adequate explanation (Mishler 1986; Plummer 1995), but his autobiography does provide a child's perspective on divorce and a vivid picture of the impact of the computer boom on men, women, and families.

10. 1972 was the last year for the draft, and the intensity of conscription had been declining for the previous few years. The war in Vietnam and the possibility of conscription were, however, subjects that the high school graduating class of 1972 had confronted during their high school years.

Chapter 2

1. Frank Furstenberg and Andrew Cherlin, in their classic review of the effects of divorce on children's well-being, suggest that marriage and parenthood are a package deal for many men (Furstenberg and Cherlin 1991: 118). In my analysis, the idea of the package deal extends beyond this link to include the elements of work and housing and to include the interconnected meanings of the four elements.

2. The first years of life may not be as critical for development as is often assumed (Kagan 1998: 83–150). Alternative views would be that the personality or character of the child is determined at birth, so experience is only a minimal influence, or that what counts for a child's success and happiness is the quality

of the social relationships, patronage, and connections negotiated for it by its parents (Riesman 1992).

3. The sociologist C. Wright Mills used the expression "vocabulary of motives" to point out that, in any particular social situation, there is a set of reasons that the people in that situation accept as explanations or justifications of their own and other people's actions. The vocabulary of acceptable motives varies over time and from place to place. Mills points out that in the West, for instance, religious motives have declined in general acceptance and are likely to be suspect if they are expressed because they are not part of the dominant vocabulary of motives. He contends, "Individualistic, sexual, hedonistic, and pecuniary vocabularies of motives are apparently now dominant in many sections of twentieth-century urban America. Under such an ethos, verbalization of alternative conduct in these terms is least likely to be challenged among dominant groups" (1963: 447). Extending and applying the situational analysis of disputes developed by Max Gluckman, anthropologist John Comaroff and legal scholar Simon Roberts (1981) described the vocabulary of motives operating in Tswana legal disputes as a "normative repertoire"—participants could invoke one or more of a variety of principles in justifying or condemning a particular course of action.

4. The approved sequence in rural Botswana was for a young man to find a job (which was frequently unconnected to his schooling), to remit to his parents and elders, to become affianced, to have children who continued to live with their mother in her parents' house, to contribute to the maintenance of that household, to finalize his marriage through bride payment, to establish (with the support of his parents and his wife's parents) a household of his own, and to live in that household with his wife and children, possibly one or more of his or his wife's younger siblings, and eventually his grandchildren. This sequence was supported by the cultural view that the young man not only had multiple responsibilities to others besides his wife and children, but was also not considered mature and experienced enough to establish his own household.

Among the educated elite, a Western (or more accurately, Northern) evaluation of the life course is common. A shift from land to capital (economic and human) as the critical factor of production, so that financial independence depends on individual employment rather than access to land, has been associated with a more individuated economic life and a greater emphasis on the nuclear family for some. It would be a mistake, however, to assume that this process is necessarily either universal or inevitable in southern Africa. The AIDS epidemic must throw any predictions about developments in African family forms into doubt. Here I am describing a set of values about family life that was widespread and dominant in a rural community in the 1990s (Garey and Townsend 1996; Townsend 1997).

5. In the United States, 60 percent of babies are born to men in their twenties, and over a third of babies are born to men aged twenty-five to twenty-nine. Less than 4 percent of births are to fathers under twenty, less than 5 percent to fathers over forty, and only .5 percent to fathers over fifty. I computed these per-

centages from published vital statistics. These percentages are for births of children of all races; the pattern is only marginally different by race. The pattern of age-specific fertility is very similar for men and women, with the men's distribution shifted upward by about two years, which is the median age difference between spouses in first marriages. The age difference between mothers and fathers varies around this figure. It is worth noting that the data on men's reproduction is much inferior to that on women—for 12.1 percent of the 3,680,537 births in 1982, the age of the father was not recorded (Townsend 1992: 13).

6. This process, whereby a social pattern is created and reinforced by, but also normalizes, individual actions, which the participants think of as choices, is a feature of social life. Goffman's "Arrangement between the Sexes" (1977) lucidly describes how social ideas about women and men are constructed through interaction, a process further analyzed in West and Zimmerman's much cited "Doing Gender" (1987). Brodkin describes the same process driving the ethnic segregation of work (1998: 58–59).

7. Howard Becker (1997: 79–119) has written about the social practice of jazz musicians as an instance of "doing things together." He emphasizes the interactive aspects of musicianship and their impact on forming in-groups and outgroups. Becker's comment on the relation between group membership and language use, on the social occasions when language is not, and cannot be, explicit, is directly relevant to thinking about men whose motivations are taken for granted:

> But every art's practitioners use words whose meanings they cannot define exactly which are nevertheless intelligible to all knowledgeable members of their worlds. Jazz musicians say that something does or does not "swing"; theater people say that a scene "works" or does not "work." In neither case can even the most knowledgeable participant explain to someone not already familiar with the terms' uses what they mean. Yet everyone who uses them understands them and can apply them with great reliability, agreeing about what swings or works, even though they cannot say what they mean.
>
> [This] suggests that they do not work by consulting a set of rules or criteria. Rather, they respond as they imagine others might respond, and construct those imaginings from their repeated experiences of hearing people apply the undefined terms in concrete situations. (1982: 199–200)

8. "When you ask why you are asking for, and will receive, given the conventions of our common speech, a justification, an explanation, a selection from the currently available vocabulary of motives. We very often want just that, but we should never mistake it for an account of how something came to pass (see Mills 1940)" (Becker 1986: 145).

Chapter 3

1. "Children" in this context are *adult* children, as they are in many places in this chapter and as they are in studies of "outcomes." To call people "children"

is to call attention to their relationship with others, rather than to their chronological age.

Chapter 4

1. The birth of children before marriage is associated with a marital disruption rate 57 to 80 percent higher than for couples without premarital births for cohorts of white women married between 1970 and 1985 (Martin and Bumpass 1989: 42). This association may be because of greater strains on the early marriage, because couples who have a child before marriage have less normative commitment to marriage, or because some of the births were the biological children of men other than the husband and so do not have an "own children" effect on his behavior. My assertion of the connectedness of marriage and children is bolstered, however, by the lack of association between premarital *conception* and marital disruption (Billy, Landale, and McLaughlin 1986).

2. Langer (1983) has analyzed the psychology of "perceived control" and its importance for both a sense of well-being and the actual outcome of events.

3. Different pronoun use is a gendered feature of speech, concealing a gendered division of labor. Compare Naomi Gerstel's comment on her research on care outside the home:

> In the process of interviewing, we found that the men (but almost never the women) would sometimes speak of "we" when they spoke about the provision of care. . . . Upon probing, it often became quite clear that the individual who did most of the labor was the wife, not the husband. Given this response, interviewers had to be trained to probe whenever they heard the word "we." (2000: 162)

4. The proportion of children living with a single-parent father rose steadily with the age of the children, and at every age boys were more likely to live with their father than were girls. The highest figure for any age or sex group was for boys aged fifteen to seventeen, 19 percent of whom were living with their father (Sweet and Bumpass 1987: 269). In the 1920s, less than 40 percent of divorces involved children. The figure was 45 percent in 1950 and 60 percent from 1960 to 1972. It had dropped to 56 percent by 1980 (Sweet and Bumpass 1987: 179).

Chapter 5

1. The significant change in work patterns over the last forty years has been in the labor force participation rates of married women—in 1960 28.8 percent of married women aged twenty-five to thirty-four were in the labor force; in 1990 the figure was 69.8 percent—two and a half times as high.

2. Cooper (2000) gives an interesting account of the way that technical expertise and dedication to completing projects have become markers of masculinity in the high-tech world of contemporary Silicon Valley.

Chapter 6

1. These are lyrics from a song by folk singer Malvina Reynolds, made popular by Pete Seeger, and inspired by the postwar developments of Daly City, between San Francisco and Meadowview.

2. I mailed a questionnaire listing twenty-nine potential forms of assistance with buying a first house to the men who had graduated from Meadowview High School in 1972. I received seventy-seven usable responses from men who had bought a home, 70 percent of whom reported one or more of these forms of assistance from relatives. Forty-five percent reported help that included direct financial gifts or loans, and another 25 percent reported only other forms of help. This 25 percent represents an aspect of kin support in the United States that is concealed by official statistics, which concentrate on financial transactions, and by the recipients themselves, who tend to downplay its importance (Townsend 1996).

3. This point is elaborated in Dudley's (2000) study of farm credit and foreclosure in the United States, in which she analyzes the varying significance of different forms of credit in determining both economic success and perceived moral worth, and is illustrated in reports of economic arrangements in societies where the role of kinship is more explicit and structured than in the United States (Benedict 1968; Shipton 1992).

Chapter 7

1. Kinship connections in industrial societies have been variously represented as characteristic of the poor and of excluded ethnic groups (Stack 1974; Young and Wilmott 1957), and of the elite or ruling class (Marcus and Hall 1992; Weatherford 1981). The importance of kinship for the middle class has been downplayed (Hansen 2001; Schneider and Smith 1973).

2. Bruno Bettelheim, a psychologist whose work has had enormous influence on parents in the United States, titled one of his books on child rearing *A Good Enough Parent* (1987). Bettelheim urges parents to realize that human perfection is unattainable and argues that this realization should reduce parents' anxiety about both their own imperfections and the imperfections of their children, encouraging them to be lenient in their parenting and their self-judgment. On becoming fathers, the men I am describing came to see their own fathers as "good enough parents."

3. Radcliffe-Brown (1950), in a classic of social anthropological theorizing about kinship in Africa, elevated the closeness of relationships between members of alternate generations to a principle of social structure.

4. Of the other thirteen cartoons, two depict an adult man with his older father and four a husband and wife (two with no children, one with two sons and two daughters, and one with a single son). The remaining seven depict a man and a woman (not married), two men, a man and his dog, children, mailboxes

labeled with family forms, a rodent couple addressing their auditorium of offspring, and a mother fish with one offspring (she has eaten her mate).

5. Only one man told me of his worry that he might find a daughter sexually attractive. The father of an only son, he told me about the thoughts he had had before his child was born:

> I was slightly concerned about having a daughter and falling in love with her and kind of, you know, being a child molester. Not that I would *be* a child molester, but just kind of fighting those urges, you know. When she gets to be fourteen or fifteen. I don't know. But I know I would have been fine.

I was struck by the conflation of emotions expressed here. To the extent that strong feelings toward women and girls are always tinged with sexual attraction even when sexual activity is clearly inappropriate there is bound to be tension in men's relationships with their daughters. On the other hand, paternal and romantic love can be experienced as very different or as incompatible. Research on sexual activity between adults and children certainly indicates that cultural norms about the inappropriateness of sexual contact between fathers and daughters do not prevent the behavior (Finkelhor 1984; Russell 1984). Adult men are much more likely than women to see children as sexual objects, and they are also more likely to act on this perception (Finkelhor 1984).

I found this man's remarks at once fascinating and frustrating. Whereas every other quotation and example I give could be multiplied from my interviews and notes and illustrates or exemplifies a common theme, this man's remark was unique. As a clear and unsolicited description of concern about sexual feelings for a child, a topic of theoretical interest and current concern, it is surely important. On the other hand, it is impossible to tell whether such a statement on a topic of extreme sensitivity represents individual aberration or a generally shared but concealed attitude.

6. *The Dick Van Dyke Show* is a classic and familiar depiction of a father as breadwinner without any of the masculine traits of strength, coordination, or decisiveness. Its long run began in 1961. Other popular television shows of the period also featured breadwinning fathers in white-collar occupations. In *Father Knows Best* (1954) the father was an insurance agent, in *Leave It to Beaver* (1957) he was a "businessman," and in *My Three Sons* (1960) he was an engineer.

7. Experience and institution are always interconnected. Adrienne Rich described women's experience of motherhood, and her own particular experience, within the institution of motherhood in *Of Woman Born* (1986), a book that has been a touchstone and point of reference for all subsequent research on motherhood and fatherhood. Rich makes it clear that not only is experience embedded in institutions, but also that understanding, resolving, and changing personal experience happens within the context of collective action directed at institutional change.

References

Amato, Paul R. 1994. "Father-Child Relations, Mother-Child Relations and Offspring Psychological Well-Being in Adulthood." *Journal of Marriage and the Family* 56: 1031–42.

———. 1998. "More Than Money? Men's Contributions to Their Children's Lives." Pp. 241–78 in *Men in Families: When Do They Get Involved? What Difference Does It Make?* ed. A. Booth and A. C. Crouter. Mahwah, NJ: Lawrence Erlbaum.

American Anthropological Association. 2000. "American Anthropological Association Statement on Race" [retrieved 18 July 2001]. Available: http://www.ameranthassn.org/stmts/racepp.htm.

Angell, Alison. n. d. "The Involved Expectant Father Script: An Examination of the Social Construction of 'Involved' Expectant Fatherhood among Middle-class American Men." Unpublished paper.

Arendell, Terry. 1995. *Fathers and Divorce*. Thousand Oaks, CA: Sage.

Baca Zinn, Maxine. 1991. "Family, Feminism, and Race in America." Pp. 119–33 in *The Social Construction of Gender*, ed. J. Lorber and S. A. Farrell. Newbury Park, CA: Sage.

Barrera, Manuel and Carolynne Garrison-Jones. 1992. "Family and Peer Social Support as Specific Correlates of Adolescent Depressive Symptoms." *Journal of Abnormal Child Psychology* 20(1): 1–16.

Beal, Carole R. 1994. *Boys and Girls: The Development of Gender Roles*. New York: McGraw-Hill.

Becker, Gary S. 1976. *The Economic Approach to Human Behavior*. Chicago: University of Chicago Press.

Becker, Howard S. 1982. *Art Worlds*. Berkeley: University of California Press.

———. 1986. *Writing for Social Scientists: How to Start and Finish Your Thesis, Book, or Article*. Chicago: University of Chicago Press.

———. 1997 [1966]. *Outsiders: Studies in the Sociology of Deviance*. New York: Free Press.

Belsky, Jay. 1998. "Paternal Influence and Children's Well-Being: Limits of, and New Directions for, Understanding." Pp. 279–94 in *Men in Families: When Do They Get Involved? What Difference Does It Make?* ed. A. Booth and A. C. Crouter. Mahwah, NJ: Lawrence Erlbaum.

Belsky, Jay, and John Kelly. 1994. *The Transition to Parenthood: How a First Child Changes a Marriage*. New York: Delacorte.

Benedict, Burton. 1968. "Family Firms and Economic Development." *Southwestern Journal of Anthropology* 24(1): 1–19.

Benedict, Ruth. 1934. *Patterns of Culture*. Boston: Houghton Mifflin.

Berger, Peter L., and Hansfried Kellner. 1970. "Marriage and the Construction of Reality: An Exercise in the Microsociology of Knowledge." Pp. 179–89 in *Recent Sociology No. 2: Patterns of Communicative Behavior*, ed. H. P. Dreitzel. New York: Macmillan.

Bernard, Jessie. 1972. *The Future of Marriage*. New York: World Publishing.

Bettelheim, Bruno. 1987. *A Good Enough Parent: A Book on Child-Rearing*. New York: Knopf.

Billy, John H. G., Nancy S. Landale, and Steven D. McLaughlin. 1986. "The Effect of Marital Status at First Birth on Marital Dissolution among Adolescent Mothers." *Demography* 23: 329–49.

Blankenhorn, David. 1995. *Fatherless America: Confronting Our Most Urgent Social Problem*. New York: Basic Books.

Bly, R. 1990. *Iron John: A Book about Men*. Reading, MA: Addison-Wesley.

Booth, Alan, and Ann C. Crouter, eds. 1998. *Men in Families: When Do They Get Involved? What Difference Does It Make?* Mahwah, NJ: Lawrence Erlbaum.

Bourdieu, Pierre. 1977. *Outline of a Theory of Practice*. New York: Cambridge University Press.

———. 1984. *Distinction: A Social Critique of the Judgement of Taste*. Cambridge, MA: Harvard University Press.

Bourdieu, Pierre, and Jean-Claude Passeron. 1990. *Reproduction in Education, Society and Culture*. Newbury Park, CA: Sage.

Brandes, Stanley. 1980. *Metaphors of Masculinity: Sex and Status in Andalusian Folklore*. Philadelphia: University of Pennsylvania Press.

Brettell, Caroline B., and Carolyn F. Sargent, eds. 2001. *Gender in Cross-Cultural Perspective*. 3d ed. Upper Saddle River, NJ: Prentice-Hall.

Brod, Harry, ed. 1987. *The Making of Masculinities: The New Men's Studies*. Boston: Allen and Unwin.

Brod, Harry, and Michael Kaufman, eds. 1994. *Theorizing Masculinities*. Thousand Oaks, CA: Sage.

Brodkin, Karen. 1998. *How Jews Became White Folks and What That Says about Race in America*. New Brunswick, NJ: Rutgers University Press.

Brott, Armin. 1997. *The New Father: A Dad's Guide to the First Year*. New York: Abbeville.

———. 1998. *The New Father: A Dad's Guide to the Toddler Years*. New York: Abbeville.

———. 1999. *The Single Father: A Dad's Guide to Parenting without a Partner*. New York: Abbeville.

Buchmann, Marlis. 1989. *The Script of Life in Modern Society: Entry into Adulthood in a Changing World*. Chicago: University of Chicago Press.

Buder, Stanley. 1990. *Visionaries and Planners: The Garden City Movement and the Modern Community*. New York: Oxford University Press.

Burnett, Jacquetta Hill. 1975. "Ceremony, Rites, and Economy in the Student System of an American High School." Pp. 43–54 in *The Nacirema: Readings on*

American Culture, ed. J. P. Spradley and M. A. Rynkiewich. Boston: Little, Brown.

Carnes, Mark. 1989. *Secret Ritual and Manhood in Victorian America*. New Haven, CT: Yale University Press.

Carrigan, Tim, Bob Connell, and John Lee. 1987. "Toward a New Sociology of Masculinity." Pp. 63–100 in *The Making of Masculinities: The New Men's Studies*, ed. H. Brod. Boston: Allen and Unwin.

Cazenave, N. A. 1979. "Middle Income Black Fathers: An Analysis of the Provider Role." *The Family Coordinator* 28(4): 583–93.

Center for Education Statistics. 1984. *Condition of Education (1984)*. Washington, D.C.: United States Department of Education.

Cherlin, Andrew J., ed. 1988. *The Changing American Family and Public Policy*. Washington, DC: Urban Institute.

———. 1992. *Marriage, Divorce, Remarriage*, rev. and enlarged ed. Cambridge, MA: Harvard University Press.

Chodorow, Nancy. 1978. *The Reproduction of Mothering: Psychoanalysis and the Sociology of Gender*. Berkeley: University of California Press.

Christiansen, Shawn L., and Rob Palkovitz. 2001. "Why the 'Good Provider' Role Still Matters: Providing as a Form of Paternal Involvement." *Journal of Family Issues* 22(1): 84–106.

Collins, Patricia Hill. 1990. *Black Feminist Thought: Knowledge, Consciousness, and the Politics of Empowerment*. Boston: Unwin Hyman.

Coltrane, Scott. 1989. "Household Labor and the Routine Production of Gender." *Social Problems* 36: 473–90.

———. 1996. *Family Man: Fatherhood, Housework, and Gender Equity*. New York: Oxford University Press.

———. 1998a. *Gender and Families*. Thousand Oaks, CA: Sage.

———. 1998b. "Gender, Power, and Emotional Expression: Social and Historical Contexts for a Process Model of Men in Marriages and Families." Pp. 193–211 in *Men in Families: When Do They Get Involved? What Difference Does It Make?* ed. A. C. Booth, A. C. Crouter. Mahwah, NJ: Lawrence Erlbaum.

———. 2000. "Research on Household Labor: Modeling and Measuring the Social Embeddedness of Routine Family Work." *Journal of Marriage and the Family* 62 (November): 1208–33.

Comaroff, John L., and Simon A. Roberts. 1981. *Rules and Processes: The Cultural Logic of Dispute in an African Context*. Chicago: University of Chicago Press.

Connell, Robert W. 1987. *Gender and Power: Society, the Person and Sexual Politics*. Stanford, CA: Stanford University Press.

———. 1995. *Masculinities*. Berkeley: University of California Press.

Contratto, Susan. 1987. "Father Presence in Women's Psychological Development." Pp. 138–57 in *Advances in Psychoanalytic Sociology*, ed. J. Rabow, G. M. Platt, and M. S. Goldman. Malabar, FL: Robert E. Krieger.

Cooney, Teresa M., and Dennis P. Hogan. 1991. "Marriage in an Institutionalized Life Course: First Marriage among American Men in the Twentieth Century." *Journal of Marriage and the Family* 53: 178–90.

Cooper, Marianne. 2000. "Being the 'Go-to Guy': Fatherhood, Masculinity, and the Organization of Work in Silicon Valley." *Qualitative Sociology* 23(4, July 21): 379–405.
Cowan, Carolyn Pape, and Philip A. Cowan. 2000 [1992]. *When Partners Become Parents: The Big Life Change for Couples*. Mahwah, NJ: Lawrence Erlbaum.
Crittenden, Ann. 2001. *The Price of Motherhood: Why the Most Important Job in the World is Still the Least Valued*. New York: Metropolitan Books.
Crouter, Ann C, Matthew F. Bumpus, Melissa R. Head, and Susan M. McHale. 2001. "Implications of Overwork and Overload for the Quality of Men's Family Relationships." *Journal of Marriage and the Family* 63(2): 404–16.
D'Andrade, Roy D., and Claudia Strauss, eds. 1992. *Human Motives and Cultural Models*. Cambridge: Cambridge University Press.
Delgado, Richard, and Jean Stefanic, eds. 1997. *Critical White Studies: Looking behind the Mirror*. Philadelphia: Temple University Press.
Demos, John. 1986. "The Changing Faces of Fatherhood." Pp. 41–67 in *Past, Present, and Personal: The Family and Life Course in American History*, ed. J. Demos. New York: Oxford University Press.
DeMott, Benjamin. 1990. *The Imperial Middle: Why Americans Can't Think Straight about Class*. New York: William Morrow.
Deutsch, Francine M. 1999. *Halving It All: How Equally Shared Parenting Works*. Cambridge, MA: Harvard University Press.
di Leonardo, Micaela. 1984. *The Varieties of Ethnic Experience: Kinship, Class, and Gender among California Italian-Americans*. Ithaca, NY: Cornell University Press.
———. 1987. "The Female World of Cards and Holidays: Women, Families, and the Work of Kinship." *Signs* 12(3): 440–53.
———. 1991. "Gender, Culture and Historical Economy: Feminist Anthropology in Historical Perspective." Pp. 1–48 in *Gender at the Crossroads of Knowledge: Feminist Anthropology in the Postmodern Era*, ed. M. di Leonardo. Berkeley: University of California Press.
———. 1998. *Exotics at Home: Anthropologies, Others, American Modernity*. Chicago: University of Chicago Press.
Dowd, Nancy. 2000. *Redefining Fatherhood*. New York: New York University Press.
Du Bois, W. E. B. 1999 [1903]. *The Souls of Black Folks: Authoritative Text, Contexts, Criticisms*, ed. H. L. Gates and T. H. Oliver. New York: W. W. Norton.
Dudley, Kathryn Marie. 1994. *The End of the Line: New Jobs, New Lives in Postindustrial America*. Chicago: University of Chicago Press.
———. 2000. *Debt and Dispossession: Farm Loss in America's Heartland*. Chicago: University of Chicago Press.
Duneier, Mitchell. 1992. *Slim's Table: Race, Respectability, and Masculinity*. Chicago: University of Chicago Press.
Easterlin, Richard A. 1978. "The Economics and Sociology of Fertility: A Synthesis." Pp. 57–133 in *Historical Studies of Changing Fertility*, ed. C. Tilly. Princeton, NJ: Princeton University Press.
Ehrensaft, Diane. 1990. *Parenting Together: Men and Women Sharing the Care of the Their Children*. Urbana: University of Illinois Press.

Elder, Glen H. 1974. *Children of the Great Depression: Social Change in Life Experience*. Chicago: Chicago University Press.

Etaugh, Claire, and Denise Folger. 1998. "Perceptions of Parents Whose Work and Parenting Behaviors Deviate from Role Expectations." *Sex Roles: A Journal of Research* 39(3–4): 215–24.

Evans, Hazel, ed. 1972. *New Towns—The British Experience*. London: C. Knight for the Town and Country Planning Association.

Fausto-Sterling, Anne. 2000. *Sexing the Body: Gender Politics and the Construction of Sexuality*. New York: Basic Books.

Ferree, Myra Marx. 1991. "The Gender Division of Labor in Two-Earner Marriages: Dimensions of Variability and Change." *Journal of Family Issues* 12: 158–80.

Fine, Gary Alan. 1987. *With the Boys: Little League Baseball and Culture*. Chicago: University of Chicago Press.

Fineman, Martha. 1995. *The Neutered Mother, the Sexual Family, and Other Twentieth Century Tragedies*. New York: Routledge.

Finkelhor, D. 1984. *Child Sexual Abuse: New Theory and Research*. New York: Free Press.

Fischer, Claude S. 1982. *To Dwell among Friends: Personal Networks in Town and City*. Chicago: University of Chicago Press.

———. 2000. "Ever-More Rooted Americans," University of California, Berkeley, November. Unpublished paper.

Fiske, Shirley. 1975. "Pigskin Review: An American Institution." Pp. 55–68 in *The Nacirema: Readings on American Culture*, ed. J. P. Spradley and M. A. Rynkiewich. Boston: Little, Brown.

Folbre, Nancy. 2001. *The Invisible Heart: Economics and Family Values*. New York: New Press.

Fortes, Meyer. 1949. "Time and Social Structure: An Ashanti Case Study." Pp. 54–84 in *Social Structure: Essays Presented to A. R. Radcliffe-Brown*, ed. M. Fortes. Oxford: Oxford University Press.

Frankenberg, Ruth. 1993. *White Women, Race Matters: The Social Construction of Whiteness*. Minneapolis: University of Minnesota Press.

Freud, Sigmund. 1965. *The Interpretation of Dreams*. Ed. J. Strachey. New York: Avon.

Furstenberg, Frank, F., Jr. 1995. "Fathering in the Inner City: Paternal Participation and Public Policy." Pp. 119–47 in *Fatherhood: Contemporary Theory, Research, and Social Policy*, ed. W. Marsiglio. Thousand Oaks, CA: Sage.

———. 1998. "Social Capital and the Role of Fathers in the Family." Pp. 295–302 in *Men in Families: When Do They Get Involved? What Difference Does It Make?* ed. A. Booth and A. C. Crouter. Mahwah, NJ: Lawrence Erlbaum.

Furstenberg, Frank F., Jr., and Andrew J. Cherlin. 1991. *Divided Families: What Happens to Children When Parents Part*. Cambridge, MA: Harvard University Press.

Furstenberg, Frank F., Jr., and Christine Winquist Nord. 1985. "Parenting Apart: Patterns of Childrearing after Marital Disruption." *Journal of Marriage and the Family* 45 (November): 893–904.

Galvin, Kevin. 1998. "Some Workers Protest Increase in Forced Overtime" [retrieved 8 May 2001]. Available: http://www.ardmoreite.com/stories/111298/mon_overtime.shtml.

Gans, Herbert J. 1967. *The Levittowners: Ways of Life and Politics in a New Suburban Community*. New York: Columbia University Press.

Garcia Coll, Cynthia, Janet L. Surrey, and Kathy Weingarten. 1998. *Mothering against the Odds: Diverse Voices of Contemporary Mothers*. New York: Guilford.

Garey, Anita Ilta. 1999. *Weaving Work and Motherhood*. Philadelphia: Temple University Press.

Garey, Anita I., and Terry Arendell. 2001. "Children, Work, and Family: Some Thoughts on 'Mother-Blame.'" Pp. 293–303 in *Working Families: The Transformation of the American Home*, ed. R. Hertz and N. L. Marshall. Berkeley: University of California Press.

Garey, Anita Ilta, and Nicholas W. Townsend. 1996. "Kinship, Courtship, and Child Maintenance Law in Botswana." *Journal of Family Issues* 17(2): 189–202.

Geertz, Clifford. 1973. "Religion as a Cultural System." Pp. 87–125 in *The Interpretation of Cultures*. New York: Basic Books.

Gerson, Kathleen. 1993. *No Man's Land: Men's Changing Commitments to Family and Work*. New York: Basic Books.

Gerstel, Naomi. 2000. "The Third Shift: Gender and Care Work outside the Home." *Qualitative Sociology* 23(4): 467–83.

Gilmore, David D. 1990. *Manhood in the Making: Cultural Concepts of Masculinity*. New Haven, CT: Yale University Press.

Gini, Al. 2001. *My Job, Myself: Work and the Creation of the Modern Individual*. New York: Routledge.

Glenn, Evelyn Nakano. 1996. "From Servitude to Service Work: Historical Continuities in the Racial Division of Paid Reproductive Labor." Pp. 115–56 in *Working in the Service Society*, ed. C. L. Macdonald and C. Sirianni. Philadelphia: Temple University Press.

Glenn, Evelyn Nakano, Grace Chang, and Linda Rennie Forcey, eds. 1994. *Mothering: Ideology, Experience, and Agency*. New York: Routledge.

Gluckman, Max. 1940. "Analysis of a Social Situation in Modern Zululand." Pp. 1–30 and 147–174 in *Bantu Studies*.

Goffman, Erving. 1963. *Stigma: Notes on the Management of Spoiled Identity*. Englewood Cliffs, NJ: Prentice-Hall.

———. 1977. "The Arrangement between the Sexes." *Theory and Society* 4: 301–36.

Goldman, Bruce, Mark Powelson, and Sally Lehrman. 1990. "Real Estate Boom or Bust? A Special Report on Bay Area Real Estate in the '90s." *San Francisco Focus* (April): 77–105.

Goldman, Debbie. 2000. "Today's Work and Family Issue: Curbing Abusive Mandatory Overtime." *HR Today*, 10 November [retrieved 8 May 2001]. Available: http://www.hr-today.com/balancingact11102000.html.

Goldscheider, Calvin, and Frances Goldscheider. 1993. "Whose Nest? A Two Generational View of Leaving Home During the 1980's." *Journal of Marriage and the Family* 55(November): 851–62.

Goldscheider, F., and C. Goldscheider. 1994. "Leaving and Returning Home in the Twentieth Century." *Population Reference Bureau Bulletin* 48(4).

Goode, William J. 1982. "Why Men Resist." Pp. 131–50 in *Rethinking the Family: Some Feminist Questions*, ed. B. Thorne and M. Yalom. New York: Longman.

Goodell, Jeff. 2000. *Sunnyvale: The Rise and Fall of a Silicon Valley Family*. New York: Random House.

Gotham, Kevin Fox. 2000. "Racialization and the State: The Housing Act of 1934 and the Creation of the Federal Housing Administration." *Sociological Perspectives* 43(2, Summer): 291–317.

Gramsci, Antonio. 1971. *Selections from the Prison Notebooks*. London: New Left Books.

Gregory, Steven, and Roger Sanjek. 1994. *Race*. New Brunswick, NJ: Rutgers University Press.

Griswold, Robert L. 1993. *Fatherhood in America: A History*. New York: Basic Books.

Gutmann, Matthew C. 1996. *The Meanings of Macho: Being a Man in Mexico City*. Berkeley: University of California Press.

———. 1997. "Trafficking in Men: The Anthropology of Masculinities." *Annual Review of Anthropology* 26: 385–409.

Hacker, Andrew. 1992. *Two Nations: Black and White, Separate, Hostile and Unequal*. New York: Ballantine.

Hackstaff, Karla B. 1999. *Marriage in a Culture of Divorce*. Philadelphia: Temple University Press.

Halle, David. 1984. *America's Working Man: Work, Home, and Politics among Blue-Collar Property Owners*. Chicago: University of Chicago Press.

Hammel, E. A. 1990. "A Theory of Culture for Demography." *Population and Development Review* 16(3): 455–85.

Hank, Karsten, and Hans-Peter Kohler. 2000. "Gender Preferences for Children in Europe: Empirical Results from 17 FFS Countries." *Demographic Research* 2(1) [retrieved February 6, 2001]. Available: http://www.demographic-research.org/Volumes/Vol2/1.

Hansen, Karen V. 1994. *A Very Social Time: Gender, Class, and Community in Antebellum New England*. Berkeley: University of California Press.

———. 2001. *Class Contingencies in Networks of Care for School-Aged Children*. Working Paper No. 27. Berkeley: Center for Working Families, University of California, Berkeley.

Hareven, Tamara K. 1986. "American Families in Transition: Historical Perspectives on Change." Pp. 40–58 in *Family in Transition: Rethinking Marriage, Sexuality, Child Rearing, and Family Organization*, 5th ed., ed. A. S. Skolnick and J. H. Skolnick. Boston: Little, Brown.

Harkness, Sara, and Charles M. Super. 1992. "The Cultural Foundations of Fathers' Roles: Evidence from Kenya and the United States." Pp. 191–211 in

Father-Child Relations: Cultural and Biosocial Contexts, ed. B. S. Hewlett. New York: Aldine De Gruyter.

Harris, Kathleen Mullan, Frank F. Furstenberg Jr., and Jeremy K. Marmer. 1998. "Paternal Involvement with Adolescents in Intact Families: The Influence of Fathers over the Life Course." *Demography* 35(2): 201–16.

Hays, Sharon. 1996. *The Cultural Contradictions of Motherhood*. New Haven, CT: Yale University Press.

Hearn, Jeff. 1987. *The Gender of Oppression: Men, Masculinity, and the Critique of Marxism*. New York: St. Martin's Press.

Henretta, John C. 1984. "Parental Status and Child's Home Ownership." *American Sociological Review* 49: 131–40.

Herdt, Gilbert. 1981. *Guardians of the Flutes: Idioms of Masculinity*. New York: McGraw-Hill.

Hernandez, Donald J. 1993. *America's Children: Resources from Family, Government, and the Economy*. New York: Russell Sage Foundation.

Hertz, Rosanna. 1986. *More Equal Than Others: Women and Men in Dual-Career Marriages*. Berkeley: University of California Press.

———. 1998. "The Parenting Approach to the Work-Family Dilemma." Pp. 767–75 in *Families in the U.S.: Kinship and Domestic Politics*, ed. K. V. Hansen and A. I. Garey. Philadelphia: Temple University Press.

Hewlett, Barry S., ed. 1991. *Intimate Fathers: The Nature and Context of Aka Pygmy Paternal Infant Care*. Ann Arbor: University of Michigan Press.

———. 1992. *Father-Child Relations: Cultural and Biosocial Contexts*. New York: Aldine De Gruyter.

Hewlett, Sylvia Ann, and Cornel West. 1998. *The War against Parents: What We Can Do for America's Beleaguered Moms and Dads*. Boston: Houghton Mifflin.

Heymann, Jody. 2000. *The Widening Gap: Why America's Working Families Are in Jeopardy—and What Can Be Done about It*. New York: Basic Books.

Hochschild, Arlie. 1989. *The Second Shift: Working Parents and the Revolution at Home*. New York: Viking.

———. 1991. "The Fractured Family." *The American Prospect* (Summer): 106–15.

———. 1997. *The Time Bind: When Work Becomes Home and Home Becomes Work*. New York: Henry Holt.

Hochschild, Jennifer L. 1995. *Facing up to the American Dream: Race, Class, and the Soul of the Nation*. Princeton, NJ: Princeton University Press.

Hogan, Dennis P. 1978. "The Variable Order of Events in the Life Course." *American Sociological Review* 43: 573–86.

———. 1981. *Transitions and Social Change: The Early Lives of American Men*. New York: Academic Press.

Hogan, Dennis P., David J. Eggebeen, and Clifford C. Clogg. 1993. "The Structure of Intergenerational Exchanges in American Families." *American Journal of Sociology* 98(6): 1428–58.

Holland, Dorothy C., and Debra Skinner. 1987. "Prestige and Intimacy: The Cultural Models behind America's Talk about Gender Types." Pp. 78–111 in

Cultural Models in Language and Thought, ed. D. C. Holland and N. Quinn. New York: Cambridge University Press.

Holland, Dorothy C., and Margaret A. Eisenhart. 1990. *Educated in Romance: Women, Achievement, and College Culture*. Chicago: University of Chicago Press.

Holland, Dorothy C., William Lachicotte, Debra Skinner, and Carole Cain. 1998. *Identity and Agency in Cultural Worlds*. Cambridge, MA: Harvard University Press.

Hout, Michael, and Melissa J. Wilde. 1999. "The Demographic Imperative in Sixty Years of Religious Change in the United States," Survey Research Center, University of California, Berkeley, 22 September.

Howard, Judith A., and Jocelyn A. Hollander. 1997. *Gendered Situations, Gendered Selves: A Gender Lens on Social Psychology*. Thousand Oaks, CA: Sage.

Hunnicutt, Benjamin Kline. 1996. *Kellogg's Six-Hour Day*. Philadelphia: Temple University Press.

Ingersoll-Dayton, Berit, Margaret B. Neal, and Leslie Hammer. 2001. "Aging Parents Helping Adult Children: The Experience of the Sandwich Generation." *Family Relations* 50(3): 262–71.

Johnson, Allan G. 1997. *The Gender Knot: Unraveling Our Patriarchal Legacy*. Philadelphia: Temple University Press.

Kagan, Jerome. 1998. *Three Seductive Ideas*. Cambridge, MA: Harvard University Press.

Karraker, Katherine Hildebrandt, Dena Ann Vogel, and Margaret Ann Lake. 1995. "Parents' Gender-Stereotyped Perceptions of Newborns: The Eye of the Beholder Revisited." *Sex Roles* 33: 687–701.

Keen, S. 1991. *Fire in the Belly*. New York: Bantam.

Kimmel, Michael S., ed. 1987. *Changing Men: New Directions in Research on Men and Masculinity*. Newbury Park, CA: Sage.

———. 1994. "Masculinity as Homophobia: Fear, Shame, and Silence in the Construction of Gender Identity." Pp. 119–41 in *Theorizing Masculinities*, ed. H. Brod and M. Kaufman. Thousand Oaks, CA: Sage.

———, ed. 1995. *The Politics of Manhood: Profeminist Men Respond to the Mythopoetic Men's Movement (and Mythopoetic Leaders Answer)*. Philadelphia: Temple University Press.

———. 1996. *Manhood in America: A Cultural History*. New York: Free Press.

Kimmel, Michael S., and Michael Messner, eds. 1995. *Men's Lives*. 3d ed. Boston: Allyn and Bacon.

———, eds. 2001. *Men's Lives*. 4th ed. Boston: Allyn and Bacon.

Kimmel, Michael S., and Thomas E. Mosmiller, eds. 1992. *Against the Tide: Pro-Feminist Men in the United States 1776–1990: A Documentary History*. Boston, MA: Beacon.

Kotlowitz, Alex. 1991. *There Are No Children Here: The Story of Two Boys Growing up in the Other America*. New York: Anchor Books Doubleday.

Kozol, Jonathan. 1991. *Savage Inequalities: Children in America's Schools*. New York: Crown.

Krivo, Lauren J. 1986. "Home Ownership Differences between Hispanics and Anglos in the United States." *Social Problems* 33(4): 319–33.

Lakoff, George. 1996. *Moral Politics: What Conservatives Know That Liberals Don't*. Chicago: University of Chicago Press.

Lamb, Michael E., ed. 1986. *The Father's Role: Applied Perspectives*. New York: Wiley.

———. 1997. "Fathers and Child Development: An Introductory Overview and Guide." In *The Role of the Father in Child Development* (3rd ed.), ed. M. E. Lamb. New York: Wiley.

Lamont, Michele. 2000. *The Dignity of Working Men: Morality and the Boundaries of Race, Class and Immigration*. Cambridge, MA: Harvard.

Lamphere, Louise. 1987. *From Working Daughters to Working Mothers: Immigrant Women in a New England Industrial Community*. Ithaca, NY: Cornell University Press.

———. 2001. "The Domestic Sphere of Women and the Public World of Men: The Strengths and Limitations of an Anthropological Dichotomy." Pp. 100–09 in *Gender in Cross-Cultural Perspective*, ed. C. B. Brettell and C. F. Sargent. Englewood Cliffs, NJ: Prentice-Hall.

Lancaster, Roger. 1992. *Life is Hard: Machismo, Danger, and the Intimacy of Power in Nicaragua*. Berkeley: University of California Press.

Lancaster, Roger N., and Micaela di Leonardo, eds. 1997. *The Gender/Sexuality Reader: Culture, History, Political Economy*. New York: Routledge.

Langer, Ellen J. 1983. *The Psychology of Control*. Beverly Hills: Sage.

Lareau, Annette. 2000. "My Wife Can Tell Me Who I Know: Methodological and Conceptual Problems in Studying Fathers." *Qualitative Sociology* 23(4, July 21): 407–33.

LaRossa, Ralph. 1997. *The Modernization of Fatherhood: A Social and Political History*. Chicago: University of Chicago Press.

Leone, Catherine L. 1986. "Fairness, Freedom, and Responsibility: The Dilemma of Fertility Choice in America." Ph.D. dissertation, Washington State University.

Levine, James A. 1976. *Who Will Raise the Children? New Options for Fathers and Mothers*. New York: Lippincott.

Levine, James A., and Edward W. Pitt, eds. 1995. *New Expectations: Community Strategies for Responsible Fatherhood*. New York: Families and Work Institute.

Levine, James A., and Todd L. Pittinsky. 1998. *Working Fathers: New Strategies for Balancing Work and Family*. San Diego: Harcourt Brace.

Levine, Suzanne Braun. 2000. *Father Courage: What Happens When Men Put Family First*. Orlando, FL: Harcourt, Inc.

Liebow, Elliot. 1967. *Tally's Corner: A Study of Negro Streetcorner Men*. Boston: Little, Brown.

Lindsey, Eric W., Jacquelyn Mize, and Gregory S. Pettit. 1997. "Differential Play Patterns of Mothers and Fathers of Sons and Daughters: Implications for Children's Gender Role Development." *Sex Roles: A Journal of Research* 37(9–10, November): 643–61.

Logan, John R., and Glenna D. Spitze. 1996. *Family Ties: Enduring Relations between Parents and Their Grown Children*. Philadelphia: Temple University Press.

Lorde, Audre. 1984. *Sister Outsider: Essays and Speeches*. Freedom, CA: The Crossing Press.

Lye, Diane N. 1990. "Where's Daddy? Paternal Participation in Child Rearing in Intact Families," Paper presented at the annual meetings of the Population Association of America, Washington, DC, March 21–23, 1991.

Macdonald, Cameron Lynne. 1996. "Shadow Mothers: Nannies, *au Pairs*, and Invisible Work." Pp. 244–63 in *Working in the Service Society*, ed. C. L. Macdonald and C. Sirianni. Philadelphia: Temple University Press.

Macleod, Jay. 1995. *Ain't No Makin' It: Aspirations and Attainment in a Low-Income Neighborhood, Revised Edition*. Boulder, CO: Westview Press.

Marcus, George E., and Peter Dobkin Hall. 1992. *Lives in Trust: The Fortunes of Dynastic Families in Late Twentieth-Century America*. Boulder, CO: Westview.

Marin, Rick. 2000. "At-Home Fathers Step Out to Find They Are not Alone." *New York Times*, 2 January, pp. 1, 16.

Marsiglio, William, ed. 1995. *Fatherhood: Contemporary Theory, Research, and Social Policy*. Thousand Oaks, CA: Sage.

Marsiglio, William, Paul Amato, Randal D. Day, and Michael E. Lamb. 2000. "Scholarship on Fatherhood in the 1990s and Beyond." *Journal of Marriage and the Family* 62 (November): 1173–91.

Martin, Teresa Castro, and Larry L. Bumpass. 1989. "Recent Trends in Marital Disruption." *Demography* 26(1): 37–51.

Massey, Douglas S., and Nancy A. Denton. 1993. *American Apartheid: Segregation and the Making of the Underclass*. Cambridge, MA: Harvard University Press.

McMahon, Martha. 1995. *Engendering Motherhood: Identity and Self-Transformation in Women's Lives*. New York: Guilford.

Merton, Robert K. 1968. *Social Theory and Social Structure: 1968 Enlarged Edition*. New York: Free Press.

Messner, Michael A. 1992. *Power at Play: Sports and the Problem of Masculinity*. Boston: Beacon.

———. 1997. *The Politics of Masculinities: Men in Movements*. Beverly Hills, CA: Sage.

Mills, C. Wright. 1959. *The Sociological Imagination*. New York: Oxford University Press.

———. 1963. *Power, Politics and People: Collected Essays of C.Wright Mills*, ed. I. L. Horowitz. New York: Ballantine.

Mintz, Steven. 1998. "From Patriarchy to Androgyny and Other Myths: Placing Men's Family Roles in Historical Perspective." Pp. 3–30 in *Men in Families: When Do They Get Involved? What Difference Does It Make?* ed. A. Booth and A. C. Crouter. Mahwah, NJ: Lawrence Erlbaum.

Mishel, Lawrence, Jared Bernstein, and John Schmitt. 2001. *The State of Working America 2000–2001*. Ithaca, NY: Cornell University Press.

Mishler, Elliot G. 1986. *Research Interviewing: Context and Narrative*. Cambridge, MA: Harvard University Press.

Modell, John. 1985. "Historical Reflections on American Marriage." Pp. 181–96 in *Contemporary Marriage: Comparative Perspectives on a Changing Institution*, ed. K. Davis. New York: Russell Sage Foundation.

Moen, Phyllis. 1985. "Continuities and Discontinuities in Women's Labor Force Activity." Pp. 113–55 in *Life Course Dynamics: Trajectories and Transitions, 1968–1980*, ed. Glen H. Elder Jr. Ithaca, NY: Cornell University Press.

Montagu, Ashley, ed. 1964. *The Concept of Race*. London: Collier.

Moore, Henrietta. 1986. *Space, Text, and Gender: An Anthropological Study of the Marakwet of Kenya*. New York: Cambridge University Press.

Morgan, S. Philip, Diane N. Lye, and Gretchen Condran. 1988. "Sons, Daughters, and the Risk of Marital Disruption." *American Journal of Sociology* 94: 110–29.

Mumford, Lewis. 1961. *The City in History: Its Origins, Its Transformations, and Its Prospects*. New York: Harcourt, Brace and World.

National Center for Health Statistics. 1986. *Vital Statistics of the United States. 1982. Volume 1—Natality*. Hyattsville, MD: U.S. Department of Health and Human Services.

Nelson, Margaret K., and Joan Smith. 1999. *Working Hard and Making Do: Surviving in Small Town America*. Berkeley: University of California Press.

Newman, Katherine S. 1988. *Falling from Grace: The Experience of Downward Mobility in the American Middle Class*. New York: Free Press.

———. 1993. *Declining Fortunes: The Withering of the American Dream*. New York: Basic Books.

Nock, Steven L. 1998. *Marriage in Men's Lives*. New York: Oxford University Press.

Ortner, Sherry B. 1989. "Community: The Question of Fieldwork in Modern Society," paper presented at the 88th. Annual Meeting of the American Anthropological Association. Washington, DC, November 15–19, 1989.

———. 1990. "Gender Hegemonies." *Cultural Critique* 14(Winter): 35–80.

———. 1991. "Reading America: Preliminary Notes on Class and Culture." Pp. 163–89 in *Recapturing Anthropology: Working in the Present*, ed. R. G. Fox. Santa Fe, NM: School of American Research Press.

———. 1995. "Ethnography among the Newark: The Class of '58 of Weequahic High School." Pp. 257–73 in *Naturalizing Power: Essays in Feminist Cultural Analysis*, ed. S. Yanagisako and C. Delaney. New York: Routledge.

Otto, Mary. 2000. "Public Housing Strategy Riles Baltimore Neighbors: Some Residents Resist Plan to Scatter Poor throughout City." *The Washington Post*, November 9, L, p. 1.

Parke, Ross D., and Armin A. Brott. 1999. *Throwaway Dads: The Myths and Barriers that Keep Men from Being the Fathers They Want to Be*. New York: Houghton Mifflin.

Parker, Richard G. 1991. *Bodies, Pleasures and Passions: Sexual Culture in Contemporary Brazil*. Boston: Beacon.

Parsons, Talcott, and Robert F. Bales. 1955. *Family, Socialization and Interaction Process*. New York: Free Press.

Pattillo-McCoy, Mary. 1999. *Black Picket Fences: Privilege and Peril among the Black Middle Class*. Chicago: University of Chicago Press.

Pleck, Elizabeth H., and Joseph H. Pleck. 1980. "Introduction." Pp. 1–49 in *The American Man*, ed. E. H. Pleck and J. H. Pleck. Englewood Cliffs, NJ: Prentice-Hall.

Pleck, Joseph H. 1981. *The Myth of Masculinity*. Cambridge, MA: MIT Press.

———. 1985. *Working Wives/Working Husbands*. Beverly Hills, CA: Sage.

———. 1987. "The Theory of Male Sex-Role Identity: Its Rise and Fall, 1936 to the Present." Pp. 21–38 in *The Making of Masculinities: The New Men's Studies*, ed. H. Brod. Boston: Allen and Unwin.

———. 1995 [1974]. "Men's Power with Women, Other Men, and Society: A Men's Movement Analysis." Pp. 5–12 in *Men's Lives*. 3d ed., ed. M. S. Kimmel and M. A. Messner. Boston: Allyn and Bacon.

———. 1997. "Paternal Involvement: Level, Sources, and Consequences." Pp. 66–103 in *The Role of the Father in Child Development*. 3d ed., ed. M. E. Lamb. New York: Wiley.

Pleck, Joseph H., and Jack Sawyer, eds. 1974. *Men and Masculinity*. Englewood Cliffs, NJ: Prentice-Hall.

Plummer, Ken. 1995. *Telling Sexual Stories: Power, Change and Social Worlds*. New York: Routledge.

Polikoff, Nancy D. 1983. "Gender and Child-Custody Determinations: Exploding the Myths." In *Families, Politics, and Public Policy: A Feminist Dialogue on Women and the State*, ed. I. Diamond. New York: Longman.

Pooler, William S. 1991. "Sex of Child Preferences among College Students." *Sex Roles: A Journal of Research* 25(9–10): 569–76.

Popenoe, David. 1988. *Disturbing the Nest: Family Change and Decline in Modern Societies*. New York: Aldine de Gruyter.

———. 1999. *Life without Father: Compelling New Evidence that Fatherhood and Marriage Are Indispensable for the Good of Children and the Family*. Cambridge, MA: Harvard University Press.

Potuchek, Jean L. 1997. *Who Supports the Family? Gender and Breadwinning in Dual-Earner Marriages*. Stanford, CA: Stanford University Press.

Prus, Robert. 1996. *Symbolic Interaction and Ethnographic Research*. Albany: State University of New York Press.

Radcliffe Public Policy Center. 2000. *Life's Work: Generational Attitudes toward Work and Life Integration*. Cambridge, MA: Author. Available: http://www.radcliffe.edu/pubpol/publications.

Radcliffe-Brown, A. R. 1950. "Introduction." Pp. 1–85 in *African Systems of Kinship and Marriage*, ed. A. R. Radcliffe-Brown and D. Forde. New York: Oxford University Press.

Reiter, Rayna R., ed. 1975. *Toward an Anthropology of Women*. New York: Monthly Review Press.

Rich, Adrienne. 1976. *Of Woman Born: Motherhood as Experience and Institution*. New York: W. W. Norton.

Riesman, Paul. 1992. *First Find Your Child a Good Mother: The Construction of Self in Two African Communities*. New Brunswick, NJ: Rutgers University Press.

Riggs, Janet Morgan. 1997. "Mandates for Mothers and Fathers: Perceptions of Breadwinners and Caregivers." *Sex Roles: A Journal of Research* 37(7–8): 565–80.

Rohner, Ronald P., and Robert A. Veneziano. 2000. "The Importance of Father Love: History and Contemporary Evidence," Center for the Study of Parental Acceptance and Rejection, School of Family Studies, University of Connecticut.

Rosaldo, Michelle Zimbalist, and Louise Lamphere. 1974. "Woman, Culture, and Society: A Theoretical Overview." Pp. 17–42 in *Woman, Culture, and Society*, ed. L. L. Michelle Zimbalist Rosaldo. Stanford, CA: Stanford University Press.

Rose, Stephen J. 2000. *Social Stratification in the United States: The New American Profile Poster, A Book-and-Poster Set*. New York: New Press.

Rothman, Barbara Katz. 1989. *Recreating Motherhood: Ideology and Technology in a Patriarchal Society*. New York: W. W. Norton.

Rotundo, E. Anthony. 1985. "American Fatherhood: A Historical Perspective." *American Behavioral Scientist* 29(1): 7–25.

———. 1993. *American Manhood: Transformations in Masculinity from the Revolution to the Modern Era*. New York: Basic Books.

Rubin, Jeffrey Z., F. J. Provenzano, and Zella Luria. 1974. "The Eye of the Beholder: Parents' Views on Sex of Newborns." *American Journal of Orthopsychiatry* 44: 512–19.

Rubin, Lillian B. 1976. *Worlds of Pain: Life in the Working Class Family*. New York: Basic Books.

———. 1994. *Families on the Fault Line: America's Working Class Speaks about the Family, the Economy, Race, and Ethnicity*. New York: Harper Collins.

Ruddick, Sara. 1989. *Maternal Thinking: Toward a Politics of Peace*. New York: Ballantine.

Russell, D. E. H. 1984. *Sexual Exploitation: Rape, Child Sexual Abuse, and Work*. Beverly Hills, CA: Sage.

Sapir, Edward. 1956. "Cultural Anthropology and Psychiatry." Pp. 140–163 in *Culture, Language, and Personality: Selected Essays*, ed. D. G. Mandelbaum. Berkeley: University of California Press.

Schneider, David M., and Raymond T. Smith. 1973. *Class Differences and Sex Roles in American Kinship and Family Structure*. Englewood Cliffs, NJ: Prentice-Hall.

Schneider, Jane C., and Peter Schneider. 1996. *Festival of the Poor: Fertility Decline and the Ideology of Class in Sicily, 1860–1980*. Tucson: University of Arizona Press.

Schor, Juliet B. 1991. *The Overworked American: The Unexpected Decline of Leisure*. New York: Basic Books.

———. 1998. *The Overspent American: Upscaling, Downshifting, and the New Consumer*. New York: Basic Books.

Scott, Janny. 2001. "Boom of 1990's Missed Many in Middle Class, Data Suggests." *The New York Times*, August 31, pp. A1, A21.

Segalen, Martine. 1986. *Historical Anthropology of the Family*, trans. J. C. Whitehouse and S. Matthews. New York: Cambridge University Press.

Segura, Denise. 1994. "Working at Motherhood: Chicana and Mexican Immigrant Mothers and Employment." Pp. 211–33 in *Mothering: Ideology, Experience, and Agency*, ed. E. N. Glenn, G. Chang, and F. R. Forcey. New York: Routledge.

Seltzer, Judith A. 1991. "Relationships between Fathers and Children Who Live Apart: The Father's Role after Separation." *Journal of Marriage and the Family* 53: 79–101.

Sennett, Richard, and Jonathan Cobb. 1972. *The Hidden Injuries of Class*. New York: Vintage.

Shelton, Beth A. 1992. *Women, Men, and Time: Gender Differences in Paid Work, Housework, and Leisure*. New York: Greenwood.

Shipton, Parker. 1992. "Debts and Trespasses: Land, Mortgages and the Ancestors in Western Kenya." *Africa—London* 62(3): 357–88.

Simmel, Georg. 1971. *On Individuality and Social Forms: Selected Writings*. Chicago: University of Chicago Press.

Smith, Dorothy E. 1999. *Writing the Social: Critique, Theory, and Investigations*. Toronto: University of Toronto Press.

Spade, Joan Z., and Carole A. Reese. 1991. "We've Come a Long Way Maybe: College Students' Plans for Work and Family Roles." *Sex Roles* 24(5/6): 273–91.

Stacey, Judith. 1990. *Brave New Families*. New York: Basic Books.

Stack, Carol B. 1974. *All Our Kin: Strategies for Survival in a Black Community*. New York: Harper and Row.

Stack, Carol B., and Linda M. Burton. 1993. "Kinscripts." *Journal of Comparative Family Studies* 24(2): 157–70.

Stearns, Peter N. 1991. "Fatherhood in Historical Perspective: The Role of Social Change." Pp. 28–52 in *Fatherhood and Families in Cultural Context*, ed. F. W. Bozett and S. M. H. Hanson. New York: Springer.

Steiner, Claude M. 1974. *Scripts People Live*. New York: Bantam Books.

Stephenson, June. 1991. *The Two-Parent Family Is not the Best*. Napa, CA: Diemer, Smith.

Stewart, Abigail J., Donna Henderson-King, Eaaron Henderson-King, and David G. Winter. 2000. *Work and Family Values: Life Scripts in the Midwest in the 1950s*. CEEL Working Paper 00600. Ann Arbor, MI: Center for the Study of Everyday Life, University of Michigan.

Suskind, Ron. 1998. *A Hope in the Unseen: An American Odyssey from the Inner City to the Ivy League*. New York: Broadway Books.

Sweet, James A., and Larry L. Bumpass. 1987. *American Families and Households*. New York: Russell Sage Foundation for the National Committee on the 1980 Census.

Tamis-LeMonda, Catherine S., and Natasha Cabrera. Forthcoming. *Handbook of Father Involvement: Multidisciplinary Perspectives*. Mahwah, NJ: Lawrence Erlbaum.

Thorne, Barrie. 1993. *Gender Play: Girls and Boys in School*. New Brunswick, NJ: Rutgers University Press.

Townsend, Nicholas W. 1992. "Paternity Attitudes of a Cohort of Men in the United States: Cultural Values and Demographic Implications." Ph.D. dissertation, University of California, Berkeley.

———. 1996. "Family Formation and Men's Transition to Adulthood: The Role of Intergenerational Assistance in Buying a Home among Men from the American Middle Class." Unpublished paper, presented at the annual meeting of the Population Association of America.

———. 1997. "Reproduction in Anthropology and Demography." Pp. 96–114 in *Anthropological Demography: Toward a New Synthesis*, ed. D. I. Kertzer and T. Fricke. Chicago: University of Chicago Press.

———. 1999. "Male Fertility as a Lifetime of Relationships: Contextualizing Men's Biological Reproduction in Botswana." Pp. 343–64 in *Fertility and the Male Life Cycle in the Era of Fertility Decline*, ed. C. Bledsoe, J. Guyer, and S. Lerner. New York: Oxford University Press.

———. 2002. "Concentration and Distribution: Father Involvement in Two Cultural Contexts." In *Handbook of Father Involvement: Multidisciplinary Perspectives*, ed. C. S. Tamis-LeMonda and N. Cabrera. Mahwah, NJ: Lawrence Erlbaum.

Turner, Margery Austin, and Felicity Skidmore, eds. 1999. *Mortgage Lending Discrimination: A Review of Existing Evidence*. Washington, DC: The Urban Institute.

Uchitelle, Louis. 2001. "Equity Shrivels as Homeowners Borrow and Buy." *New York Times*, January 19, pp. C1–C2.

United States Bureau of the Census. 1972. *1970 Census of Population and Housing: Census Tracts, San Jose, California, SMSA: PHC(1)-190*. Washington, DC: United States Department of Commerce.

———. 1983. *1980 Census of Population and Housing: Census Tracts, San Jose, California, SMSA: PHC80-2-322*. Washington, DC: United States Department of Commerce.

———. 1992. *Statistical Abstract of the United States: 1992*. Washington, DC: U.S.G.P.O.

———. 1996. *Statistical Abstract of the United States: 1996*. Washington, DC: U.S.G.P.O.

Uttal, Lynet. 1997. "'Trust Your Instincts': Cultural and Class-Based Preferences in Employed Mothers' Childcare Choices." *Qualitative Sociology* 20(2): 253–74.

Vinitzky-Seroussi, Vered. 1998. *After Pomp and Circumstance: High School Reunion as an Autobiographical Occasion*. Chicago: University of Chicago Press.

Vogel, Dena Ann, Margaret A. Lake, Suzanne Evans, and Katherine Hildebrandt Karraker. 1991. "Children's and Adults' Sex-Stereotyped Perceptions of Infants." *Sex Roles: A Journal of Research* 24(9–10): 605–16.

Waite, Linda, Gus Haggstrom, and David Kanouse. 1985. "The Consequences of Parenthood for the Marital Stability of Young Adults." *American Sociological Review* 50: 850–57.

Walker, Karen. 1990. "Class, Work, and Family in Women's Lives." *Qualitative Sociology* 13: 297–320.

Walzer, Susan. 1998. *Thinking about the Baby: Gender and Transitions into Parenthood*. Philadelphia: Temple University Press.

Waters, Mary C. 1990. *Ethnic Options: Choosing Identities in America*. Berkeley: University of California Press.

———. 2000. *Black Identities: West Indian Immigrant Dreams and American Realities*. Cambridge, MA: Harvard University Press.

Weatherford, J. McIver. 1981. *Tribes on the Hill*. New York: Rawson, Wade.

Weber, Max. 1978. *Economy and Society: An Outline of Interpretive Sociology*. Berkeley: University of California Press.

Wellman, Barry. 1999. "The Network Community: An Introduction." Pp. 1–47 in *Networks in the Global Village: Life in Contemporary Communities*, ed. B. Wellman. Boulder, CO: Westview.

West, Candace, and Don H. Zimmerman. 1987. "Doing Gender." *Gender & Society* 1(2): 125–51.

Weston, Kath. 1997. *Families We Choose: Lesbians, Gays, Kinship*. New York: Columbia University Press.

White, Lynn, Alan Booth, and John Edwards. 1986. "Children and Marital Happiness: Why the Negative Relationship?" *Journal of Family Issues* 7: 131–48.

Wienberg, Howard. 1988. "Duration between Marriage and First Birth and Marital Stability." *Social Biology* 35: 91–102.

Williams, Brett. 1988. *Upscaling Downtown: Stalled Gentrification in Washington, D.C.* Ithaca, NY: Cornell University Press.

Williams, Joan. 1999. *Unbending Gender: Why Family and Work Conflict and What to Do about It*. New York: Oxford University Press.

Wilson, William Julius. 1996. *When Work Disappears: The World of the New Urban Poor*. New York: Knopf.

———. 1999. *The Bridge over the Racial Divide: Rising Inequality and Coalition Politics*. Berkeley: University of California Press.

Wisensale, Steven K. 2001. *Family Leave Policy: The Political Economy of Work and Family in America.* Armonk, NY: M. E. Sharpe.

Wolgemuth, Robert D., and Ken Blanchard. 1999. *Daddy@Work.* Grand Rapids, MI: Zondervan Publishing.

Woolf, Virginia. 1966 [1938]. *Three Guineas*. New York: Harvest/Harcourt Brace Jovanovich.

Yanagisako, Sylvia Junko, and Jane Fishburne Collier. 1987. "Toward a Unified Analysis of Gender and Kinship." Pp. 14–50 in *Gender and Kinship: Essays toward a Unified Analysis*, ed. J. F. Collier and S. J. Yanagisako. Stanford, CA: Stanford University Press.

Young, Michael D., and Peter Wilmott. 1957. *Family and Kinship in East London*. London: Routledge and Kegan Paul.

Zeller, Tom. 2000. "Calculating One Kind of Middle Class." *New York Times*, 29 October, p. 5.

Zussman, Robert. 1987. "Work and Family in the New Middle Class." Pp. 338–46 in *Families and Work*, ed. N. Gerstel and H. E. Gross. Philadelphia: Temple University Press.

Index

Note: Interviewees are indexed under their first names.